Frances Awdry

The Miz Maze

A Story in Letters

Frances Awdry

The Miz Maze
A Story in Letters

ISBN/EAN: 9783744687881

Printed in Europe, USA, Canada, Australia, Japan

Cover: Foto ©Thomas Meinert / pixelio.de

More available books at **www.hansebooks.com**

THE MIZ MAZE

OR

THE WINKWORTH PUZZLE

THE MIZ MAZE

OR

The Winkworth Puzzle

A STORY IN LETTERS, BY NINE AUTHORS

'Many hands make light work.'

London

MACMILLAN AND CO.

1883

Printed by R. & R. CLARK, *Edinburgh.*

PREFACE.

IT had sometimes occurred to two of the writers of the ensuing correspondence that novels in letters generally were unsatisfactory because the various characters could only be the same person under different masks. They therefore resolved to try the experiment of putting the representation of each correspondent into different hands (as far as possible), so that there may be the difference that real life might produce in style and way of thinking. The result is here given to the public. We give our real names, but leave as an enigma for the readers which parts we have taken.

PERSONAGES INTRODUCED

Who write or receive Letters.

(DATE, 1858-1859.)

SIR WALTER WINKWORTH, Baronet of the Miz Maze, Stokesworthy, Wilts, age about 64, residing, when the book opens,
at High Scale, a small property in Westmoreland, which was
his in right of his second wife, Sophia Ratclyffe, recently
deceased.

DOROTHEA WINKWORTH and ELIZABETH WINKWORTH, his sisters,
aged 62 and 56, living at the Dower House, Stokesworthy.

MARY (MRS. HOME), another sister, settled in Australia.

BERTHA, his daughter by his first wife, aged 39, married to
Luigi Marini, an Italian patriot.

MILES and RATCLYFFE (CLYFFE), Sir Walter's twin sons, aged
22. Miles at Oxford; Ratclyffe in the army, quartered in
Canada.

FRANK, 12, youngest son; at school.

SOPHIA (called ZOE), 20, MARY (called POLLY), 14, and ELIZA-
BETH (called LISA), 10, Sir Walter's daughters.

EMILY WARBURTON, 21, an heiress, whose property is chiefly in
coal mines, renting Triermain, High Scale.

MRS. WARBURTON, her mother.

EDGAR FANSHAWE, 27, her cousin, whose father was an English
gentleman, his mother an Italian lady. He is an artist by
profession.

CARLO MONTI, his cousin and correspondent in Italy.

REV. JOSHUA BOOTLE, Rector of High Scale.

MRS. BOOTLE, his wife.

ALGERNON BOOTLE, his son, age 23, having just taken his degree.

MISS MADGEWICK, governess to Polly and Lisa, having been transferred to them from Emily.

FANNY, schoolroom-maid at Sir W. Winkworth's.

ANNIE, kitchen-maid at Mrs. Bootle's.

REV. H. BERNARD, Vicar of Stokesworthy.

MEYRICK, Sir Walter's agent.

CONTENTS.

PART I.

HIGH SCALE.

PART II.

IN THE MIZ MAZE.

PART III.

A DAY AT DALLINGTON, AND WHAT CAME OF IT.

PART IV.

OLD LACE.

PART V.

THE CAPTIVE KNIGHTS.

PART VI.

THE RESCUE.

PART VII.

THE BARONET ABROAD.

PART VIII.

Love Birds.

PART IX.

WOO'D AND MARRIED AND A'!

PART I.

AT HIGH SCALE.

B

If he's only an excellent person,
My dear Araminta, say no !

1.—Aunt Dora's Doubts and Deliberations.

Miss Winkworth to Mrs. Home.

THE DOWER HOUSE, STOKESWORTHY,
November 30, 1858.

MY DEAR MARY—There is not much external news
for you by this budget, though, I suspect, you care
more for little home circumstances than anything else,
such, for instance, as that the white-headed jackdaw I
told you of last year is safe and sound, and chattering
on one of the churchyard trees to a gray-headed friend
on one of the battlements. I hope he may escape
another year, but he is a sore temptation to strangers,
and I fear we may have them at the poor old Miz
Maze, for the lease will be out this winter, and
Meyrick tells me that Mr. Pratt does not mean to
renew it, finding himself in better health at Torquay.
Even Ratclyffe could hardly keep his hands or his gun
from the poor bird, though he was very good about it
when he found that it would be a great grief to his
aunts to lose it.

Dear Clyffe, it was a kind visit of his when he
came to wish us good-bye before starting for Montreal.
You know he always has been the most demonstrative
of the twins, and when he was here without his
brother, he let out a good deal about the state of
things since his mother's death—quite enough to make
me thoughtful.

For instance, on Mrs. Pratt lamenting that the
Vicar is unmarried, he answered : " People don't know
their blessings." She answered, rather heavily: "Surely
you are not an advocate for the celibacy of the clergy ;"
to which he responded : "I only know the Romans may
be thankful that the Pope isn't married." We laughed
at the quaint idea ; but afterwards, when walking with
him, I found that the boy was speaking from his
annoyance at the masterful spirit of the clergyman's
wife at High Scale. " If she would only be content
·with bullying her husband, who isn't half a bad
fellow," said Clyffe, "there'd be no damage done ; but
it is rather too bad that the girls can't do a thing
without father's asking her advice ! Actually, when
Mrs. Warburton would have taken Zoe to hear Jenny
Lind at Carlisle, the woman must needs persuade
father that it was worldly !" I gathered further that
this Mrs. Bootle had been a great friend of his mother's,
who, as you know, always saw the best of every one ;
and that ·poor Walter fancies that by consulting her
about his girls he shall best carry out Sophia's wishes.
" You've never been at High Scale, Aunt Dora," says
Clyffe. " I do wish you would go. It would do father
ever so much good !"

Do you know, I have really begun to think that I
ought to take the boy's hint. Bessie is better than
she has been for years, ever since the great shock of
her youth ; and if Kate Thorburn could come and stay
with her, I think I might go. I yearn to see Walter
and his children. How little we guessed when Bessie
and I sailed for Madeira, that it would be such a
parting, that a trouble so unexpected should fall on
the Miz Maze, causing Sophia, in the first brunt of the
matter, to bear the whole family off to her Westmore-

land home.   Then Bessie's health became all-absorbing
to me, and Sophia's was an equal detention at the
other end, while Walter himself has had a growing
distaste to renewing painful recollections; and thus
we have only seen one another when he has been down
here on business, or the boys have come for a few
days' shooting.   I can't help thinking Sophia was glad
to keep us apart; and that, not unnaturally, she
dreaded Stokesworthy, and all influences there.   Perhaps her desire to be buried at High Scale among her
own people, instead of ours, was connected with that
feeling; anyhow, it is sad to see the dear old place
made over to strangers, and to feel ourselves drifting
away from our brother and the children.   I think I
ought to make an effort to throw a line across the
space, if Bessie can spare me.   There, I have built up
such a rigmarole on the white-headed jackdaw, as
rather reminds me of the catalogue of catastrophes
prefaced by "the old magpie's dead, sir."

Tuesday.—There certainly is something in the
atmosphere that makes people's plans occur to them
simultaneously.   Not that I am going northward, but
what is far better, the dear Walter is coming south.
He will come to us for three days on business next
week, so I close my letter with good news.—Your
loving sister,   DOROTHEA WINKWORTH.

2.—EMILY'S COLLIERY CASTLES.

Emily Warburton to Zoe Winkworth.

DURHAM, *December* 1858.

My dear Zoe—I wish you were with us.   It was
a capital plan of my dear old trustee, Cousin Charles

Fanshawe, to have us to meet him here, Edgar and all.
Edgar is quite wild about the Cathedral. He says
that it is unique, placed, indeed, somewhat after the
fashion of those in the quaint old Italian cities, but
with an English severity peculiarly its own. It is a
glorious place, particularly the Galilee. Fancy St.
Cuthbert banishing even Our Lady's Chapel to the
west end, and we poor women coming no farther than
the pillar at the end of the nave, just like the wild
Borderers. We saw the great knob or knocker that
gave security to a Border thief when he once touched
it.

However, Durham may wait till I come home. I
wanted to tell you that I got Cousin Charles to take
me to Black Joe's pit, the place where all Uncle
Brooke's money was made. My dear, you never saw
such an awful place, all blackness and ashes by day,
and fire and flame by night. Not a scrap of a church
for miles and miles, and full of wild rough men and
women and little grimy children, who evidently never
saw a primrose, or a lady, or a clergyman.

Now I know what is to be my work in life, and
Cousin Charles says he will not hinder me. We will
begin with a school chapel, and a mistress and a
clergyman, and as time goes on have a church. Could
it not be like the Galilee? Then those poor men are
always getting killed with water or fire-damp, so I will
have an orphanage at High Scale, and bring up the
children among the mountains and foxgloves. There
may be some sisters to nurse a little hospital, and you
and I and Madgy may find our nest there when our
fathers and mothers have given up their plans about
us. Poor mamma, I am not the daughter of her ideal
hope. She would give me up gladly to be married.

Why not to better things ? You may show this to
Madgy, but to no one else. Most likely we come
back on Monday, but we are to have one Cathedral
Sunday free from Bootledom.—Your affectionate

EMILY.

3.—ZOE'S SYMPATHY.

Zoe to Emily.

HIGH SCALE, *December* 1858.

Dearest Emily—*How* glad I shall be to get you
back I cannot tell, for I have no companions just now
but the two little girls, and the confidence might be
too much for Polly ; besides that I have not leave from
you to speak to her,—so that I have had to keep all
to myself till now, when I can write to you some of
the thoughts I am so full of. What a beautiful thing
it is to have such a path marked out for you, and to
be able to enter on it without doubt that it is really
your own vocation ! I wonder if I should feel the
same in your place, but you were always so much
braver than I, and so much less disposed to depend
on home opinions, that Mrs. Warburton's want of
sympathy would be a much greater drawback to me.

But then, whenever dear mamma did not sympathise
with me, I always found myself wrong. I wonder
what she would say now, if she were only here. She
would persuade Mrs. Warburton to like the work, and
then you would be more sure that there would be a
blessing on it.

However, this is nonsense, for the way is sure to
become clear if it is really a *call*, as I hope and believe
it is. Do you remember Mrs. Bootle declaring that
" vocations only meant self-will," and how dear mamma

answered that she could not quite think so, but that
she believed that family circumstances were providen-
tially overruled, so as to point out where the summons
was a real one.

And then don't you recollect the two pictures of us
that Clyffe drew, each with a lily in our hand, such
dreadful frights that Mr. Fanshawe did them over again
and made us far too pretty ? There was the brook
and river meeting, and you with your big arum-lily
just going to jump in and swim both ; and I, with my
little lily of the valley, putting one foot to the edge,
as if I did not like it at all.   That is just like us two.

I wish you had let me tell Miles ; he is beginning
to brighten now that we have had letters from Clyffe.
We have had some long rides together, and he really
utters about a sentence a mile, which is gratifying,
though of course nothing can supply the companionship
of Clyffe, his other half.—Your loving   ZOE.

4.—MISS MADGEWICK'S LOOKING ON AT THE GAME.

Miss Madgewick to her sister, Madame Saisset, at Geneva.

HIGH SCALE, *December* 1858.

My dearest Annette—You say I never tell you
anything about myself and my surroundings, but only
comment on your letters and the home news. But
you see there has been so much to comment on for
the last year, that I always find my letters coming to
at least three sheets before I have finished answering
yours. When one's sisters take it into their heads to
marry Swiss professors, and their husbands break their
legs in the cause of science on Alpine heights, while
one's brothers are reported lost at sea, and then turn

up again, one gets out of the habit of thinking that one's own little matter-of-fact routine of life can be interesting to anybody but one's self.   If it were not for having the Warburtons so near, I don't know what I should do; but that makes all the difference.

Considering how long I had known the Winkworths, of course it was not like coming into a perfectly strange family; still one never really *knows* people till one has lived in the house with them.   Since Lady Winkworth's death, this house has been very unlike what it used to be, and I was quite prepared not to find the Triermain atmosphere here.   "High and squirish" Sir Walter always was, but now his stiffness and chilliness are really beyond description.   His wife's death seems to have petrified him altogether, and very wretched it is for his children.   It has been much worse since Clyffe went off to Canada, and Miles feels the separation from his brother terribly; besides which there is something else to make him gloomy, poor boy.   That "very desirable arrangement," of which I told you before I left Triermain, seems more unlikely than ever to come to anything.   I always said there was no chance of it, and Mrs. Warburton's attempts at furthering it would ruin the plot, even if Emily was as willing to be wooed as Miles is to woo her.   More willing than able, poor fellow!   He does more harm than good to his own cause, and knows it; consequently he is in the depths of despondency, and if he does chance to make a remark, it is to disagree with the last thing said by anybody else, especially by Zoe.   You say I never gave you a distinct idea of Zoe, but somehow she is one of those people whose character you only take in very gradually.   I suppose I should not understand her as well as I do even now if it were not for having had

Emily as interpreter.   She is shy, like Miles, and,
indeed, all of them except Clyffe and Lisa.

Sir Walter's unapproachableness may possibly be a
form of shyness.   Such is the theory of some of his
most charitable neighbours, Mrs. Warburton among
them.   Poor Zoe gets the credit of being proud and
ungracious when she is only in a perfect quiver. of
shyness.   " Such a haughty young lady," one of
Emily's old women said to me.   " So different from
Miss Warburton ! "   And so she is in her manner to
them, because she feels shyer than if they were of her
own class ; whereas Emily plunges into sympathy with
them at once, in her impulsive, warm-hearted way, and
talks as naturally as she would to her mother.   But
Zoe stiffens all over, and assumes a severe stateliness
which gives an utterly wrong impression of her feelings.
She makes a very dignified mistress of the house, and
no one who did not know all her different shades of
manner would guess how constrained and nervous she
is when her father is in the room.   If Emily had been
his daughter (but that is almost beyond even imagining)
she would have been on quite different terms with him.
Zoe's timidity, and her way of distrusting herself and
seeing both sides of the question at once, are all points
which tell against her with her father.   Emily has
none of these.   Zoe is painfully sensitive to other
people's opinions, while Emily is a little bit inclined
to be too reckless about them.   Emily has not learned
to be reticent *enough* about her feelings and opinions
as yet, while Zoe is so afraid of criticism that she can't
bring herself to speak out when she really wishes to
express what is in her mind, except to the people she is
most intimate with, of whom Emily is of course the chief.
She has her enthusiasms, too, and Sir Walter calls her

romantic and excitable, only she can keep them pent up generally; while with Emily out they flash, whether or not the audience is sympathetic. I wish she had a little more of Zoe's repose. When she and Mrs. Bootle meet there is always more or less of a skirmish. But Zoe is too loyal for that. Mrs. Bootle was really fond of Lady Winkworth, and Sir Walter defers to her now on every occasion in a way that I *cannot* understand. There never was a more odious woman. She even lays down the law as to the girls' reading and amusements, putting a stop to Mary's finishing *Kenilworth*, and Zoe's going to Carlisle to hear Jenny Lind. She actually took upon herself to warn *me* against that dangerous writer Kingsley, whose *Two Years Ago* she heard Mr. Fanshawe offering to lend me. She had seen a criticism of his works, which " proved him to be a foe to Christianity and morality." I did not say that *Westward Ho !* was my delight, and that I am sure there is Gospel truth in *Yeast*. She certainly has a faculty for making one feel *un*-Christian. Coming out of church the other day, she told me that she was going to " give Mr. Fanshawe a piece of her mind," which I had an instant presentiment would concern Zoe. Mrs. Warburton and I have long been aware that he worships the ground Zoe treads upon, and I suppose that fact is beginning to dawn upon other people. She has no idea of it herself, but there is no doubt that she talks to him in a more natural, unreserved way than to any man except her brothers, and that his opinion has a strong influence upon her. We have had a great many sketching and boating expeditions with him this autumn, and he has educated her a good deal, directly and indirectly—lent her Ruskin, and so forth. Poor little girl ! I hope her eyes won't be opened, for

her father would as soon think of bestowing his
daughter's hand upon the piano-tuner or the man who
winds up the clocks as on " that idle sketching fellow,"
as he calls him.   I have often spoken of Zoe's beauty
to you, I am sure, if not of her character.   She has
grown lovelier even than she promised to be.   Her
hair is darker than it was, though there is some golden
brown in it still, and she has that pure, wild rose
complexion that the Winkworths all have, but her eyes
are not so dark as the others.   They are those deep
gray that sometimes look almost hazel.   The children
are clamouring for me to go in the boat with them, so
good-bye !   Don't accuse me of reticence about myself
and my surroundings another time.   I hope the Pro-
fessor is upon his feet again.——Ever your affectionate
sister,   ESTHER MADGEWICK.

5.—SIR WALTER'S VISIT TO STOKESWORTHY.

Miss Winkworth to Mrs. Home.

December 1858.

Good news, my dear Mary.   It is not " he came,
he is gone:" we have him, but the spell is broken.   He
is going to bring his children to the real home.   The
Pratts don't mean to come back at all, and their people
and Meyrick are up to the ears in inventories.   As
soon as they are cleared out, Walter and Co. are
coming back !   Yes, really and truly.   Bessie says I
said " Coming back !" in my sleep last night.   Can't
you fancy how we went poking about in the planta-
tions, and don't you wish you had been there, Mrs.
Mary?   Wouldn't you give all your cockatoos—black,
white, and spotted—for one honest jackdaw, and a

forest of eucalyptus for the stubby old maybush in the
lane ?   It shows how greedy and discontented is human
nature, that, no sooner had we three closed round the
fire, and felt ourselves Wat, Bess, and Doll again, than
we began sighing for Molly.   Walter says you must
come some of these days to show your corn-stalks your
English home.

It was good to see the old fellow so much his
original self, and so enjoying the sight of everything
here, and the welcome from all the people.   I am
doubly certain that it was not of his own free will
that he has banished himself these weary eighteen
years.   His loss has aged him; he is gray, and more
than ever like old Sir Miles by Sir Peter Lely.   Sophia
was the best of wives; but the sister that is in me
will bound up as I feel I have mine own old Wat
again.   Isn't it horrid in me, so much older as I am
than when I felt it before, when he turned to me in
his sorrow for Bertha's sweet young mother.   Imagine,
the children have been kept in complete ignorance that
ever they had a half-sister.   Even the twins, who might
have been expected to remember her, know nothing.
Walter has never heard of the Marinis since the day
he traced them to London, and he has never forgiven
either the deceit or the conduct to his wife, nor is this
a time, while he is still wearing crape, to whisper the
extenuation that the two natures were incapable of
understanding one another.   I almost wonder so good
a woman as Sophia did not make some move towards
reconciliation at last; but the end came suddenly, and
she may have said something on which Walter is silent.
I might with equal justice wonder at ourselves, but
when Bessie begged me in Madeira to let her write to
the poor girl, I said that the advance ought to come

from herself and to her father. And when time went on, and we came home, heard more, and began to yearn after her, the clue was lost.

Walter talked openly about his children, and wishes me to chaperon Zoe, whom he calls a dear, good, affectionate girl, but young for her age, excitable, and too liable to passing impressions. Then he said that he should have been very unwilling to remove her from the influence of her mother's excellent friends, the Bootles, if it had not been that he was bringing her to us; besides, there were influences that—hum—haw—he was sorry to say, went far to neutralise the beneficial ones. I am sure he had put on his High Scale manners, poor old man, but suddenly descending from them when he saw sententiousness disposed me to laugh, he declared that it would be a blessed thing to get into a sensible ugly country not infested with tourists. Bessie told him he was like Guy Mannering, and it proved to be too near the truth, for there really is a "sketching fiddling scamp of an artist, of good family, more's the pity," sighs Walter, "for you can't get rid of him though he has gone and taken to art." Not that there have been any demonstrations, and he believes Zoe to be perfectly sincere so far, but he has been warned by a person qualified to judge (Mrs. Bootle, no doubt. It is odd how the High Scale note gets into his tones when he talks to her), and I can see that poor Bertha has bequeathed a distrust of young girls. If he goes on like that at home, I should wonder at the daughter who could be free and open with him.

This same scamp is, to complicate matters, cousin to Zoe's bosom-friend Miss Warburton, a damsel, with whose £5000 a year this match-making brother of ours hopes to see Miles set up at High Scale. The girl's father belonged to the Warburton-Scotney family, and has long been dead. He married into one of the great coal-proprietors' families in the north, and fortunes have a tendency to flow in upon the young lady. Of the mother, Walter only says she is very tolerable, and will give no trouble. There is no land, only a villa on the lake in High Scale parish, and the young things have been always together. Little Mary and Elizabeth have the reversion of the Warburton governess. I fancy Walter hardly likes her, but that he thinks the ills one knows better than those one does not know.

The artist is the object of my gratitude for driving him south, where he can choose his visitors and send Miles in pursuit of the heiress. It is beginning rather young, but those boys are really twenty-two, though their coming of age was neglected in their mother's illness. No doubt Miles will seem older without Clyffe, who spoke for both, and is evidently preferred, for Walter does not speak enthusiastically of his heir.

Bessie reminds me of post time.—Your loving

D. W.

6.—MILES'S VIEWS ON LEAVING HIGH SCALE.

Miles Winkworth to Lieutenant Ratclyffe Winkworth,
120th Regt., Montreal.

HIGH SCALE, LANGMERE,
Dec. 31, 1858.

Dear Clyffe—Great things are about to happen. My father has made up his mind to go home and to live at Stokesworthy, as the lease is out, and the Pratts are going away. I'm very glad of it. I think people ought to live on their estates, and though this place is very pretty, there's nothing in the world to do here, no shooting to mention, and the place isn't big enough to make occupation even for my father, and certainly not for me—all very well for holidays, for walking and boating; but now, if I am to live at home, I must have something to do with myself. If I'm to be "nothing but a country squire," I think I'd better learn the business, as one can't do in a made-up place like this. I don't see but what looking after your land and your tenants is just as useful and sensible as cutting people's throats, or splitting hairs in a law-court. And everybody can't write books and paint pictures. And as for the friends one has to leave behind, why, I'm not sure that there isn't more satisfaction in an occasional visit to people than in seeing them constantly. At least, the more I see of some people, the less I have to say for myself. *You* always had a tongue in your head, and can talk sometimes to Zoe. Of course she will miss Emily very much, and she is very fond of High Scale, and of all its associations. But I think I feel more with father that the whole place is sad and empty now. With all its beauty and finish, it is a lady's place altogether, and when Oxford is over it wouldn't suit me to live here at all, so hurrah for the Wiltshire turnip tops! Well, there's one piece of news for you. I hope you'll like it. Now for another. It's hard to get thumps from both sides at once; to be considered so very dull and narrow-minded in some quarters, and then to get into disgrace with Sir Walter for my dangerous acquaintances. Now, did Fanshawe come over here after me especially? You asked him in the first instance. Certainly I think he's a capital fellow, and though we differ on every conceivable subject, and fight over everything, I know there's plenty of good stuff in him. Though his mother was an Italian, he chose to be an Englishman himself, though his Roman relations would have made it quite worth his while to give up his Church and country.   He has a trifle of money of his own, and no one dependent on him, so why shouldn't he paint pictures and sell them if he can?   I did think at one time that he must have had an object in being here so much, but we had it out, and he said if I couldn't see that the scenery was object enough for any one, I had no eyes in my head.   However, I'm much mistaken if he hasn't found another object now. When he was always here sketching the waterfall in the autumn, he saw a good deal of Zoe, and then father took fright, and blamed me for encouraging him to come over.   He hasn't been so much here lately; perhaps he sees that he isn't welcome.   Poor little Zoe!   I hope she hasn't taken a fancy to him; of course it isn't the sort of thing one expects for her, but he is a capital fellow.   What do you think?

I shall have no opposition to encounter.   My father has given me to understand that he has perceived my views with regard to Emily, and approves. Much good that is.   But I can't go on in this way. I may be a fool in her eyes, but I won't be a coward, and before the move I mean to speak out.   I don't believe in favourable opportunities.   If she cares for me, she'll say so; and if not, no sort of family encouragement will do any good.   And in that case, I shouldn't care where we went, as long as it was far away from here.   She doesn't often give me a good word, but sometimes I think perhaps girls go by contraries.   She wouldn't be the creature she is, if she cared for position, or money, or good looks, or any of a

fellow's " advantages," as they call them ; and I'm
such an idiot, that if there's any remark she doesn't
like, any view she despises, it comes uppermost when
she's there.   Sometimes I think if you were at home
you'd manage it all better.   But I'm going to take the
fence, and in my next you'll hear if my neck's broken.
I never uttered a word to Zoe on the subject, but,
strange to say, she has found it out.   That's the worst
of being near one's own people on these occasions.

Mr. Meyrick is rejoiced at our coming back to
Stokesworthy, and he and my father exchanged a
great many compliments when he was here the other
day.   Certainly I expect he is a thorough good agent,
and he was always jolly to us when we went down to
shoot.

I may as well mention that your little piece of
business will be concluded very soon, but I cannot
manage it till after next quarter, and as the last
"account rendered " was directed to you, there was a
very narrow escape of Sir Walter's opening it.   I don't
quite like keeping him in the dark, but it will soon be
settled now.   And do recollect in future that twenty
shillings are worth a sovereign, and don't let them run
out without being counted.   Do you recollect Mr.
Meyrick saying once that you never had any small
change in your pocket, nor I on my lips ?   So we did
best together.   I am a little afraid of Mrs. Warburton,
and she does encourage one in such a barefaced way
that it is enough to disgust Emily altogether.—Ever
your loving brother,   MILES WINKWORTH.

The best times we had were looking at the comet;
I am sure it was a lucky star for me.   There was one
night—but never mind all that now.

7.—MISS MADGEWICK'S ANTICIPATIONS OF WILTSHIRE.

Miss Madgewick to Emily.

HIGH SCALE, *January* 1859.

My dear Emily—Why haven't we seen you here for the last three days ? But on second thoughts, never mind ! I don't want to know. One may have one's reasons for things, and at the same time object, like the hostler at Tattersall's, to "put one's name to paper." But "to return from this digression ;" you will agreé with me that three days are not to be treated lightly, when you hear what I have to say. In a little while we shall not be in the least surprised if we don't meet for three *months.* I am as sure as if Sir Walter had told me (which he hasn't, in so many words) that he has made up his mind to go back to Wiltshire to his mouldy melancholy Miz Maze.

In the first place, I heard him say to Miles, at breakfast, not long ago, that the lease of the place was out, and the present tenants going away shortly.

Secondly, every now and then lately he has asked Zoe what she recollects of the house and grounds ; evidently wishing to find out if she remembers enough to have any affection for the place. I think he was half disappointed when it dawned upon him how completely rooted they are at High Scale, and how very little Stokesworthy is to her now, and yet half relieved that her memory was not very clear about it.

I suppose he connects it a good deal with the first years of his marriage. Well, not long after this, he asked me whether, " supposing that he should at any time contemplate leaving High Scale to settle nearer London, I should have any objection to accompanying

his daughters." That was last week, and now—to-day
he starts to see his sisters at Stokesworthy. Isn't this
circumstantial evidence? It is not wonderful that he
should find this place painful, poor man! but there is
another reason. Your cousin *does* come to call upon
Miles very often; and. Sir Walter is not blind to the
fact. (Do you know, I have a shrewd suspicion that
Mrs. Bootle has been giving him a hint of it.) He
would not object to Miles going to see Mr. Fanshawe,
neither would Miles himself; but probably Mr. Fanshawe might not take kindly to that arrangement. I
don't think poor little Zoe has quite taken in the
position of affairs; but I am afraid by the time we
are all transported from the "warm precincts of the
cheerful day" into the dark labyrinths of the Miz
Maze, she will be only too clear as to what her feelings
are. As to my own feelings, there is no doubt about
them. First and foremost, there is the having to leave
you behind; and putting that out of the question,
when one has lived seven years amongst such scenery
as this, one doesn't exactly rejoice in the prospect of
Wiltshire, which I believe to be, of all the counties in
England, the most ugly and the least interesting.
Bare downs for mountains, and for lakes the "hundred
waves of mangel-wurzel that ripple round the lonely
Grange." Then the aunts! What must it be to have
about one two more editions of Sir Walter (which of
course they will be)! I have an exact portrait of
"Aunt Dorothea" in my mind's eye.

But I am writing as long a letter as if I was
already three hundred miles away instead of one.
Come soon, and let us make the most of our short time
together.—Always your affectionate

                                        ESTHER MADGEWICK.

P.S.—It is borne in upon me that the Miz Maze will be like an old château in Bretagne in one of Balzac's novels, out of which my brother once read me some chosen bits. (I certainly shall *not* choose it as a lesson-book for Mary and Lisa.) There was a most vivid description, I remember, of the life at this château.

The baron, his wife, an old maiden sister, an old chevalier, and an old curé, used to sit down every evening to a round game called *mouche.* They always had the same jokes, and always went through the same phrases of triumph and despair; and when the curé held *mistigris* (the knave of clubs, and *the* card of the game), it was invariably found out by the effect upon his nose. *Monsieur le Curé blanchit au bout du nez! Il a mistigris!*

Yes, we shall play *mouche,* or the Wiltshire equivalent; let us say Pope Joan.

8.—EDGAR'S PICTURES OF HIGH SCALE.

Edgar Fanshawe to his friend and cousin, Carlo Monti, at Rome.

HIGH SCALE, *January* 1859.

Dear Carlo—Your letter made me laugh, though in a hollow fashion; but, as you don't know by experience, one may "smile and smile" and be a wretch very worthy of pity. I have not written to you for months you say, but my last letter was so brilliant that you forgive me; you conclude that I am far too pleasantly engaged among charming English friends, painting immortal pictures, and winning besides what, if not so immortal as my fame, is better worth having, to remember you and your dull patient work in the old atelier at Rome. You are such a sarcastic man that you won't believe me when I tell you that the Windermere picture is finished, though it was horribly cold work in the garret of my lodgings where I paint, and I have another little picture nearly finished from the sketch of the old barn at High Scale House I described to you in my last letter. For an English winter, the weather has been splendid, and I have only just begun to wish myself in Italy, but that is not because of the weather. Flatter yourself that I can live no longer apart from you, my friend.

This country is even finer in winter than in summer; it has all the elements of the sublime. I wish you could see it, and I wish you knew Emily Warburton. Her eyes are as brilliant, and her soul as enthusiastic as ever, and she is looking out for philanthropic ways of spending her fortune. Her mother tells me I make her enthusiastic, and is very angry when she drops in upon our talks, but you know I am quite innocent and the most matter-of-fact creature in the world. My aunt thinks, however, that because I paint, I am encouraging Emily to snub Miles Winkworth. On the contrary, if I ventured to hint at the subject to my cousin, I should tell her that an excellent, uncultivated, honest English boy like Miles is the very foil wanted by all her attractions. The fellow is a good fellow really, and he and his sister and brother have been Emily's companions from childhood. He likes me and I like him ; the former is the most remarkable fact, for I can understand how hard it must be to like a mongrel. Yet mongrels have their privileges. At this moment though, I hardly know what they are, for you would not count

among them perhaps being shown by Sir Walter
Winkworth, as plainly as a gentleman can show
another (being a mongrel), that he does not want him
in his house and would like to kick him out of it.   I
thought in the autumn that he was merely a grumpy
old fellow all round, but a mutual friend, as I suppose
she would call herself, has hinted to me that he is
afraid of me,—you know why, I told you enough in
my last letter,—and that he thinks I come too often
to see Miles, and that people are beginning to talk;
their talk seems to matter more in England than in
Italy, Carlo.   I feel melodramatic about it, don't you?
and yet if you saw her, I do not believe you would
understand me.   Such an English girl, dutiful, child-
like, simple and single-thoughted,—very like Miles in
some ways, but as much deeper and wider as a girl
is than a boy,—such a soul of obedience to her father,
and to the memory of her mother, that Emily's
generous vagaries frighten her, because they would
shock them.   A poet could not describe her, because
she is beyond men's imaginations; one can only look,
and feel the influence of such a girl.   I send you a
sketch of her profile, from memory of course, let
nobody see it; I suppose very soon I shall have
nothing but these scraps left.   You have seen angels
with all their own beauty and a child's beauty too;
they are Zoe.   I am going to town directly, for Miles
is going back to Oxford, and it is better for her sake
to take the hints people give one.   When I come
back to High Scale it will be empty.   Sir Walter
Winkworth is going to carry them all off into Wiltshire
to his old family place there.   Emily says that Zoe
will not forget us, but of course she speaks for herself,
and no one could easily forget Emily; besides, girls

are always writing to each other. It is fortunate for me that I have not irretrievably made a fool of myself.

At this moment I hear all the bells in Rome ringing, and wish myself with you. How is the violoncello going on? Do you mean to throw away your palette and fight the Austrians? Sometimes, Carlo mio, I forget I am English, and think that all my strength belongs to our beautiful mother, Italy. Shall I go back? there is after all nothing to keep me here. Write again and tell me all your news, and remember me to your people.—Ever yours,

EDGAR FANSHAWE.

9.—EDGAR'S DEPARTURE.

Edgar to Miles.

HIGH SCALE, *January* 1859.

Dear Miles—It might be better for me to go off without saying anything, but I think we have been too friendly for that. I suppose I am not likely to meet you or any of your people again for a long time; this move to Wiltshire would have separated us thoroughly, even if I had not discovered that it is better for me to run away. There are gossips at High Scale and mischief-makers, and I cannot bear that they should cause any annoyance to your sister. I do not think it is my fault, for I have restrained myself, as you may have guessed. I see there would be great opposition, for, to begin with, I am not considered her equal, and what is worse, I have no reason to believe that she wishes things were otherwise. Even fame would not do me much good, I suspect, and that seems just

now far enough away.   I shall not forget our many
pleasant hours.——Yours most truly,

EDGAR FANSHAWE.

10.——ALGERNON'S LUCUBRATIONS ON THE FUTURE.

Passages from Algernon Bootle's Diary.

HIGH SCALE VICARAGE, January 1859.

At the commencement of my twenty-third year I
now intend to begin a regular diary of my life.   I feel
that it is destined to be a remarkable one, and though
my good father too often shows himself unappreciative
of my present, and incredulous of my future, my dear
mother's sympathy invariably confirms that faith in
myself which all great men have been conscious of in
their youth.

All great careers have had humble beginnings,
and have begun among humble surroundings.   I will
therefore not apologise, even to myself, at inserting in
this my silent companion——my diary——the small
events of every day.   The future will show what effect
they have had upon the career of him who was so
calmly and unobtrusively waiting among them for the
moment which was to reveal what he really was to the
world.

I will record as accurately as I can the events of this
morning, which indeed has not been wholly uneventful.

10 A.M.——I was sitting by the fire with a book in
my hand,——I am not ashamed to say that it was a
classic author,——when my dear mother came up to me
looking flustered and flurried, and evidently intending
to disturb my studies.   I strive ever to be mindful of
my duties to· my parents, whose only son ought to

combine in himself the comfort which might have been
produced by a larger family. (Query, could a larger
family produce more comfort to them than I do?)   I
at once put my book down and listened to what she
had to say.

"My dearest Algernon," she began, "Sir Walter
has been here.   And do you know they mean to give
up the house here and go away to Stokesworthy, and it
is all because of that young Fanshawe.   I'd Fanshawe
him, if I had my way!"

"Gently, gently, my dear mother," I said, seeing by
this turn of expression that she was much irritated.
"What can Fanshawe have to do with it?"

"Why, he's after Zoe, that's what it is.   I thought
that was it when he went on here so long, and at last
took Miss Postlethwaite's lodgings and turned the loft
into a studio, as he calls it ; why can't he say study,
like other people?   So I had Miss Mixton to tea the
day you were out."

"Who is Miss Mixton?"

"Why that old maid cousin of Emily Warburton's
who stays so often with Mrs. Warburton ; and she
tells me that Mr. Fanshawe's always hanging about the
place, and he and Miles and Emily and Zoe, in the
autumn, were always playing that new game, with
balls that you push through hoops, and she notices
it's always Miles and Emily against Mr. Fanshawe
and Zoe.   And one wet day he drew her and made her
push her hair back and show her ears in a way that,
as Miss Mixton says, isn't modest ; and she believes one
day he gave her a rose, and she wore it in the band of
her frock.   And once, Miss Mixton says, they had a
fire on a wet afternoon, and Zoe went too near it in
her great big crinoline, and as near as possible set

herself on fire, and Mr. Fanshawe started up looking as white as a sheet, and pulled her back just as her frock was beginning to scorch, and when they said good-bye, Miss Mixton heard Zoe say, " I shan't forget what you saved me from to-day," and he said, " Please don't do it again," and they both got red and stood holding each other's hands ever so long.   So I thought it was only right by you to tell Sir Walter all this as strongly as I could."

I cannot say that I was pleased to hear this little narrative from my mother.   I have always intended to marry Zoe myself some day, and I shall be extremely angry if a mere superficial young fop, like Edgar Fanshawe, engages her affections before I think it well to speak.   On the whole, I agree that nothing could be much better, under the circumstances, than that Zoe should be removed from the neighbourhood of this young artist, if it were not also the fact that she would also be thus removed from my influence, and in me from the only person who can give her character that feminine solidity which it requires.

" So," my mother went on, " I spoke to Sir Walter seriously as to what Miss Mixton had told me, and he told me that he was very much obliged, for, as it was his full intention that Miles should marry Emily Warburton, there was danger that the intimacy between Miles's sister and Emily's cousin would increase, as they were all living in the same place, and to-day he comes up and tells me that for many reasons, among which not the least was my kind warning, he had made up his mind to leave High Scale and to return to the Miz Maze at Stokesworthy."

As I was unwilling to hear my mother dilating on the misfortune that Sir Walter's departure would be to

High Scale in general, and to me in particular, I now
resumed my Horace, and she went off. I studied the
poet with apparent assiduity, but

> " My eyes
> Were with my heart, and that was far away." .

Before very long a bell rang, and I went into the
drawing-room. The visitor, whom I had seen through
the trees coming up the drive, was pretty Zoe Winkworth herself, with a clothing club book in her hand,
about which she had come to speak to my mother.
My mother sent word that she was occupied at that
moment, but would come if Zoe would wait a little.
She did not come for three-quarters of an hour, during
which, as she no doubt intended, I entertained Zoe in
the drawing-room. Zoe never seems to have much to
say to me ; is it modesty or deficiency of intellect ?
After we had remarked on the weather, she began
turning over the club-books on the table. One was
Westward Ho ! ordered unfortunately by Miss Madgewick, and intended to be passed on by my mother
immediately, and I need not say, *unread*. She looked
at it with envious eyes. I asked if *she* had read it.

"I mayn't," she said ; "papa says he's a Chartist,
and won't let the book come into the house."

"Sir Walter," I said, "is perfectly right. No
young lady should defile her hands with the works of
one whose aim is to sap the foundations of all
government, whether in politics or religion."

"I don't believe his aim is any such thing," she
said, indignantly ; "I believe he sympathises with the
oppressed against the oppressors, if you like, and so do I."

"That is the cant phrase," I observed, wishing to
instruct her in a more practical view of life, "which

produced such acts as those of which the so-called
Italian patriots are, I regret to say, too often guilty.
Take, for instance, Orsini's diabolical (for I can call it
no less) attempt on the life of the Emperor Napoleon only
last year.   If I were you, Zoe, I would not utter words
which implied that I sympathised, in however small
a degree, with such atrocious crimes.   Think of your
family, thorough true blue Tories from time immemorial,
and do not say things which sound as if they had been
inspired by an Italian drawing-master."

"Thank you," said Zoe, with a little bow, and a
smile on her lips which I could not understand, though
I hope she understood the delicately veiled allusion to
Edgar Fanshawe, whose mother is an Italian, and who
has been brought up much in Italy.   "I have no
doubt you have a wide acquaintance with Italian
drawing-masters, and I am afraid they must have been
unfavourable specimens.   I never came across one
myself.   Do you think Mrs. Bootle will be at leisure
soon ? if not, I must go home."

As this moment my mother entered, and Zoe
performed her business with her in a very brief space
of time.   As I let her out at the garden gate, her
silent and evidently displeased manner led me to say :
" I hope, Zoe, that you do not resent my frank avowal
of my political views ?"

"Resent ?" she said, laughing ; "why should I ?
They are exactly what I should have expected from you."

Yes, she knows I am solid and consistent !

" But I suppose," she went on quietly, " it is only
natural that you should think as you do.   If you had
ever been to a public school, like Miles and Walter,
you would have had a chance of learning to stand up
for any one who was bullied.   I hope you will learn

it soon, for it seems to me the chief use of life. It
must be a great disadvantage to you to have to begin
to learn it at your age."

Why is it that I dislike Zoe to speak of my never
having been to a public school ? and why do I also
feel inclined to dislike *her* when she speaks to me as
she did then, as if we were upon an equality ? Some
say that all women are conceited. Can Zoe share this
foible ? I do not wish to think so. Yet if not,
would she not perceive more truly the great gulf
between her intellect and mine ?—mine, which has
carried me through a second class in honours, which I
firmly believe would have been a first but for the
partiality of the examiners.

As she went down the steep lane below, I paced
along the grass on the top, and I heard a girl's voice
greeting her with, " There you are at last, Zoe !" I
believe it was Emily Warburton. To which she
replied something which I could not hear, but it
sounded like, " That idiot !"

What idiot, I wonder ?

11.—WARE MILES !

Emily Warburton to Zoe Winkworth.

TRIERMAIN, HIGH SCALE,
January 1859.

O my dear Zoe ! if you ever cared for me, don't
let him do it. Tell him I can't bear baronets, or eldest
sons, or handsome men, and that I detest grooves.

Tell him that I love one, and love no more, and
that is Amyas Lee, the blind giant. Tell him my
vocation is to Black Joe's Pit, and that it would be

base to desert it. Tell him that there's nothing so
stupid as going and marrying, and that I shall never
forgive him if he sets on Sir Walter and mamma to
worry me, and destroy all our peace and comfort.

We four have run about together, plagued Algy
Bootle, and "paidlit in the burn from morning sun
till dine," and got into deadly disgrace for it too, much
too long for anything so stupid to come between us. I
like the dear old slow and steady fellow much too well
to endure his taking such nonsense into his head. I
am sure it is all Sir Walter's doing. Now isn't it ?—
Your devoted old savage,   EMILY.

12.—MILES'S VENTURE.

Miles Winkworth to Emily Warburton.

CHRIST CHURCH, OXFORD,
Jan. 1859.

My dear Emily—It did not need your letter to
Zoe to show me how little encouragement you are likely
to give to the hopes, which you must know are not new,
but are entwined with every memory of that childish
time which *you* seem to think ought to make such feelings unlikely or impossible. You avoided me when I
was at home, and made it impossible for me to speak.
When you ran away from me and treated me coldly,
Zoe endeavoured to "account for your conduct" to me.

There is one line in your letter that gives me a ray
of hope. You say "it is all Sir Walter." No, no; if
my father would not hear of it, it would make no
difference. What had my father to do with the hours
we spent together, with the rides and walks when I
learned to love you ? Never dream for a moment

again that I have fallen in with anyone's wishes. So I write when away from home, and to yourself, to tell you that I have loved you all my life, and shall love you for ever. I ask you to be my wife. I will leave in your mind no possible doubt of my feelings and intentions. Don't fancy the continuation of our childish friendship could ever content me again. And I did hope last summer when you listened to some of my plans, when you saw how much I missed Clyffe, and was at a loss without him, that something more than kindness——

I don't suppose I have put into words half what I feel, but if I wrote for ever I could say no more than that you have always been my star, and will be to my life's end. Whatever you think of me, never doubt the true and faithful love of

MILES WINKWORTH.

13.—EMILY'S REFUSAL.

Emily Warburton to Miles Winkworth.

TRIERMAIN, HIGH SCALE,
January 1859.

My dear Miles—I suppose you could not help it, but I did hope my letter to Zoe would have settled the matter, and that you would not have been deluded by what they say of commonplace young ladies. Indeed, it cannot be. People don't marry playfellows exactly like brothers to them, as I trust you will still remain when all this folly has passed away. Please put it out of your head, and let us all be comfortable again. If you tease me about it, or make mamma do so, I shall have to keep out of your way, and really dislike you.   If anything could make me glad of your all leaving High Scale, it would be this.   I do so wish you had not done it.——Your (I don't know what, except not your)   EMILY B. WARBURTON.

14.——EMILY'S ENTREATY.

Emily to Zoe.

January 1859.

There ! he has been and gone and done it !   Could not you stop him ?   But I forgive you !   Only, Zoe, my dear Zoe, remember how lonely I am, and do not let it keep you from me ; I think that would break my heart.   Let us leave it all as one of the little follies of those old " grown-ups," and be the same Zoe and Em. as ever.   E. B. W.

15.——MILES'S DISAPPOINTMENT.

Miles Winkworth to Zoe Winkworth.

CHRIST CHURCH, OXFORD,
Jan. 27, 1859.

Dear Zoe——It is all of no use, as indeed I feared it must be ; but I was determined to leave no stone unturned.   Never let your friendship for her be interfered with.   Remember she has behaved perfectly well to me ; but I am not made of stuff fine enough for such as she.

Don't mention the subject again, and don't let father do so.   And don't worry about me, for I shall get on perfectly well, I have no doubt.——Ever your loving brother,   MILES WINKWORTH.

D

16.—Zoe looking at the Flats.

Zoe to Emily.

HIGH SCALE, *Jan.* 28, 1859.

Dearest Emily—You need not be afraid. I cannot help being grieved and disappointed, but though we cannot be sisters, we can be friends as much as ever. We have lived as one, and shared too many thoughts and resolutions, for the double strand of our life to be easily untwisted.

Only, my dear, never think that Miles did not act of his own accord. Clyffe would tell you the same, for Miles has been ridiculous about you ever since he began to be a man. Papa never put it into his head; indeed, papa would much rather he had waited till he had taken his degree. It would have been more *selon les regles.* I don't think that papa knows what has come to pass.

He is in haste to get away to Stokesworthy, and seems hurt to find that I cannot look forward more to it. The Miz Maze is his home, and the having seen it and his sisters seems to have revived all his love for it; and yet we are leaving my dear mother's grave here. I cannot tell you how I dread it. I know he is going back, because I have failed in being such a head of the house as he would like; and when I am watched by two critical pairs of eyes, besides his own, I shall lose my powers altogether. I shall do worse than ever, and they will think it all perverseness.

Do you know, I sometimes wish I were as tiny as you. If I wasn't so tall and stately, people would pity me; but as the shyer and more wretched I am, the more dignified and grim I look, they think it is all pride and obstinacy, and so perhaps it is. I wish there was any understanding one's self, or making one's self better. Of course I do not mean that there is not grace and help to enable one to do so, but I wish I could feel myself improving, or being a comfort to papa, and a guide to my sisters. But life seems to me all flat, like the "good turnip country," instead of our mountains and lakes.

I have all those water-colours, that Mr. Fanshawe helped us with, framed to hang round my room. How many happy days they will recall! I never seemed to have really seen anything before he showed us how to look at it. There is one that is all his—of one of our great boulders, with the sunset reflected in the lake, which is *too* beautiful. It must be very valuable; I wonder whether he meant me to keep it. Do find out.—Your ever affectionate   ZOE.

17.—EMILY'S MURMURS.

Emily Warburton to Miss Madgewick.

TRIERMAIN, *Feb.* 4, 1859.

My dearest Enchantress—You always told me that no true woman need ever receive an offer which she meant to decline. Either your sorcery is at fault or I am not a true woman, or else the parental pressure was too strong. That poor old Miles has been and perpetrated a lumbering letter to me. Why could not his father and my mother have let us alone? It is very hard that all this should come between us to spoil my comfort in those who have best made up to me for the want of brothers and sisters. I think Zoe

does understand that I have higher aims than propping
up a stupid old baronetage. She is very dear, and
promises that this tiresome affair shall not interfere
with us. But I dread the effects of that lot of old
aunts, and the general pressure of county! So I look
to you to keep them from poisoning her mind; and I
am sure you will tell me what every one is like, and
whether you are lost in the Miz Maze or can find a
clue to escape the Minotaurs—*i.e.* the old aunts, who
are no doubt Sir Walter in petticoats. I hope they
won't devour my Zoe; but no doubt all plans for
parish work will be as effectually stifled as in Bootledom. Any tidings of the "Thing of Life" will be
welcome if I can convey them to poor Edgar.—Your
affectionate   EMILY.

18.—MISS MADGEWICK'S CONSOLATIONS.

Miss Madgewick to Emily.

HIGH SCALE, *February* 1859.

My dear Child—I am neither going to unsay my
dictum, nor to let you accuse yourself of not being a
true woman. This is a case in which a much more
experienced woman than you are could not well have
managed better. If Miles had been older he would
have been more manageable; but, after all, he is only
a boy, and boys will be blundering and wrong-headed.
You could not help it; you did all you could to keep
·out of his way, and make him understand you, and he
can't feel that he has been badly used. But I must
say one word in his favour. It is not *all* his father's
doing. I believe his love for you is as genuine as
everything else about him; though perhaps if he had

been, as you say, left alone, he would hardly have put his fate to the touch in such a hurry. But there is no reason that this should make any difference in your friendship with the rest of the family. Sir Walter may be vexed and disappointed, but he can't blame you, and time will cure Miles. He is a thoroughly good fellow, and one must like and respect him, but there is not *enough* of him for you; he is born to be a Wiltshire squire. I am indeed sorry that you should have to give such pain to him and to Zoe just at this particular time; but one can't get through the world without saying "No" sometimes; and there ·is no doubt, in this case, that you have done what is really best for all of them, as well as yourself. Good-bye, my dear child, never forget our watchword: *Zum höchsten Dasein immerfort zu streben,* and never marry a man who can't help you to act up to your ideal.

I will send you full particulars of our life at the Miz Maze, and do my best to keep your Zoe from withering under the baleful influence of "the aunts" and "county respectability."—Ever your affectionate
                                            ESTHER MADGEWICK.

19.—SIR WALTER'S PLANS.

Sir Walter Winkworth to Miles.

HIGH SCALE, WESTMORELAND,
February 1859.

My dear Miles—When I last spoke to you of my hopes for your future, nothing was said of any arrangements which I might be able to make in case you should be so fortunate as to secure Miss Warburton's affections. I do not wish you to hurry her choice, or to take action before you feel that the way lies open;

but I should be glad to be assured of your own intentions, as I have just received a very advantageous proposal for letting High Scale, which, however, I should certainly keep in my own hands if I thought it probable that you would marry and wish to reside there; and I hope, my dear boy, that you will not allow any youthful distaste to the responsibilities of life to prevent you from making every effort to secure the happiness which, I am convinced, it is in your power to attain. Such a hope should add zest to all your studies, and be a safeguard against many temptations.—Believe me, my dear boy, your affectionate father,

WALTER WINKWORTH.

20.—OVERTHROW BY MILES.

Miles to Sir Walter.

CHRIST CHURCH, OXFORD,
February 1859.

My dear Father—There is nothing to prevent your letting High Scale. Miss Warburton has already refused me, so I am not likely to wish to live there. It is perhaps as well that you should know that the matter is at an end, to prevent any further discussion on the subject.—I am, my dear father, your affectionate and dutiful son,   MILES WINKWORTH.

21.—THE DRAGON OF HIGH SCALE.

Edgar to Emily.

EBURY STREET, LONDON, *February.*

My dear Emily—As you insist, with what is firmness in you, but what would be obstinacy in another

woman, in knowing my full reason for running away
suddenly the other day, I will confess that it was Mrs.
Bootle. · I know that you and I had talked it over,
and grumbled, and despaired, and yet found a few
husks of hope to feed upon.   It was left for Mrs.
Bootle ·to collect these in her parochial basket and
carry them with tracts to feed some other prodigal.
Don't lose your patience, I won't be poetical.   I will
copy Mrs. Bootle, who certainly was prosaic enough ;
the dullest mind could not have misunderstood her.
She met me in the road; stopped me resolutely, and
spoke—I need not say, as a friend—warning me that
the whole neighbourhood was talking, and assuring me
that my constant visits were the chief reason of Sir
Walter's going away.   Most inconsiderate, she said,
for Miss Winkworth ; in fact she went on for some
time.   I did not hear all she said, for there was an
effect of red sun and dark clouds across the lake which
took off my attention.   It came back just in time to
catch her last words : " Well, good-bye, Mr. Fanshawe !
I see advice is wasted on you."   She was gone.   Now,
you may despise me for being influenced by Mrs.
Bootle, but I thought the matter over, and it seemed
that the best thing was to take myself off.   I am not
so foolish as to think that my doings make any difference to anybody, and I certainly don't think myself
important enough to move a whole household from
Westmoreland to Wiltshire. , That way of putting the
case is thoroughly Bootle.   But if people will " talk,"
the only way is to remove the subject of discussion.
I will come back by-and-by, if your mother and you
care to see me, when the Winkworth move is over.

I am sorry about Miles, but you are of course the
best judge in your own affairs.   I don't quite agree

about grooves, though I know I am inconsistent. In
this restless world it is good to have a rock under one's
feet. After all, sun, moon, stars, mountains, are the
foundations of life. Don't think I am going to turn
Tory, but a soul quite loyal to heaven and home is rare
and beautiful. There is some family likeness between
Miles and his sister.

What do you think of this improved sketch for the
school chapel ? My uncle may call it fantastic, but
you want something. as different as possible from the
children's own homes. We-must raise a little wonder
in their minds. Would painted windows make the
room too dark ? I know a fellow who would work
out thoroughly well any designs we gave him. He
has a feeling for colour, and it would be a kindness to
him, as well as an advantage to ourselves, to send him
to Belgium to look at windows there.

Tell me any news you can. Did I ever say that
one of my sketches, the one with the hair pushed back,
reminds me of an English lady I met in Italy the last
time I was there ? It is an unusual outline. This
lady knew something of the Winkworths. I forget
how their name came up, for I did not know them well
then, or care particularly about them ! I might have
mentioned it before, but you know I never have more
than one thing in my head at a time. The Windermere picture is messy, and I feel half inclined not to
send it in. I like the Barn-door better myself, but
the R.A. may not agree with me, as I very often don't
with them, and it is perhaps as well to have two
strings to one's bow. My love to your mother.—
Yours affectionately,   EDGAR FANSHAWE.

22.—SIR WALTER UPON GROOVES.

Sir Walter to his sister Dora.

HIGH SCALE, *February* 1859.

My dear Dorothea—As I told you my hopes for my eldest boy's future, it seems but right to inform you that they are not likely to be realised at present. Miles has proposed to Miss Warburton, and she has refused him.   Such reasons for the refusal as have been mentioned to me appear to my mind utterly insufficient and absurd; but there may be some more cogent reason in the background—an unavowed preference for another suitor, for instance.   In that case, of course Miles has no chance, but if, on the other hand, the motives Miss Warburton assigns be the real ones, I do not think he need despair.

Zoe has carefully explained to me : "You see, Emily thinks it would be too *groovy* to marry Miles ;" but I confess this conveys nothing to my mind beyond the fact that Miss Emily must be more foolish than I thought her.   There was no talk of things being "groovy" in our young days; not merely because we were contented to use words which were to be found in the dictionary, but because it seemed to us an advantage rather than an objection when anything proposed to us came in the natural course of things, and had the sanction of parents and friends.   I fear the young people of the present day are bitten with a desire to do something out of the common way, no matter whether that something be bad or good.

I confess it makes me anxious to find Zoe sympathising with any feeling of that kind, so on this and other accounts, I have determined to hasten our move, and you may expect to see us at the Miz Maze very shortly.

There must necessarily be some pain to myself in the revival of old associations, but it will be outweighed by the benefit of the change for my children, and the pleasure of being near you and Bessie once more. I have felt very acutely of late the want of some one near me to whom I could speak quite freely, and you, my dear sisters, will supply this want in the best and most natural way.

Hoping that Bessie's cold has left her, and with Zoe's love to you both,—I am, your affectionate brother,
WALTER M. WINKWORTH.

23.—PACKING UP.

Lisa Winkworth to Frank Winkworth, Harrow.

HIGH SCALE, *March* 10, 1859.

My dear Frank—Every one is packing, and Miss Madgewick wants the lesson-books, as they have to go to-morrow, so I have got a holiday ; but it is horrid and uncomfortable, and everybody is so cross, and always taking away the things one wants.   I can't see why we may not stay on here ; I am sure it must be much nicer than that stupid old Wiltshire can be.

Zoe is always crying up in her room (*she* says she has got a cold, but I am sure it is crying), and I *know* Polly cries, because I hear her at night, but she hardly speaks at all all day, and is quite cross if any one says anything.   She says : "Papa was born in Wiltshire, and we were born here, so of course he likes it best," and snaps at me if I talk about it.   And then there is some secret, I know, and Emily has got something to do with it. She hardly comes to see us at all, and she is crosser than any one else when she *does* come. I don't think that is fair, for us to have all this bother going away, and Emily to make it worse by being cross. *She* has not got half so much to make her unhappy as we have.

I am sorry to say papa won't let me take any of the rabbits, and only one kitten,—the black one. He said at first there were plenty of such things in Wiltshire without bringing them; but I persuaded him to let me bring just Blackie. The ponies and all the dogs, except poor old Jock, are coming with us. I have no more to say, and it is getting dark.—I remain, your affectionate sister, LISA.

P.S.—Don't tell any one I said that about Emily.

PART II.

IN THE MIZ MAZE.

I remember, I remember !

24.—Aunt Dora's Gladness.

Miss Winkworth to Mrs. Home.

Dower House, *March* 14, 1859.

Dearest Mary—Here are all the dear ones! We all met on the Hall steps, and the old rooms are ringing once more with the Winkworth voices, and Walter sits in his proper place again under our great-grandfather's picture, and Bessie and I feel twice ourselves and quite young again, in spite of the new generation. They are fine handsome creatures, these children, though Miles will be better looking by and by, when he has overcome the heaviness that clings about fine young men in the undeveloped stage. He has honest brown eyes, but is dull and silent to a disappointing degree. The poor fellow has gone through a great deal this year, and they say he has never been the same without Clyffe, his double. There was his rejection, too, though he seems too boyish and loutish to feel such a thing much. He is shy, for, though courteous as his father's son must be, he never opened his lips voluntarily all the evening. As to his sister, I don't wonder the name puzzled you. It is Sophia, but Sophy became Goee on her brother's baby lips, and Zoe, in spite of her father's dislike to nicknames, adheres as part of the fitness of things. For she has the same delicate Greek profile as poor Bertha, and the new way of doing the hair sets it off. Her complexion is very pretty, and her eyes lovely. She does the honours prettily, only shyly, and as if she were afraid of her father; and he has the High Scale manner, as I feared, when he sits at the head of his table. He seems to expect so much of his children, and to be always pulling them out to his standard, till the elastic young nature recoils into as small a space as possible. Only Lisa, as they call Elizabeth, can do no wrong in his eyes, and he seems to think Zoe hard on her. The governess is young for a widower's family, small, pale, keen, and very modern, Miss Madgewick by name, but the children seem fond of her. We shall get on best with the young ones; the others cannot be quite as if they had grown up with us, and we must not be unreasonable or exacting.

Zoe asked about parish work, and looked astounded (as I felt) when Walter, like imperial Jove himself, decreed: " Understand, Zoe, that you do nothing with-. out your aunt's directions. I will discuss the matter with her, and she will let you know what you may undertake."

Thursday.—Walter came in and interrupted my letter. He is so much more natural down here than in his big house. He stands on his dignity with his children; he can't with us, but he is perplexed, and afraid of the girls' heads being turned by "Mr. Bernard's vagaries," wishing them safe back with his Bootles. We assured him that it was Mr. Bernard's sister, not himself, who was unscrupulous, and that the vagaries of eighteen years ago were the ordinary practice now. I had some trouble to avoid a flat promise that Zoe should never be left alone with the Vicar; but he was tolerably satisfied on Sunday that things had not gone much beyond what he left them ; and some advanced Church he saw a few weeks ago has shown him that Mr. Bernard does not go all lengths. So Zoe may teach, visit, and help in general under me. Poor little maiden ! I can see how that stipulation takes out all the zest of it ; I won't be very obnoxious, or make her feel the leading-strings.

Miles is to be sent to read abroad with a tutor. He has kept his terms, and his father does not want him to go back to Christ Church, but thinks he will do better with some one to keep him up to his work. He is rather a perplexity to his father, and there is some unexplained mystery about money matters that makes my brother anxious, and sure that he is not treated with confidence. If I could only get him to unbend or show those children the side we knew in him, how good it would be for all !—Your loving

D. W.

25.—POLLY'S FIRST SIGHT OF WILTSHIRE.

Mary to Frank.

THE MIZ MAZE, *March* 17.

My dear Frank—Zoe sends you her love, and bids me tell you that she cannot write this week, she is so very busy.

We have been here about three days, but it seems much longer. It is nicer than I expected, but it is all dreadfully tidy. The house is very big, and there will be plenty of room to play battledore in the gallery when it rains.

Aunt Dora and Aunt Bessie are very kind, but I always feel afraid of breaking Aunt Bessie ; she is just like an old china cup, only prettier.

E

The stables are very grand, nearly as large as the
house.   They say this is because there is such good
hunting here.   People talk about hunting as if it were
the only thing to be done here.   The gardens are all
very trim, and there are straight rows of hyacinths
and tulips all down each side of the straight gravel
paths.   There are no nice holes and corners like
what we had at High Scale, and all the people look
stupid, and wear smock-frocks, as they call them.
It is rather a pretty church, with a painted east
window in memory of papa's first wife.   I did not
know he had been married before.   Poor papa, how
much trouble he has had in his life !   Good-bye, dear
Frank.—I remain, your very affectionate sister,

MARY WINKWORTH.

26.—ZOE IN A BUSTLE.

Zoe to Emily.

THE MIZ MAZE, *March* 14th.

One line, dearest Emily, to say we are safely arrived.
Salisbury spire is the only beautiful thing that has
met my eyes yet.   It is not flat· here, but dreary,
lengths of white road rising over hedgeless green hills ;
and when you get to the top, there's just such another
white stage between you—not a single thing meets the
eye that Mr. Fanshawe could make a picture of.

This is a great white house, the fitting growth of
such a country.   That is all I know yet, for I am
stealing a moment to write to you before breakfast,
when what the boys call the bear-fight of settling-in
will begin.

The aunts were here to greet us ; I can hardly
believe that Aunt Bessie is the youngest.   Anyway, I

am sure Aunt Dora is the *husband* one—she has *such*
a pair of eyes. I know now where Lisa got hers
from. They seem to look one through and through
and through, and she is as alert as if she were sixteen.
I tremble, but papa looks at rest with her—rather as
Polly used to do when she had got her own nursery
and her own Nana after the horrors of company downstairs. If he is happy, I'll bear anything. Aunt
Bessie is a gentle, tearful, old downy pussy-cat, minus
claws, made to pet and be petted. Gong sounding.—
Your loving   ZOE.

27.—EMILY'S OTHER SIDE.

Emily to Zoe.

TRIERMAIN, HIGH SCALE,
March 1859.

My dearest Life—Now you are gone, and we shall
not meet at once after it, I must say something that
stuck fast while everybody was fussing about. I mean
how much I owe to that dear mother of yours. If it had
not been for her, I should have gone on thinking religion
only something that made Sunday dull, and that was
embodied in Bootledom. But if anything so shocking
could befall me as being stitched into a tract, and dis-
tributed by Mrs. Bootle, my conversion would certainly
be dated from that day—don't you remember it?—when
we were caught playing at being at church; Clyffe, in an
old black waterproof as Mr. Bootle's gown, preaching a
sermon, chiefly consisting of " Beloved, I say, beloved
brethren, there's a black sheep in the corner ;" the said
black sheep being Miles, who would have nothing to
do with it, though at every pause we shouted Amen.
I shall never forget how dear Lady Winkworth talked

to the spoilt, ill-taught girl so gently and tenderly, and how, when I looked into those sweet true eyes, things grew real to me. Then there were those Sunday hours when I stayed with you between services, and she read us Mrs. Sherwood's *Stories on the Catechism*, and thought she asked us the questions; but I see, on looking at the book, that she made them her own, and altered them. She could assimilate nothing that was not good, and true, and wholesome, and even Mrs. Bootle was never her real self with her, for she drew out the best, and repressed whatever jarred. Then there were those readings before our Confirmation! How she made soül and self long to be devoted! I am afraid she was vexed with me afterwards, when she could not sympathise with all the new vigorous hopes of Church life I brought from the Fanshawes, and which seemed to us the natural outcome of her own teaching. I never could understand it, for she was above Mrs. Bootle's style of prejudice ; but Cousin Charles told me that she had had a great shock from some one who Romanised, and that made her dread all such ideas. Then I hardly saw her during the last sad year; yet even the very looking at her window woke up all that was good in me, just as Mrs. Bootle stirs up all that is spit-fire and flippant. Do you remember that saying of mine, the nine days' horror of High Scale, that it was very nasty not to be worldly ? If I were left to unmitigated Bootledom, I fear it might become my motto. Mrs. Bootle is ever so much worse now that there is no one to keep her within bounds. Nothing but the thought of Black Joe's Pit, and my dear little orphans that are to be, keeps me in any order at all. I wonder if I may call the place St. Joseph's.

We are going to the Fanshawes in March, and
thence to London, so I shall have some good Lent services. I'm sure I want good done to me. For oh,
Zoe mine, a course of *ryling* is not wholesome for the
moral constitution. I am going to look at your
mother's photograph to subdue myself withal.—Your
loving   EMILY.

28.—MILES ON HIS REJECTION.

Miles Winkworth to Ratclyffe Winkworth.

THE MIZ MAZE,
STOKESWORTHY, *March.*

Dear Clyffe—Here I am in a maze, literally and
figuratively. It is uncommonly odd to find one's self in
this new old home. I always did like the place when
we came down to the aunts. I like the old-fashioned
gardens, and the shrubbery walk down to the Dower
House; and I think I remember the back premises,
the stable yard, and farm buildings. There is a pond
into which I recollect pushing you, and getting into a
scrape accordingly. The village of course we have
often seen, and people make many inquiries after you,
and can't quite tell which of us has turned up here.
It seems to be rather a large neighbourhood, and the
place is beset with callers and invitations. Zoe is in
an excitement of delight at the chance of doing the
young lady of the village, and is full of schools and old
women My father takes me about; he seems to enjoy
renewing old acquaintances, but I hate strangers, and
have .nothing to say. If things had been different
indeed! Of course you have guessed that I had no
good news, or I shouldn't have left you so long without

a letter.   It is all up with me, and I don't see that
there is much use in saying any more about it.

Perhaps if I had waited, and not forced myself upon
her after what she said, it might have been better;
but I was determined she should not think that my
father was the chief mover in the business.   Zoe came
to me mysteriously, and gave me so many hints, and
was so horridly sympathetic, that I got savage, and
made her explain herself.

"Emily had other views," she said.   Then I said
she ought to have warned me; she knew how it was,
and she should have told me who had come in my way.

"Oh," she said, "Miles! don't be so fierce; there's
no one in particular."

"What do you mean by ' other views,' then ?" I said.

Then she said that *I* wasn't Emily's ideal.   "How
do you know that ?" I asked her.   And she said Emily
had always described quite another sort of person to her.

"Well, but who is this person; where has she met
him ?"

"Oh, only in her imagination," said Zoe.   "She
never expects to meet him, but she never means to
marry unless she does.   I don't think she ever will
marry."

I laughed, and Zoe was shut up.   I *did* think that
her imaginations had given way to reality when poor
Fanshawe was here; but I don't know.   I think girls
haven't much heart.   As long as they think no one can
blame *them*, they don't care what a poor fellow feels;
he may go to the dogs as well as not.

The end of it was that I made her show me a letter
Emily had written to her.   There had been one day of
skating and going home together afterwards, when I had
hoped there was a chance for me.   But I suppose she

found me out, and writes to try to get Zoe to prevent
me from speaking; as if she thought that if I didn't
speak, I could go on being *friendly*.   Well—never
mind—there was no mistake about her refusal, and
she would treat it as a sort of aberration which my
slow, easy-going nature would get over in no time.   It
was very hard work to get through the term; but I
don't mean to justify the opinion she has formed of
me, and get plucked if I can help it.   I think I should
have stayed up and read, if I hadn't been wanted here
" to take my place in the county," as father says.   I
must say I think I never met a more stupid, dull set
of people.   I have kept all my terms now, so my
father wants me to stay down for this term and read
with Algy Bootle; but if I can, I shall get him to let
us go abroad together.   Algy is more of a muff than
ever; but he *can* coach one, and in other matters of
course I can make him do as I choose.   I only wish
we could go with Fanshawe.   He would do all the
talking, and he enlivens one's ideas; but such is the
prejudice that I can't suggest it.   Of course I must
take to Stokesworthy some time.   Just now I feel as
if I hated everybody there.   The only comfort is that
no living soul knows about Emily; but how can I go
making new acquaintances, when I feel as if I should
like to hang myself?   Well, she may despise one for
being *groovy*, as she calls it, but I shall stick to my
grooves all the same in the long run.   I couldn't write
about it before, even to you, and I *could* not read last
term.   I got more stupid than ever.   Zoe says that
you and I have only one tongue between us, and she
wishes you would send it home by the next post.   I
wish I could go after it.—Yours ever,

MILES WINKWORTH.

29.—A Schoolroom Maid's View of the Miz Maze.

From Fanny Martin, schoolroom maid at the Miz Maze, to Mrs. Warburton's housemaid.

My dear Annie—I take up my pen according to promise to tell you of our journey, and how we likes this place. It is a fine large place,—thirty-three bed-rooms and twelve sitting-rooms,—so that we has three housemaids, which the two youngest is nice genteel girls, though I will never forget you, dear Annie. They says it is called the Miz Maze because of a long wind-about walk with the sun-dial in the middle in the old walk. I am sure it is a miz maze of rooms, and the one that would be nicest of all for my young ladies is kept spare.

It is a nice country here, with fine fields as would do father's heart good to see, with no great mountains and nasty rocks sticking up everywhere to be of no use. But then it is mortal dull. There are no gentlefolks, nor holiday folks coming down, and if there was, we are in the middle of a great big park where we can see nothing, and has nigh a mile to walk to church or to shop, and Mrs. Parsons, the housekeeper, is horrid particular about our coming in early. However, thank goodness the parson is a bacheldor, so there baint no pious lady to be spying about and telling tales on one. There is two old ladies, sisters of Sir Walter, but one is an invalid, and the other, Miss Winkworth they calls her, but I shall always call her Miss Dora, which seems quiet and artless enough. If not, I would give warning next day, as I found her at that game, though I likes my young ladies and Miss Magic very well; but my Miss Winkworth is a nice innocent sort of a missus if she was let alone, but what can a poor young lady do when there's one outside always driving at her and her pa. Miss Elthwayte says she will stand none of that no more, one missis is enough. No more will I, for it is dull enough, and Mr. Winkworth goes about looking more mopey than ever now he is away from his young woman. I don't know as my spirits will stand the place. They say it was gay enough in the first lady's time, but she died leaving one daughter, and then Sir Walter married again. And my Lady was so pious, and Miss, having been bred up worldly, was so jealous of the young gentlemen putting her nose out of joint, that what does she do but run away with a Popish Italian music-master. And Sir Walter was that angry that no one has dared name her to him since. But I must conclude, for Miss Lisa will be coming to bed.— Your affectionate friend, FANNY MARTIN.

30.—THE OLD GENERATION *versus* THE NEW.

Miss Winkworth to Mrs. Home.

April 1859.

My dear Mary—"Human nature," you will say, but even the having the Miz Maze full again does not make up for the eighteen lost years out of our lives. The odd thing is that Walter should have two selves. He is our own original Walter when down here at the Dower House, but in his own he instantly rises to his High Scale manners, and treats his children, except Lisa, with the dignity of a heavy father, which so far impresses me that I have not yet begun to laugh him out of it.

He does so perpetually refer Zoe to me about every question about household, village, or company, that I ended by telling him that I did not think it wholesome for either of us, and that Zoe, having plenty of good sense, would do much better acting on her own judgment than being kept in leading-strings; I was afraid it would make her dislike me. He looked dreadfully shocked, and trusted she had shown no unbecoming want of deference, etc. I made haste to assure him that it was no such thing; I was only thinking how I should feel in Zoe's place. To which he responded that the young people of our day were very different from these, and that at High Scale he had always been grateful to Mrs. Bootle for her advice to his motherless girls. And he looked so sad that I could not tease him further by asking if the girls were equally grateful to this same clergywoman, whose son, by-the-bye, is to be Miles's tutor. "Papa swears by Mrs. Bootle," observed Polly one day, by which means she brought on herself a most thorough snub from her brother. It is quite refreshing to see his loyalty to his father. We get on better with the younger ones than with the two elders. Miles is always silent, they tell me, and there is a certain atmosphere of cloud about him, while Zoe seems to be reserved, though with plenty of outward talk. One never gets beyond a certain point, and when she is evidently in full career, my entrance seems to check her, as if I were an interloper. In fact I never knew before how old I was. The children were all playing at "adjectives" the other day, and when I offered to join them, they seemed as much amazed as if their great-grandfather's

picture had made the proposal. When we had done
they thanked me, as if I had not been playing for
my own amusement. I wish I knew how to get
rid of all this constraint. Perhaps it is only my
old impatience, and it will wear off in time; but it
would be a real delight to see Zoe give way to a little
wholesome nonsense with me, as I see her, at a safe
distance, doing with the other children and Miss
Madgewick, who, by-the-bye, has a satirical eye and
lip that keeps back a good deal.

We had a discussion over Kingsley. It seems
that all his books are prohibited on the Bootle authority, but Miss Warburton has told Zoe all the stories.
She evidently expected me to be frightfully shocked
when her second-hand knowledge of *Westward Ho!*
oozed out; but when Miss Madgewick stood up for
the earlier books as equal to the later, I could not say
that I liked their tone. Their sympathy is great, but
reckless; and there is a want of reverence and refine-
ment, which one does not feel in the later stories. The
writer himself has evidently become chastened by experience, but any such dispraise of her first favourites
plainly numbered me among the hopelessly prejudiced.

So much from your naughty, discontented old soul,
ungrateful for the wish of her heart fulfilled.

D. W.

31.—Sir Walter's Request to Algernon.

Sir Walter to Algernon Bootle, Esq., B.A.

Miz Maze, *April* 1859.

Dear Algernon—I write to ask if your engagements
would permit of your undertaking to read with Miles
for his degree. He has kept all his terms, and as I

have some reason to fear that longer residence at Oxford might tend to confirm him in habits of extravagance, my idea is that he should now go abroad for a time and settle down in some quiet village in Switzerland, where he would be able to pursue his studies uninterruptedly. I should prefer his being in one of the *Protestant* Cantons, but if you are so good as to accept the post of tutor, I will leave the choice of the place to you. It will be a great satisfaction to me if you can undertake the charge of him, and should you at all see your way to do so, perhaps you will come to us here for a day or two that we may arrange terms and so forth together. I think the sooner he starts the better, and I feel sure it will prove a great advantage to him if he can have the assistance of so good a classical scholar as yourself, not to mention other advantages which he may derive from your companionship.

Pray give my best remembrances to your parents, and believe me, yours truly,

WALTER M. WINKWORTH.

32.—ALGERNON ACCEPTS.

RECTORY, HIGH SCALE, *April.*

Dear Sir Walter Winkworth—I shall be happy to accept your flattering proposal of becoming tutor to your son Miles, whose abilities, I feel sure, will respond to the individual cultivation I feel myself competent to bestow, and whose character has always been such that I could wish it no otherwise.

I fully agree with you respecting the Protestant Cantons of Switzerland as a suitable situation for the cultivation of the Muses, where the mind will be at

once ennobled by the contemplation of the grandest
landscapes, and at the same time out of the risk of
contamination by the so-called priests of the Romish
Church.—I remain, yours obediently,

ALGERNON BOOTLE.

33.—MISS MADGEWICK IN THE MIZ MAZE.

Miss Madgewick to Emily.

THE MIZ MAZE,
STOKESWORTHY, *April.*

My dear Emily—As Zoe seemed to be sending
you a tolerably full budget last week, I thought I
would put off the pleasure of telling you " all about
everybody" till we had shaken down a little, and
taken stock of each other, as it were.   On the whole,
it is better than I expected.   There is something really
rather grand about the house.   It is solid and dignified
—much more of a place than High Scale; but the
country does certainly answer to my forebodings.
However, we don't play *mouche*, and Mr. Bernard, the
vicar, does not forcibly remind one of Monsieur le
Curé of the Knave of Clubs.   Nor are the aunts altogether Sir Walter in petticoats, though there is a good
deal of him in Miss Dorothea; only she has such a
much brighter, more genial manner—not what somebody (probably Sydney Smith) called " that *landed*
manner."   She must have been—indeed, she is—a
very handsome woman; very like the Winkworths in
general, but more, I think, like the twins than like
Zoe.   But none of the family have her eyes.   They
are very dark gray, with thick lashes; and, as Zoe
says, they are desperately critical eyes.   She is taking

notes of us all, and observing everything in a quiet
way; and so, I fancy, is her sister, though she is rather
an invalid, and seems very amiable and gentle.   The
moment at which I felt most drawn towards Miss
Dorothea was when Sir Walter handed her a note
which he had this morning from Mr. Algy Bootle.
She said, as she gave it back, " I did not think there
could be any human being extant who could write so
like Mr. Collins in *Pride and Prejudice.*"   I longed
to jump up and shake hands with her.   By the way,
Zoe tells me that it is arranged that poor Miles is to
go to Switzerland and read for his degree with Algernon
Bootle.   Poor fellow ! he has been very morose and
melancholy of late, and consequently has not made a
favourable impression on his aunts, or on people in
general.   He will go through a meal sometimes without
speaking a single word, and I can see that Sir Walter
is horribly annoyed.   Nothing could be better for him
than this plan of going to Switzerland, if his father had
pitched upon any other man as a travelling companion.
It *is* hard on the poor boy to have his first glimpse of
"foreign parts" poisoned by an Algernon Bootle. I wish
Sir Walter would nominate *me* travelling-tutor !   This
place makes me yearn for Switzerland again as I never
did at High Scale.   The atmosphere certainly is very
"county," and at times somewhat stifling.   As to the
society here, I have not seen very much of it yet ; but
there is a sameness in the people you do come across.
They talk hunting incessantly.   Old men and young
are always bursting into minute descriptions of "runs,"
which seem to me eternally the same thing over again.
But Sir Walter evidently appreciates those fine dis-
tinctions which are beyond Zoe and me ; and even
Miles becomes roused to a gloomy interest.   But the

politics! The rabid Conservative opinions I have heard expressed here make even Sir Walter's seem rational and moderate. The Protectionist sentiments, the abuse of the Free-Traders, would really make your blood boil. Well! now I must go to my children, who, I fear, have not managed to bring me favour in the eyes of the aunts. They don't approve of me— that is quite clear! Miss Dorothea only said, "Oh, indeed," but her eyes were very expressive, when Lisa remarked at lunch the other day that "Miss Madgewick could swim like a duck, and was giving her and Mary lessons;" whereupon Mary followed it up with reminiscences of the day "when Miss Madgewick and Ratclyffe had a canoe-race." Wretched children! why do they never refer to the many weary hours Miss Madgewick has spent in explaining Mary's harmony exercises, and Lisa's German declensions? One subject I have not touched upon, simply because there is nothing to be said. No one but the children ever talks of Mr. Fanshawe, and even Lisa seems to have an instinct that he is not a safe subject of conversation. Nevertheless, I suspect Zoe has fulfilled my prediction. Now, good-bye, my dear child.—Your ever affectionate

ESTHER MADGEWICK.

You will be glad to hear that we have a ghost; that is to say, there is a room (and a very good one) which, for some mysterious reason, is used for nothing. Ergo, "the place is haunted." But, of course, the Winkworths would possess a familiar banshee.

34.—THE BEGINNING OF THE PUZZLE.

Zoe to Emily.

THE MIZ MAZE, *March 25th.*

At last, dearest, I can sit down with some chance
of not having to jump up again instantly, so that I
have some chance of writing a letter to you. The
children are settling into regular ways,. and papa is
indoctrinating Miles with farms, turnips, and sheep,
and no one is likely to want me for some time.

This is the first day I have felt able to breathe,
there has been so much to do, and whatever seemed
settled one day, was sure to be unsettled the next
Moreover, the people who come up and speak to me
seem always to be in Aunt Dora's black books, whereas
Aunt Bessie sits by the fire in her lace cap and Shet-
land shawl, and has a good word, or at worst a pitying
one, for everybody.

I suppose it is the same with us; for if there is a
thing the children had better not mention, they invariably detail it, Mary especially. I am afraid she has
impressed Aunt Bessie with the notion that time was
spent at home between the rocks and the lake, and
that Mr. Fanshawe did all my water-colours. Moreover, her crape is always in the wars, and altogether
she is a great deal too genuine a dear old Mary to be
a pattern of decorum. I like Aunt Dora. Do not
fancy that I am prejudiced and foolish; I see she is
very kind and sensible, only she is more critical with her
eyes than her words, and I feel convinced she does not
approve of me. My belief is that she did not get on
with my dear, dear mother. Perhaps that was the
reason, together with her strong influence over papa,

that made darling mamma wish always to live away from here. It would account for a great deal, and perhaps would explain my strange feelings that we are walking side by side, apparently meeting, but not really touching one another. She thinks she understands what I say, and answers it by combating some notion that never entered my head at all.

The greatest comfort is that papa is really content, and I try not to be jealous for High Scale when I see how thoroughly busy he is, as if he were in his true element. Lisa says we never see him, "for he is out all day after turnips, and farmers, and Union workhouses." I am thankful to have him thoroughly occupied and off my mind, instead of feeling cut to the heart by hearing him give that heavy sigh, and not knowing what to do for him. He and the aunts seem as if they could go on for ever in the evening about who has married and who has died, and who has that house or this, and he thinks them worth talking politics to, as he never did to us, and I see Miss Madgewick bridle and compress her lips, till I wonder whether she will explode.

Now as to the place. It is really fine, though not quite equal to Clyffe's report, when he told you and Algy Bootle that Lowther Castle was nothing comparable to it, and that the park was a hundred miles round, and had herds of wild boars in it! There is something worthy and respectable about, though it is not beautiful, or pretty, or picturesque, only solid and well kept; and I can fancy its getting home-like, now that it is strewn with all our own things. Besides, there is a strange sense of familiarity with it. Miles and I have been comparing notes, and find that we knew our way about as if by instinct, and the sounds

of the doors and the bells bring such curious half-
memories to us, that we sometimes feel as if we were
dreaming.   There is a sort of vision of a beautiful
young lady which comes over us both in many parts
of the house, especially in the old nursery and in a
bow-window room at the end of the corridor.   I
remember turning out somebody's jewel-case on that
window-seat, and nurse scolding me, and that beautiful
somebody taking me in her arms, and saying I had
done no harm.   I think she was dressing, for I recollect
a white robe, and long black hair down her back.   In
the nursery, too, I see her building a tower with our
little bricks, but it only comes in gleams.   Was she
only a visitor, or could we have had an elder sister ?
Miles knew that dear mamma was papa's second wife.
I am sure there must be some sad story connected with
that room, for it would be the obvious one for the little
girls, if not for me ; but when I proposed to use it,
Aunt Dora said : " I think you had better not, my
dear ;" and when I asked what was the objection, she
said : " Your father would not wish it."   It did not
seem to be a thing to tease him about, so I said no
more ; but I cannot always yield if Aunt Dora meddles
with my household arrangements.   To do her justice,
it is the only time she has interfered in home matters.
As to the village, I see she is the sovereign mistress of
schools, clubs, and all the rest of it.   The rector, Mr.
Bernard, is an old bachelor, and she has been the lady
of all work nearly all her life.   All I do is to be under
her inspection, I find, and I perceive that duties are
picked out for me, in which I can't do much harm—
such as teaching the second Sunday school class, and
visiting the old women in the prim row of almshouses,
just to try my prentice hand.   What a contrast to your

work! It is like feeding barn-door fowls instead of
reclaiming eagles! Moreover, I don't fancy these Wiltshire folk; their speech is slow, and lacks the racy
variety of our "north countree." The people are solid
and heavy, like their own elms. They call the elm-
tree the weed of Wiltshire, you know, and though it
has a beauty of its own, I do get tired of it, the foliage
is all so gray a green, and there is so little variety. It
seems to me there is as little variety in people's ideas.
Miles says he is sure he is a Wiltshire moon-raker to
the backbone—another term of abuse for himself—as
if he had not enough already.

The village lies about the park gates and the church.
The aunts have a pretty flowery garden and house
bordering on the churchyard. One thing is really a
great improvement on High Scale, and that the chief
of all. The church is beautifully kept, and the services
such as dear, good Mr. Bootle never dreamt of, and
indeed they would drive Mrs. Bootle distracted. I
have just been to church this morning with Aunt Dora,
and thought how you would have enjoyed it.

The strange thing is that papa is stiff with Mr.
Bernard, and does not seem to wish me to have more
to do with him than if he were a young curate. Much
love.—Your ever affectionate

SOPHIA WINKWORTH.

Aunt Dora objects to the public use of Zoe. She
says "it is very pretty, but surely you do not wish to
be known by a nickname all over the county." Certainly not; but I have as yet seen no one anywhere
near Christian name terms. However, as, alas! there
can be no confusion now, I am trying to get into the
habit of signing my proper name.

35.—ALGERNON'S CONDOLENCE.

Passages from Algernon Bootle's Diary.

THE MIZ MAZE, *April.*

I reached this place yesterday afternoon, and now, as no one seems to be in the way, I take this opportunity, in the solitude of the drawing-room, of recording my impressions of it.

Before I reached the station I had made up my mind upon the course of conduct I intended to pursue. As a man and as a Christian, I conceive it to be my duty always to strive to make myself agreeable to my fellow-creatures ; and as a man of the world, I conceive this to be much more incumbent upon me in the case of Sir Walter Winkworth, who has patronage to bestow, and a fair daughter whom I desire in time to make Mrs. Algernon Bootle. My duty, therefore, will be at once to strive to please and to improve the fair Zoe ; to condole with Miles upon his rejection by the wealthy Miss Warburton, of which my mother has kept me duly informed ; to assent to all Sir Walter's remarks, as far as my conscience will allow ; and generally to keep my own personality well before the minds of the company, lest chill Oblivion should (as a poet would say) annul all the advantages which Fate at this moment has to offer.

No one was in when I arrived, and I immediately began to stroll down the garden walk. Here, before long, I observed Miles and Zoe so deep in conversation that they positively did not see me. They were talking very earnestly, and I heard Zoe say, " Mr. —— will be the person to tell you all about it, no doubt; but he is such an old bore that I would just as soon get an opinion from ———." She ended her sentence with a name, I could not quite hear what. If the sentence had been turned another way, such as "I would *sooner* get an opinion from ———," I should have said she uttered my own name; but probability forbids me to believe that she would have said, "I would *as soon* get an opinion from Algernon Bootle." No, I think better of Zoe!

Zoe started when she saw me, and turned scarlet, looking very much confused.   I believe well-brought-up girls invariably turn red and look confused when they suddenly see those to whom their inmost hearts are most susceptible, and I therefore augur well from Zoe's conduct upon this occasion.   She walked down the path to the house with us, and then slipped in by the garden door.   Modesty, doubtless!   Miles turned round and walked back down the garden, and I thought that this was a good opportunity for condoling with him on his rejection by E. W.   Alas! his temper appears to me terribly uncontrolled, and it will need all the firmness and wisdom of which I am master to keep him in due subjection during our proposed tour.

"I am very much grieved," I began, "to hear that you have had a disappointment lately."

"Disappointment?" said Miles, colouring, and looking the other way.   "Well, yes; I hoped old Baker would have let me have that gray cob, but it seems he can't."

"I did not refer to the gray cob, my dear Miles; indeed, I did not know about it.   I referred to the family alliance you were contemplating.   But though no one could be more sorry than I am that you should lose the chance of securing a wealthy heiress, yet there

may be consolations. That Fanshawe might not be
a desirable connection, and perhaps her partiality for
him——"

"Confound you!" said Miles, suddenly stopping
short; "what business is it of yours? Look here,
Bootle, if ever you mention her name to me again, I
vow I'll speak to my father and tell him no power on
earth shall make me go abroad with a fellow who has
got so little of the feelings of a gentleman. I mean
it."

"My good fellow," I said, "you are surely hasty,
and entirely undervalue the feelings of sympathy and
condolence which, with the kindest intentions, I was
about to offer you."

"I don't care what your intentions were," said
Miles, red and angry; "I only know that unless you
give me your word of honour that you will never touch
upon the subject again, no earthly consideration shall
make me consent to go abroad with you. Now, then,
will you or won't you?"

Rather than wreck my hopes of future prosperity
from Sir Walter's hand, I accepted Miles's conditions.
But his anger was not yet allayed, for as we walked
along together he hit the bushes so savagely with his
stick that I felt it might be dangerous further to
irritate the lion. When we reached the house, however, he seemed to make a great effort. "Mind,
Bootle," he said, "I expect that compact to be kept.
I suppose you meant no harm, but I shall consider
any allusion to that subject a personal insult. Now,
we will say no more about it."

He went in. He is certainly a masterful young
fellow, and I feel that I shall have to use all my force
of character to keep him in his proper position while

we are abroad together.   But one who, like me, feels himself destined for a high position in Church or State, need not shrink before the ungoverned temper of a Miles Winkworth.

36.—MYSTERIOUS RECOLLECTIONS.

Zoe to Emily.

THE MIZ MAZE, *Saturday, April.*

The longer we are here the more Miles and I are haunted by recollections, which will never stay to be examined.   We have talked it over, and feel almost certain that there must have been a time of great trouble before we left this place.   Little things which we accepted while baby-children could, we see, only have happened under great grief to our elders; and we are sure the mysterious lady never appeared at High Scale.

Just here, Miles, who had been roaming about the library, pulling out a book here and there, brought me what he had found squeezed in between two great quartos—a nursery picture-book of *The House that Jack Built*, with half the cow with a crumpled horn torn out.   He said he quite recollected that he and Clyffe were being shown the pictures by *some one*, and that Clyffe wanted to turn over before she had worked back to the malt, and he (Miles) held the page fast, and it was torn.   We looked at the first page, and read : " Ratclyffe Winkworth from Sister Birdie."   So she really must have been an elder sister.   Then it came back on Miles that Clyffe had asked for " Sister to come and play," and that nurse said she was gone away, and always called it naughty to talk about her.

Yet it is very strange there is no monument, nor even
any mention of her upon the tablet to papa's first
wife, which is in the wall over our seat.   Then Miles
said, "Look here, Zoe !"   He had found a *Peerage
and Baronetage ;* we never had one at High Scale.   I
remember when I read *Persuasion*, thinking how
superior we were to Sir Walter, who was always
studying his own name in the *Baronetage*.   Well, this
was a very old one, the date 1838, but it contained
what we were looking for ; and we really had a sister
Bertha Dorothea, and, as papa was married in 1830,
she might have been eighteen when we remember her.
I think she must have died in some sad, strange way,
that made this place distressing to papa and mamma ;
yet it is puzzling that Miles can remember nothing,
except that the words Sister Birdie brought her face
and voice and pretty caressing ways back strongly to
us both.   Some of the old people could tell me more,
I am sure, for I have heard them say, "How like she
is to poor Missie !" and that it is like old times to
have me about among them ; but then one old woman
hushed up the other, as if there were a mystery.   I
ought not to ask them questions, but if I can screw
up my courage I will ask Aunt Dora, and she can tell
me or not, as she thinks fit.   That will be the most
direct and straightforward way of dealing.   I long to
know, for these rooms seem full of the presence of
one who made everything pleasant to me.   What is
strangest of all is, that Miles has a strong impression
of some one kissing and crying over him on the stairs
leading to the nursery in the dark.   We wish Clyffe
was here to help us to piece out our memories.

I am almost sure there must have been some
terrible accident, or an infectious illness, from which

we were taken away. Poor Birdie! that we should
have so forgotten her.—Your loving   Z.

37.—AUNT DORA APPLIED TO.

From Aunt Dora to Sir Walter.

Monday.

My dear Walter—I feel that I must tell you that
yesterday, when walking back from church, Zoe suddenly said (it was suddenly to me, I don't think it was
to her), "Did my sister Bertha die away from home?"

I answered on the spur of the moment: "Don't you
know, my dear?"

"No," she said. "Do tell me about her."

So I answered: "It is a painful story, and I should
wish to have your father's consent before telling you."

She said no more. And now, dear Walter, tell me
what I shall do. My own impression is that it would
be better that you or I should give Zoe and her
brother the whole account simply as we knew it, than
that they should pick it up from the old folks in the
village or indiscreet neighbours. If it will save you
pain, I will tell Zoe the story myself. I do not think
she would ask questions or gossip with strangers, but
it might come out at unawares and puzzle her.—Your
affectionate   D. W.

38.—SIR WALTER GIVES CONSENT.

Sir Walter to Aunt Dora.

MIZ MAZÈ, *Monday.*

My dear Dorothea—I find it easier to answer your
note in writing than in person, as I could not enter

into conversation on the subject without great pain.
You are at liberty to tell Zoe as much about her
step-sister as you think necessary ; and I feel sure that
(without throwing needless blame on poor Bertha) you
will be careful not to drop a word that might imply
blame to her mother.

My dear Sophy acted for the best in every way,
and if her motives were sometimes misunderstood, and
wise restraint was construed into studied harshness,
the fault did not rest with *her*.   The position of a
step-mother towards a grown-up step-daughter is one
full of difficulty, and Bertha's disposition was such as
to make the difficulty even greater than it would
naturally have been.   There is always *some* excuse for
a motherless girl ; but I should fail in loyalty towards
her who tried so conscientiously to fill the mother's
place, did I admit that there was any extenuation but
this for Bertha's conduct.   Zoe must not be allowed
to think of her as a victim, nor to suppose that the
changes which time has wrought have at all given me
reason to alter my resolution never to re-admit her to
intercourse with myself or my more dutiful children.—
I am, your affectionate brother,

WALTER M. WINKWORTH.

39.—INVITED TO DALLINGTON.

Miss Winkworth to Mrs. Home.

April 18th.

My dear Mary—Such an afternoon as we had at
the Miz Maze on Saturday.   It was as if all the
county had by one consent agreed to call !   At least
all who were at home, and the nicest were away.   In

they came, one upon the other, the little nodding
Misses Perrott, who actually observed on Zoe's likeness
to her sister, but Bessie nervously drowned that by
turning on the flood of Miss Perrott's cook stories.
Then came the Bardolphs, raving about a fox that one
of the tenants is supposed to have shot; and, besides
three or four more, arrived George Thorburn, who
thundered us all deaf about exclusive dealing in
preparation for the next election.   I was vexed, for I
am sure Zoe and the governess recoiled, and it is not
wholesome to see too much of the seamy side of the
maintenance of principle.   I should like to talk it over
with them, if they would only give me the opportunity
and let me into their world of youth.   It is a pity
that loyalty and constancy to Church and State should
be made to sound like narrowness and persecution of
the vacillating butcher.   "I warned him," says Mr.
Thorburn, "and I had him warned, but says the
fellow, 'What can I do, sir? Mr. Boozer and the rest of
them are worth a dozen carcases a week to me.'"   I
tried to make the girls observe that such being the
average tradesman's line, what could be expected from
farther extension of the franchise to more ignorant
people still.   But Zoe evidently thought it no affair of
hers, and probably Miss Madgewick sneered in private.

Mr. Thorburn is delighted to have Walter back
again, and insists on our all coming over to spend a
day at Dallington in the old fashion, since his wife
cannot take so long a drive.   Poor George Thorburn!
I believe he fancies we can be all boys and girls
together again, and he wants his grandchildren to strike
up a friendship with Mary and Lisa.   So we are all to
go to luncheon, and Walter is to see the shorthorns,
and be persuaded to set up a farm-engine, horrid thing!

I told them it was base in Tories to spoil all the
picturesqueness of farming, and make us say,

> "The whistle shrieks the knell of parting day,
> The humming engine coughs along the lea,
> The driver lets the steam puff forth its way,
> And leaves the world to ugliness and me."

On which he soberly replied, "Dora, you are at your
old tricks, but don't you understand that it is a duty
to keep pace with those fellows ? "

And actually Bessie is to be of the party. You know
she has never been at Dallington since the day we all
spent there just before Charles Thorburn went away to
Oxford for the last time, when Sophia was so annoyed
at the Bernards bringing Signor Marini over. How
little we thought that we were all on the verge of a
changed life. George was very nice and tender with
her, and asked her very gently as a favour to himself,
and she is bent on going, and declares it will be good
for her. I really think it will, and that, after all this
softening of time, she will be happier for having visited
the old scenes. The day is not fixed yet ; I suppose it
will be in Easter week.

Saturday, Easter Eve.—The inevitable has come to
pass. Zoe has put things together and made out the
fact of Bertha's existence and disappearance, but like a
good girl she has not gossiped, only asked me. I have
made her wait till I can ask her father's consent to
telling her, but *tête-à-têtes* are hard to achieve—now
especially, when the schoolboy Frank is just come home,
a fine fellow, galloping up and down, in and out, with
his little sisters and two or three dogs after him.

The tutor, Mr. Algernon Bootle, is also come. My
dear, if you could only see the curl of his whiskers
and the shine of his boots, you would know what

a phœnix is like. I confess that my fingers tingled
to box his ears all the evening; above all, when he
patronised Bessie by explaining the Latin scrolls on
the stained windows in the hall. My brother says he
is an excellent scholar, and what young men call an
excellent coach, but I can't help pitying Miles. However, Mary and Lisa are full of tales of tricks played
on him by their brothers, so perhaps my pity ought to
go in the other direction.

"A very superior young man," pronounces Walter;
"perhaps a little self-satisfied, but very well bred.
Those who respect themselves also respect others."

"I don't know that," I said; "I never respect you
so little as when you are sententious."

And as all the young people were out of the way,
he could descend from his dignity and threaten to box
my ears for my sauciness.

We go to Dallington on Wednesday, Miles's last day
at home. George Thorburn views him as a future
county member, and means to fascinate him with
Southdowns, prime pigs, and haymaking machines.
He need not take the trouble. The boy is staunch
and loyal to the core, though I can't say he makes himself agreeable, and his young brother moans for Clyffe,
and says Miles is as dull as ditch-water without him.

I must leave off; I am wanted for the decorations.
We durst not ask for the children's help or the Miz
Maze flowers, for fear of reviving old associations.
But Walter accepts much in silence, though I think it
must be purposely that he has taken all his flock over
to see Salisbury Cathedral to-day. Here is Miss
Madgewick come down to offer her services, and half
the parish with baskets of primroses.—Your affectionate
                                         D. W.

40.—EDGAR ON THINGS IN GENERAL.

Edgar to Carlo.

LONDON, *April.*

Dear Carlo—As to Dandolo's funeral, it must have
been a grand spectacle, and the consequences make one
wonder how much longer Milan will endure the sight
of these white coats.   You have stirring times before
you in Italy.   If Louis Napoleon gives his hand to
Sardinia now, we shall forgive him all his sins.   His
motive may not be unmixed enthusiasm for Italian
unity, but whose motive is pure ?   It is at least a step
forward into daylight, a hearty push to our old world
as she rolls towards freedom.

Thanks for your welcome, but I shall not avail
myself of it now.   I have pulled myself together, and
found out that there is a great deal to keep me in
England.   Emily will not let me give in ; she has a
faith in her useless cousin which astonishes him.   Is
it not a good joke ?   She declares that I shall soon
make a name, and that Sir Walter Winkworth will
wake up some morning and find me famous, so that he
will have no further excuse for tabooing me.   In fact,
she will not let me lose hope at all, and tells me things
I dare hardly believe, but of which she is " perfectly
certain."   Very amiable, but she has acted selfishly,
and not improved my chance by refusing Miles
Winkworth.   I cannot, however, put the matter in
that light to her.   I speculate a good deal about
Emily, and wish you knew her.   There is a chance,
however, that even *you* might not be her ideal.   I
believe she will never meet him, or if she does, he will

be a humbug, and his real attraction will be *les beaux yeux de sa cassette.*

You ask indignantly the name of the mutual friend who drove me away from High Scale. As she is a woman, we will say no more about her; besides, I might write pages without making you realise her in the least, as you don't know the species. And I will not do her picture for you as it would be caricature, and you told me long ago that this was a degraded form of art. I agree with you, and yet I could; but I won't. So rest you happy, and be thankful that yours is an unmarried clergy. I shall be here for the present; the Warburtons are coming up shortly.— Ever yours,   EDGAR FANSHAWE.

41.—EMILY'S SECRET.

Emily to Miss Madgewick.

HATCHETT'S HOTEL, *April.*

N.B.—Read before you speak, or give this to Zoe.

My dear Madgie—Here we are actually coming into your parts, more's the pity. Mamma has engaged us to go to the Thorburns at Dallington in Easter week. The eldest son of your Tory squire married a Fanshawe, and the relationship was resuscitated by an encounter at "Israel in Egypt," in Exeter Hall, to which Edgar was escorting us. So they asked him too, though they consider it rather disgraceful to have his name in the catalogue of the R.A., as I glory in saying it will be. He is coming down with us, which is a mutual comfort. I hate myself when I think of the *mauvais quart d'heure* to which I treated my poor

parent; but then I should hate myself a dozen times
more if I allowed myself, like a helpless ball, to be
projected at the head of an estimable youth.   So I
absolutely refused to accompany mamma unless she
would solemnly promise not to let a creature know of
our coming, nor to drag me over to Stokesworthy to
spy out the land if she chooses to go there herself.   I
trust the ill-assorted pair of travellers may be off before
we get to Dallington.   Let me know, and I shall not
have to drag back so hard, or be so like a sulky puppy
in a string.   There's a good Madge.   Keep my secret.
—Your   E. W.

(Enclosed.)

Zoe, my dear, here's a discovery for you.   Edgar's
Anglo-Italian friend must be your sister.   He met her
at Signora Monti's at Rome two years ago.   She asked
if he knew Wiltshire, and when she found he was connected with the Thorburns, she spoke of having been
at Dallington, knew all their names, and seemed as if
it was a great blow to her to find that Sir Walter had
left Stokesworthy ; but as he then hardly knew you all,
he could not tell her much.   He did not see her husband, and was not sure of his name, but thought he
was a marked man, who could not venture to Rome.
He was struck by her fine profile, and says yours is
like it.   There, my dear, make what you can of that !
—Your loving   E. W.

42.—MISS MADGEWICK'S POLITICS.

Miss Madgewick to Emily.

MIZ MAZE, *April 27th*, 1859.

My dear Emily—Knowing your calm, deliberate,
and entirely dispassionate way of forming your judg-

ments, I can feel confident that you are not at this moment pronouncing me " faithless," " gone over to the enemy," etc. etc.   So, though of course I would have prevented this if it had been possible, and though I am most sincerely sorry for you, poor child ! still I will confess that I am a little inclined to laugh at the contrariness of things in general.   When I got your letter yesterday, by the second post—too late to answer—the expedition to Dallington had just been arranged for to-day, in order that Miles might not be left out, for he starts on the 27th.   But I assure you that not one of the " twelve precious souls " that set out from here this morning had the slightest suspicion of your being with the Thorburns, so you need not flatter yourself that you are the cynosure.   Ah, my dear, you young folks have not a monopoly of romance.   I find poor old Miss Bessie was once engaged to a clerical Thorburn, who, after waiting for years for a college living, had just come in for it when he managed to get drowned in the Isis, while saving a senseless undergraduate.   Her health broke down, and she has been the subject of her sister's devotion ever since ; nor has she ever been to his home at Dallington, so that it is a marvel to all that she should have yielded to his brother's persuasions, and agreed to be of the party.   I doubt whether Miss Winkworth will have eyes for anybody else.   So anxious is she about her Bessie that she could not help telling me the whole story.   I really thought she was beginning on your affairs when she said this expedition was a peculiar anxiety to her ; but you see you are not the only person in the world. This expedition has been a floating scheme for some little time—ever since Mr. Thorburn first came over here.   Strange that he should turn out to be a con-

G

nection of yours! Now you will see some specimens
of our "county respectability," and have the opportunity
of improving your mind by observing the unprejudiced
tone and lofty morality of our politics. I daresay you
have heard the case of the Dallington butcher discussed
by this time. Curious, the cool way in which men,
who are punctiliously honourable in every other respect,
will talk of putting pressure on their butchers' and
bakers' and candlestick makers' consciences! That sort
of thing jars upon Miss Dorothea, I can see; but I suppose people's minds get thoroughly saturated with class
prejudices! I believe she was trying to excuse the
practice to Zoe and me the other day when she asked
what good would come of lowering the franchise, if the
average tradesman is willing to sell his vote. I did
long to make the obvious retort, that if there was no
demand there would be no supply, but discreetly
refrained. She would probably consider politics out of
my province, and besides, when people have been born
and bred and lived all their lives in an atmosphere of
old Toryism, it can do no good to argue with them.

It is rather pleasant to find myself in an empty
house, with the day before me. To say the truth, I
always have a certain sense of relief when Sir Walter
is out of the way. There is something about him
which I *cannot* get on with; and it is almost irritating
to see how he is worshipped by those two sisters of
his, though he has not the brains of either of them—
certainly not of Miss Dorothea. Mrs. Bootle would
never have ridden rough-shod over *her!* I should
like you to see the effect of Algy Bootle's speeches on
her face sometimes. It is a curious and interesting
spectacle. Now, as I want to make the very utmost
of my holiday, I must not spend any more of it in

letter-writing. A most pleasing innovation has actually been made, *by Sir Walter himself*, in the shape of a Mudie-box; and I have succeeded in getting Macaulay's last volume, which is lying by me on the table; so, good-bye. Is there any chance of my seeing you while you are at Dallington? I am afraid not. You will be surprised to hear that I like the aunts well enough to feel vexed that they are not seeing you to advantage to-day. I can vividly imagine how you are flouting them, and how they will confide to one another that it is evident what poor success Miss Madgewick's system must have had in forming the character and manners of her late pupil. But most of all, I am sorry for Miles. It is a thousand pities that he was not off before seeing you again. Zoe has been a little grave and abstracted lately; but I should not wonder if she came back looking brighter. This unlucky *contretemps* will be a case of the " ill wind."——Ever your affectionate   MADGE.

One word more before I betake me to my Macaulay. Though I remember your mother telling me that Sir Walter had been married before, I never knew that he had another daughter. Yet, the other day, a communi-cative old lady, who was calling at the Dower House, when I went in with the children and Zoe, whispered to me that Zoe was " so like her poor sister." Then came a lull in the conversation, and she said no more. It is odd that I never heard any of them allude to it, and also that there is no tablet in this church, as there is to Sir Walter's first wife. But this is gossip! the direful result of living so long under the shadow of Mrs. Bootle.

43.—MEYRICK ON THE MYSTERY.

Miles Winkworth to Ratclyffe Winkworth.

THE MIZ MAZE, *April* 19.

Dear Clyffe—You take an entirely wrong view of the matter, and you utterly fail to appreciate her ; you always did. Your advice unluckily comes much too late to be of any use, and as for " letting her alone till she grows wiser and knows what I'm worth," I might have let her alone long enough. You will know soon the result of my attempt. But waiting would have made *no* difference in *her* case. She isn't that sort of girl ; nor am I a fellow to be bowled over by any girl with a pair of eyes in her head, and who knows how to use them. I daresay the French Canadians *are* very pretty, but what can you know of a girl from meeting her at two balls ? Do look out, there's a good fellow, and don't do anything foolish.

Algy and I are off in a few days, and he is down here with us. What a *duffer* he is ! I don't know how I shall endure him. I think I've put a stop to his sympathy, though, for the future. I shall try if I can't get him out of some of his absurd ways ; he would never get on with strangers, and he isn't such a bad fellow at bottom. I told him the other day that you would have been a more creditable pupil, and he became natural on the spot and said : " I wouldn't have undertaken him for a thousand pounds." I believe he'd expect you to inveigle him to the top of an iceberg—I mean glacier—and leave him there, as we used to do on the top of the loose-box at home. Shall you ever forget him holding on by the morella-

cherry, and struggling down by degrees, declaring that
he'd tear his new jacket? Poor old Algy! after all
one can't help liking him better than a stranger. He
says, however, he is a pedestrian, and has got a knapsack with about fifty straps and no end of pockets.
I know I shall have to carry it; it'll tire him out.
And he is going to keep a diary. I think I shall set
up one too, for your benefit. Wouldn't it be a joke to
compare the two?

Fanshawe writes very jolly letters. He has told
me all the fine things I am to look out for. His
picture is in the Academy this year. They wouldn't
have the large one of Windermere, but have accepted
what he calls a "bit," which is our old gray barn
where Emily and I hid the rabbits, with the fell
behind and the door open, and Lisa, very untidy,
feeding the chickens. At least it was Lisa really, but
father didn't like her to be recognised, so he dressed
her up like a farm girl.

We are to go first to Lucerne, because Algy says it
is in a Protestant Canton, which is considered essential.
Such folly! My father seems to think that one can
go through Oxford and never hear anything different
from Bootledom. I cannot understand the sort of
prejudice he has against Mr. Bernard, the rector here,
who seems to be a thorough good sort of fellow and a
gentleman. The aunts seem to like him; but I think
there must have been a quarrel formerly, for he is very
slow in making advances to Zoe and me, and father is
so awfully civil to him. I wish he (father I mean)
wouldn't lecture me on making myself pleasant and
my want of manners. I can't help it, and really some
of the ladies do make themselves so desperately
agreeable; they take the words out of one's mouth.

There'll be more chance of quiet abroad, for Algy *can*
be shut up.   You know the children have got Miss
Madgewick for a governess.   I never did like her much,
and now she is so distant and respectful, and calls me
Mr. Winkworth ; but I think she takes it out somehow,
she looks so odd sometimes.   She and Emily correspond
constantly.   I get on very well with the aunts, better I
think than Zoe does.   I like Aunt Dora.   Zoe doesn't
quite make her out, and is afraid that she'll object to
the children tearing their clothes and getting dirty; but
I shouldn't wonder if Aunt Dora had torn hers in her
day.   She is very proud of the family, and showed me
lots of black shades of our ancestors.   She's very clever
too, and the handsomest old lady I ever saw, though she
goes about in a wonderful mushroom hat as big as an
umbrella.   She talked a great deal about you the other
day, and asked me questions, and said she had never
seen us apart before since we were born, and I had an
M. inked on my foot, so that they might not confuse
us.   I think it's rather a pity they didn't.   Evidently
the aunts were very sorry when we all went north.
Aunt D. says that you could speak long before I could,
so you ought to remember better what happened when
we were babies.

Easter Tuesday.—I have been a week writing this
long letter, and I think I shall tell you what Zoe and I
have our heads full of.   Directly Zoe came here she began to have what she calls "impressions" connected with
the place, and one day she told me quite in an excited
manner that she was sure that we had an elder sister who
must have died.   I haven't been caring enough about
anything to take up with new ideas very quickly, but
at last I began to think that I did remember a lady,
not mother, who used to play with us, and sing to us.

Zoe recollected or imagined more and more, and at last I looked in an old *Baronetage* and found her name— Bertha Dorothea, married Marini, 1841; but her death is not given, nor is there any tablet to her in the church, as there is to her mother.   The first Lady Winkworth really had such a daughter.   And now that the clue is given, I see that something must have gone very wrong about her, or why has there been such a mystery made of it?   So I stopped Zoe's investigations, and told her on no account to speak of it to any one but Aunt Dora, who, I suppose, knows what to say. But I think I ought to know the history of my father's eldest daughter, and I should ask him to tell me, only I suppose it is a painful subject, and besides he never realizes that one is grown up and can have a right to ask such a question.   But as I am sure it is no secret to any one besides ourselves, I shall speak about it to Meyrick, who may not be interesting to Zoe, but is a tried friend and has plenty of sense.   I shall walk over and do it at once.

10.30 P.M.—Well, I've heard Meyrick's story.   I met him in the Park, and asked him a plain question: could he tell me what had became of my half-sister?

"Ah," he said, " poor Miss Winkworth, she was a beautiful creature, and Sir Walter was very proud of her.   A sad disappointment!"

"How?" I said.

"Her father spoiled her sadly," he answered, "and your mother, the second Lady Winkworth, did not get on well with her; Miss Winkworth was headstrong and very hot-tempered and enthusiastic.   She had some Italian lessons from Signor Marini—he stayed with Mr. Bernard.   He *said* he was a man of family in his own country; but a political refugee may be

anybody.   Lady Winkworth disapproved very much of
the intimacy with the Bernards.   The Rector had a
sister living with him then.   Puseyism, you know, was
just coming up, and Mr. Bernard made himself very
unpopular by having daily service and wearing his
surplice in the pulpit.   It was even said that he dis-
seminated the *Tracts for the Times.*   Lady Winkworth's
principles were, as you know, entirely against these
innovations."   Then he hummed and hawed a little, and
at last told me that there was a great explosion.   Miss
Bernard went over to Rome, and Miss Winkworth
insisted on following her example.   " For my part,"
he said, " I never thought the rector was in the plot,
and he looked broken-hearted.   But there was great
anger, and much double-dealing was discovered."
Then it appears that Bertha was shut up and watched,
and that she behaved very ill to mother, and at last
she ran away and left a letter behind her, saying that
she had joined the Roman Church, and that she was
going to marry Signor Marini.   She was just of age,
and they were married, Mr. Meyrick says, in some
Roman Catholic Church in London.   I suppose the
priests managed it.   Then father was so angry that he
would never forgive her, and mother insisted on our
all going away, as she could never attend Mr. Bernard's
church, or let us grow up under his influence.   Mr.
Meyrick says nothing was ever heard of Bertha
afterwards.

I thanked him for telling me, and came away
without saying anything about it.   But *I* think, that
though turning Roman Catholic and eloping was very
wrong, and no doubt she was a deceitful girl and would
have been a very bad companion for Zoe, she ought
not to have been treated as if she had utterly dis-

graced the family. She couldn't have done us any
harm in Italy, and if we had always heard of her, we
should have thought nothing of her. Now Zoe will be
apt to think of her as a martyr. Besides, after all, she
was Miss Winkworth, and who knows what misery
she may have brought on herself. I think some
inquiry should be made about her, and if you agree, I
think some time or other I shall tell Sir Walter that
we think so. I shan't tell Zoe; if the elders choose
her to know they may tell her themselves; and, indeed,
on Thursday we start, and to-morrow we are to lunch
at Dallington. How I hate those intolerable lunches
and dawdling afternoons, playing pool perhaps with a
set of girls who don't even know how to handle a mace.
And to drive twelve miles for it!

Wednesday night.—Half-a-dozen lines more. We
found the Warburtons at Dallington. And Fanshawe.
Mrs. Warburton most gracious and easy; Emily spoke
to no one but Zoe; and Fanshawe was quite shy and
savage. We were a nice party. A detestable girl
would talk to me at lunch. Well, seeing her only
shows me how hopeless it all is. We are off the first
thing. I shall write from somewhere, and tell you how
we get on.—Yours ever,   MILES WINKWORTH.

Bootledom and many other things are now
accounted for.

PART III.

A DAY AT DALLINGTON, AND WHAT CAME OF IT.

A Tory to the quick. —TENNYSON.

Edgar to Carlo.

DALLINGTON, *April* 27.

DEAR CARLO—It is past midnight, and I am going to inflict my tediousness on you—write myself to sleep perhaps, as I have done before now. Do you ever find yourself get entirely out of hand? What spiteful demon is it that takes hold of one sometimes, and plunges one headlong into happiness, so that one is bewildered and dizzy, and perfectly miserable, and then takes the happiness away in an hour, quite unappreciated, and leaves one much worse than before? The meaning of this allegory is that I came down here for a few days with my aunt and Emily, to stay with some stupid old cousins called Thorburn, who mean to be good-natured, but think it a condescension to ask an artist to their house. I make the best of it, however; old George has a good heart, and can't help his prejudices. Emily is in a very bad temper. Miles Winkworth and all his relations were asked to luncheon to meet her to-day. They live in this neighbourhood, you know, and they came, a dozen of them, great and small. A luncheon party of old family friends is an institution likely to remain quite English, and you need not have wished yourself here. I entertained the Winkworth children, who are jolly little things, and hardly spoke to the others, not even to Miles, who

looked savage, and skulked about by himself. There
were several old ladies trotting about with Mrs. Thorburn. They seemed happy, and talked tremendously,
and looked at me with a sort of fierce curiosity. One
of them had a handsome pleasant face ; they are Sir
Walter's sisters, and seem more lively than himself.
His pleasure, poor old boy, was evidently quite spoilt
by finding me there. I did not intentionally make
myself a bore to him ; the whole thing was more pain
than pleasure to me. Emily monopolised her friend
the whole afternoon, and I could only look on at a
distance, till by some wonderful chance—I cannot to
this moment tell how it happened, but it was done by
nothing better than that demon I mentioned just now
—I found myself alone in a garden-walk with Zoe.
What had become of all the others I did not know, and
certainly did not care to ask. Her face was sad and
troubled, and she began asking me some questions in a
breathless, confused way, which I hardly heard or
answered. I could only look at her, and try to realise
that she was there, and I was haunted in a maddening
way by the sound of wheels coming up to the door. I
said something, I forget what, and then came a voice
calling Zoe, and I lost my senses just then, and
begged her to let me have one moment more, but she
only looked frightened and hurried away. I cannot
remember anything that she said, but I know I said
more than I ever ventured on before, and I am afraid
she was angry. Afterwards I realised what she was
talking about. Do you know or remember anything
of an Englishwoman married to an Italian, whom I met
at your poor mother's house two years ago ? We had
a little talk about England, and she asked me if I knew
Wiltshire and the Winkworths. I now see that she

was very like them. Emily has been making me brush
up my memory about her this evening, and we think
she may possibly be Sir Walter's daughter by a former
marriage, who it seems displeased her father beyond
forgiveness by running away with an Italian. I think
that lady's husband was a patriot. I do not remember
seeing him. Poor Sir Walter! I feel quite sorry for
him. The knowledge of people's past troubles has a
tendency to soften one's heart. Emily, however, will
not pity him, and has no doubt that the whole thing
was his own fault. Possibly, but one may pity him
all the same.

There is a very pretty sketch of that runaway Miss
Winkworth in the study here, in a group of less interesting heads. It would make a good portrait, but
I don't suppose George Thorburn would let me carry
off the group. He would expect never to see it again.
I will tell you more another day. I am falling asleep
gradually, and you have begun to yawn long ago.

. The R.A. agreed with me, for a wonder; rejected
the Windermere, and accepted the barn-door. Of
course it will be skyed. Who said that genius was
patience? He was a sharp fellow, and knew the
world.—Yours always, EDGAR FANSHAWE.

45.—ALGERNON'S DIGNITY.

Algernon Bootle's Diary.

April 27, 11 P.M.

The other day some plan was talked of for going to
lunch at a Mr. Thorburn's of Dallington, not far from
here. To-day Sir Walter at breakfast turned to me
and told me in his most polite manner that Mr. Thor-

burn hoped I should accompany the party. I assured
him that it would give me great pleasure to make the
acquaintance of his friend ; and it was then arranged
that I should sit upon the box of the barouche, in the
place the footman would ordinarily occupy. I felt
somewhat startled at this suggestion, and looked round
the table to see if there were any covert slight intended;
but even young Frank was unconcernedly eating his
bread and jam, and I thought that on the whole my
claims to social and intellectual rank were such that, in
spite of appearances, I need not fear being confounded
with a footman.

We started. I endeavoured at first to make myself
agreeable to Zoe by constantly pointing out to her, from
my seat on the box, objects of interest in our route ;
but she responded only faintly, and at last told me
that as she was sitting with her back to the horses, it
was impossible that she could see the same points
which I did. In this confession I read a maidenly
acknowledgment of my manly superiority, and thought
how sweet it would be to go through life with one so
appreciative of the difference betwixt us.

We arrived at our destination, and were warmly
greeted by our host and hostess ; and I was preparing
to shine in conversation, when, to my horror and disgust, two persons appeared upon the scene, who always
have upon my spirits the effect which, to borrow a
metaphor from my native mountains, a fog has upon
the summit of Helvellyn. These two were my rival
—the painter Fanshawe, and his cousin, that little
impertinent Emily Warburton, from whom Miles has
had so happy an escape. I resolved, under these circumstances, to take refuge in the dignity of silence,
and did so. I feel that the change in my deportment

was not unobserved, for one of the young Thorburns observed in my hearing to Walter : " I say, is that sulky chap your coach ?   He's swallowed a poker, and no mistake."   This convinces me, though uttered in the common slang of the average schoolboy, that my bearing produced the effect I intended it to do.

These Thorburns seem to me to treat Fanshawe with far too much consideration.   I could see no sign that they had less esteem for him than they had for a person in my position.   He wisely forbore to stir my sleeping jealousy by any demonstrations towards Zoe, and for the most part devoted himself to the children. Towards the end of the visit, however, something happened which made me doubt whether this affected indifference were not a cloak for sinister and dark designs.   Zoe was missing when we were all assembled in the hall waiting for departure, and, to my horror, one of the young Thorburns announced that she was with his Cousin Edgar in the Espalier walk.   The very name of the place brought up before my mind treason, plots, and conspiracies ; one can well imagine that the Gunpowder Plot may have been hatched by men in slouched hats and long cloaks in an Espalier walk !   I was considering whether it would be well to draw Miles aside and propose to go to search for the young lady, and was only deterred by knowing how rough he can be on such occasions, when Zoe appeared. She has then escaped from his toils !   Doubtless the consideration of the open and manly love of one I will not name, and the fear of forfeiting his good opinion, wrought with her so that she refused to listen to his wiles.   It was, however, evident that her father and her aunts were much displeased at her conduct, and I observed in the evening that she was evidently in dis-

H

grace. This is well ; one who has to enjoy the honour
of at some future day becoming my wife, should, as my
mother observed, be as far above suspicion as the Queen
of Spain's legs. (I felt sure that she intended to refer
to Cæsar's wife, but she assures me that it was an incident in modern history which was in her mind.) At
the same time I cannot but be sorry for poor Zoe, even
while I feel that this treatment is for her eventual
good.

46.—POLLY ON PAST AND PRESENT.

Polly to Clyffe.

THE MIZ MAZE, *April* 28.

My dear Clyffe—I had not time to write and wish
you a happy Easter ; but I hope you will forgive me.
We have been having a little Easter holiday whilst
Frank is at home, but it is not so much fun in the
holidays here, as we cannot do any of our old things.
I do not think anybody seems very happy here except
papa and Lisa (who likes new things, you know). Do
you remember that Mr. Thorburn with a loud voice
and great big freckled hands who once came to High
Scale ? Well, he lives near here, and comes over
rather often to see papa. His brother was going to
marry Aunt Bessie, but he got drowned instead. I
wonder if Aunt Bessie's Mr. Thorburn was like his
brother ; it would be a pity, I think, for she is so delicate and pretty, and he is just like Mr. John Bull in
the *Punch* pictures, only not quite so fat. So yesterday we all went over to Dallington. It is a big house,
not so big as this, and uglier. The hall is full of dogs
and hunting-whips and foxes' tails. One of the dogs
I liked very much, a beautiful St. Bernard, with such

a noble face; I thought he looked much more like a gentleman than Mr. Thorburn, and *he* did not fuss at all. There are a great many young Thorburns, but the boys are all alike, and say the same things, and seem to think of nothing but hunting or ferrets. There is a girl called Charlotte, who is my age, but she looks quite as grown up as Zoe does. Frank and Lisa said she was very pretty, and that I was stupid; but she is horrid, I think, and she made Lisa talk about all the grown-up things at home, which was not good for a child like Lisa. I hope we shall not go there again. And do you know, Mrs. Warburton and Emily were there, but it did not feel like *home* a bit. Mrs. Warburton was very kind in that way of hers which we don't like, and Emily was not kind *at all;* she nearly bit Miles's head off, all for nothing. I wish she would not! Miles is very fond of her, and he does not like it. Mr. Fanshawe was there too; and the nicest part of the day was luncheon, when he sat with us young ones at a side-table, and made fun. Charlotte was not silly whilst he was there, as she was afterwards. I don't like this letter; I am afraid it is cross, but I am very tired to-day, and I have not time to write it over again. How I do wish we were all back at High Scale!—Your loving sister,   MARY WINKWORTH.

47.—AUNT DORA'S GUESSES.

Miss Winkworth to Mrs. Home.

April 29.

Well, dearest Mary, our expedition is over, and a very odd day it has been! I will begin by saying that Bessie bore it very well, and says she is all the

happier for it. To her George Thorburn is something
quite different from the big, loud-voiced squire he is to
other people.

We went crammed into the barouche — all the
women-folk, I mean—Mr. Bootle outside, and Walter
riding with his boys—a pleasant sight. Miss Madgewick was thankful to get a holiday, but I fancied
mischief in her eyes as she saw us off, and it is my
belief that she knew what was coming.

When Mr. Thorburn had met us at the door with
some of his clan, and had given Bessie his arm across
the slippery oak floor, and we were safe in the drawing-room, up flew Zoe to a small creature we found
there. I thought it remarkable precipitation in swear-
ing an eternal friendship with Alice Thorburn, but,
behold, Walter was beaming, and Miles sheepish, and
I found myself being introduced to Mrs. and Miss
Warburton.

The mother is as broad as she is long, and that is
not saying much for her size. She is a perfect ball
of good humour, not over-wise ; but the young lady is
what in our day was called a sylph, exceedingly tiny,
all but her eyes, which are hazel and rather over-
whelming, as mademoiselle took no pains to conceal
her displeasure at finding herself in a trap. At least,
such is the charitable interpretation of what young
Frank tersely described thus : " Emily was so cross, it
was a caution !"

Moreover, when we had been paired as for a dinner-
party, and had filed into the old dining-room, who
should appear but a foreign-looking youth, at sight of
whom Miles's heavy looks lightened, even as his father's
darkened. There was a general hand-shaking, and he
proved to be the redoubtable " scamp of an artist,"

though he seemed inoffensive enough. He disposed
of himself among the young fry at the side table,
whence we heard occasional titterings, especially from
Lisa. It seems that both the young man and Miss
Warburton are relations of Mrs. James Thorburn.
Certainly, if a Dallington luncheon was ever enlivened
with by-play, it was this one; but I was too anxious
about Bessie to think much of the young folks. After
luncheon George Thorburn took Bessie into his study
to show her a framed photograph of Charles's cross in
the cemetery at Oxford, and also the only likeness
they have of him—a sketch of the whole group of
heads that Signor Marini made on that last day, I
believe, as an excuse for drawing Bertha. For there
was the pretty profile twice over, poor child, and
Bessie's head, and mine, and Charles Thorburn's, only
done a week before his accident.

After a time, when we thought every one gone to
adore the steam-engine except the two matrons, who
were putting on their things for a sober-sided stroll to
exhibit the Cochin-Chinese monstrosities, Bessie took
me in to see it. Behold, whom should we find there
but Miles, lounging disconsolately in Mr. Thorburn's
magisterial chair! He turned crimson, muttered something unintelligible, and was dashing off, when, with
an afterthought, he turned round, and said in an odd
sort of desperate voice down in his throat: "I say,
Aunt Dora, who is that? Not Zoe?"

"No," I said, "it is Bertha. It was drawn the
last time we were here all together, and that is the
reason we came to see it."

I think his father must have told him what Charles
was to his aunt, for he begged our pardon in confusion,
and hurried away. Poor fellow! I fear this is a

renewing of the sore.   Only there may be hope in the
young lady's avoiding him so desperately.   It is not
sublime indifference.   But is she worth wishing for ?

Well, we prowled about.   Mrs. Thorburn purred
to Bessie, who answered at intervals, and Mrs. Warburton expatiated to me on the loss High Scale had
suffered in my brother's family, and the unaccountable-
ness of young people, till I began to think her daughter's
fortune might be dearly bought.   She also seemed
afraid I might think Mr. Fanshawe a lover of her
daughter's, and took care to explain to me that it was
no such thing.   He knew better, poor fellow!   I
gathered from the two ladies that his father was one
of the Fanshawes of Carbiland, a *dilettante* sort of man
who, on the plea of health, spent his life in dawdling
about Italy, and married an Italian lady, who died
soon.   His son was chiefly educated in England, but
never cared for much but art.   His uncle, a banker at
Rome, would have taken him up, but he could not
bring his mind to stick to business, and chose to be
an artist, "though there's no harm in him, no harm
at all in poor Edgar," says the good lady; "and he has
got a picture in the Royal Academy."

"Dear me !" says another of the party, "I did not
know it had gone so far.   Is it not a great annoyance
to Sir Raymond ?"

Then came the one incident that vexed me.   The
stirrup-cups of coffee were drunk, the carriages had
come round, and the party flowed into the hall in
detachments, the two fathers discussing sheep, Mr.
Bootle advising Mrs. James Thorburn on his mother's
method with her parish, the children bubbling over
with laughter, Miss Warburton apart in a window,
bristling all over—every one there except Zoe, and I

was anxious not to have Bessie kept out late. A young Thorburn volunteered that she was in the Espalier path with Cousin Edgar. Her father ordered off Frank to desire her not to keep her aunts waiting; but she appeared the next moment very red and rather fluttered.

"Your aunts have waited, Zoe," said her father, almost in the tone of Louis XIV.: "See, I have almost been made to wait."

She coloured still more, meekly said she was very sorry, and we took leave; but all the talk all the way home was left to Mary and Lisa. There may be nothing in it, but she seems preoccupied. She had seemed so nice and simple, that I am much disappointed at this, and we were beginning to draw nearer when I told her about Bertha.

Yes, I did tell her all only the day before. She said nothing; but I think she cried a little. It ought to be a warning to her, but if this were her first step in the same path, how would it be with her father?

Oh, if nobody would ever fall in love!

There, I know how you and even poor Bessie would laugh at me for a poor, benighted old maid. But you see there's plenty of love for other people from your stupid, old, affectionate   D. W.

Miles is gone.

48.—A SCOLDING FROM CLYFFE.

Ratclyffe to Zoe.

BARRACKS, MONTREAL, *April* 14.

Dear Zoe—Now you see what comes of being so very high-flying. I have no patience with Emily, and

if you have encouraged her to sacrifice Miles to any of
the fine schemes which you and she were always so
full of, it is a great shame.   As if she couldn't do a
great deal more good with her fortune with his steady
old head to guide her, if that's her notion.   And as
for thinking herself too good or too clever for him,
nobody knows what there is in Miles.   Certainly, he
doesn't himself, and when people make nothing of
themselves, they'll always find plenty to agree with
them.   And now, if he is miserable and wretched, he's
quite sure to be plucked.   He would have been a great
deal more likely to do well, if papa had sent him out
to see *me*, instead of condemning him to a *tête-à-tête*
with Algy.   I know just how he will mope and fret
with no one to stir him up, and very likely with every
one finding fault with him because he is bored with all
the Stokesworthy strangers.   You don't know how
much he minds father finding fault with him.   It
rather amuses you and me to have our own ideas
and strike out new lines; but if he is obliged to do it,
and feels himself all across with people, he hates it.
He never said anything when mother was vexed at
new notions in Church matters, and he hated taking
them up; but when he once gets to think a thing
right, he'll make himself stick to it.   So mind you're
kind to him, and don't encourage Miss Emily in any
nonsense.

I wish I was at home.   What fun all the settling-in
must be !   Afraid of the aunts ?   Nonsense !   I'll be
bound I'd get on like a house on fire with them.
Miles says the neighbours are stupid.   I daresay there
are plenty of jolly ones.   How I should like to see
Algy up a glacier, and sticking there !   I enclose a
sketch of his probable appearance.   Miles will show

him far too much mercy. I do hope he'll do something extravagantly silly one day, and let the *pater* find him out.

I am very well, and find this place very jolly. Couldn't you work on father to send Miles out when he has taken his degree to see the world? And just write me a line to say how he gets along.—Ever your affectionate brother,   RATCLYFFE WINKWORTH.

Tell Aunt Dora I recollect the jolly visit I had before I sailed last year quite well.

49.—A HEAVY FATHER.

Sir Walter to Miles.

MIZ MAZE, *May.*

My dear Miles—I was glad to receive your letter of the 1st inst. announcing your arrival at Lucerne. No doubt the change of scene will prove good for you, and help you to shake off the depression produced by your disappointment with regard to Miss Warburton. I try to look upon that as the sole cause of your altered manner and evident want of spirits, but an uneasy feeling takes possession of me when I remember your extreme reticence on the subject of your money affairs, and recall one or two little indications that you were short of money when last with me, though you ought to have had in hand a large portion of your half-year's allowance.

I am convinced that what I allow you is enough for every reasonable want, and remembering how well my dear Clyffe has always managed with a smaller allowance, I cannot help fearing that you have been careless and extravagant. You are not, I hope, too

proud to take example from a younger brother, and
you will now have the advantage of Algernon Bootle's
excellent advice, so I confidently look for an improvement in you, and I trust, my dear boy, you will not
disappoint me.

Zoe is, I believe, writing to you, and will tell you
the local news.   Your aunts are kind enough to say
that they miss you, and I think they would consider it
a mark of attention if you were to write to them now
and then.   Remember me kindly to Bootle.—I am
always your affectionate father,

WALTER M. WINKWORTH.

50.—MILES UNDER REBUKE.

Miles to Sir Walter.

LUCERNE, *May.*

My dear Father—I have never had the slightest
desire to complain of my allowance, with which I am
quite satisfied.   I never wished to have more than you
gave Clyffe, and I know quite well how he managed.
I have no reasons for being out of spirits particularly,
and I wasn't aware that my manner was altered.
Nobody noticed it when Clyffe was there, or considered
us separately.   I can quite believe now that Miss
Warburton was right in thinking us unsuited to each
other, so I have no ground for complaint on that score,
and I don't wish it to be considered as a grievance.
Algy is enjoying himself; he does all the sights properly.
We read in the morning, and I think he really does
know something about Latin and Greek.

Lucerne reminds me a little of Derwentwater, or
Ullswater, but it is larger and bluer.   Pilatus is close

by. Very few English are travelling as yet. Algy thinks
we had better go on soon to a place called Engelberg.

It is more difficult to read steadily when one is
travelling than at home, and the weather is getting
very hot.

With love to the aunts and the sisters,—I am, your
affectionate and dutiful son,   MILES WINKWORTH.

51.—SIR WALTER TO HIS FAVOURITE.

*From Sir Walter Winkworth to his son Ratclyffe in
Canada.*

THE MIZ MAZE,
STOKESWORTHY, *May.*

My dear Ratclyffe—I have two letters of yours to
acknowledge, and was glad indeed to receive them.
Every detail of your Canadian experiences is full of
interest to me, and the little etchings on the margin of
the second letter were very graphic, and helped one to
realise your surroundings. I found *Hochelana* in the
library, and have been reading it with great interest,
though Zoe says we must get down some newer books
on Canada in our first Mudie-box. I am going to
subscribe partly for her sake and partly for Miss
Madgewick's; as your aunts, who are themselves sub-
scribers, tell me they can select many readable books
from the catalogue, without venturing upon those three-
volume novels of which your dear mother had such a
horror. Zoe is well, and I think begins to take more
kindly to this place than she did at first. She has a
curious constraint of manner when talking to her Aunt
Dora; and I noticed the same thing in Miles when he
was at home. Had you been here you would have

contrived to set them more at ease, and help them to
show themselves to my sisters in a more engaging light.
Aunt Dora always speaks of *you* with the greatest
affection.   There were other things besides this constrained manner which distressed me about your brother
before he went abroad.   Some gloom was of course
natural in a disappointed man, but there was a reserve
about his money affairs and a sparingness in his
expenditure which led me to think that he was in
money difficulty.   I alluded to my fears on this subject
in my first letter to him at Lucerne, but in his answer
he rather evaded the matter, merely saying that he
was quite satisfied with the allowance I gave him.   I
shall not, of course, mention my suspicions to others,
but I cannot help telling them to you, who are Miles's
second self as it were, and his good genius to boot.
Perhaps by some well-directed word in your next letter
to him you might lead him to be open with me.

I have the steward's accounts to look over to-day,
and I must not prolong this letter.   The little girls are
well and send love.—Accept, my dear son, the love of
your affectionate father,   WALTER M. WINKWORTH.

52.—THE TUTOR'S PRECAUTIONS.

Passages from Algernon Bootle's Journal.

May 1.

We reached Lucerne this morning after travelling
by the night train from Freiburg in the Black Forest.
We went immediately to the hotel, washed and
breakfasted, and then went out.   The morning was
beautiful, and the lake was of an emerald green.   We
contemplated Nature with satisfaction for some time.

I observe that there is a difference between myself and Miles in our method of communicating with the natives. When I speak French I speak it with great fluency, as my mother accustomed me to do when I was a child; but (owing, I suppose, to the fact that German is the mother tongue here) I find it well nigh impossible to render myself understood. And yet I hear other people speaking French who do not seem to find the same difficulty as I do, although they run their words into each other and ring their r's in every other word, so that I do not find it easy to understand *them!* Miles, on the contrary, goes into a shop, and says, pointing to a carving or a view, *Combien?* or even sometimes *Wie viel*, and gesticulates and points till he obtains an answer. In my position as tutor I do not consider that this would be a sufficiently dignified method of proceeding, and I therefore leave it to him.

I remained sitting on one of the benches by the lake while Miles explored the town. After a time he returned to me. "I say, Algy, I don't believe they are Protestants here a bit. I've been into the Cathedral, and it's a regular Roman Catholic one."

"My good fellow," I replied, "this does not show that we are not in a Protestant canton, but that the Protestants of Lucerne are extremely liberal-minded."

"You are sure it is a Protestant canton?" Miles said.

"Of course. Do you not hear the people around you speaking German, and is not that a sufficient proof?"

"Why should it be?" said Miles.

"Why? I should have thought that question could be asked by no educated man. The Reformation spread exclusively among the Teutonic races, and was rejected by all those who spoke languages derived from the Latin."

" I thought the Tyrolese spoke German," said Miles ; "and I am sure I've been told they were Roman Catholics."

"They speak Italian," I replied. "There may be a slight amount of German *patois* mixed with their Italian, but the foundation of their language is Italian. In the Italian Tyrol the language is spoken pure."

Where did I read this ? Miles asked me, but I could give no answer. The stores of my mind refuse to be labelled, as those of some inferior minds are.

53.—AUNT DORA'S VERSION.

Zoe to Miles.

THE MIZ MAZE, *April.*

Dearest Miles—Our last days were spent in such a whirl, that I let you go without having said half what was on my mind. What an ordeal it was at Dallington, but you made a Spartan of yourself, and no one could have guessed anything.

It was dreadful to have our last day consumed in such a manner, when I was burning to tell you all about my talk with Aunt Dora, and now I have had to let you go without hearing. I watched and watched for an opportunity when you went up to bed ; but how could you let Algy Bootle come after you to your room! Oh, I remember, he said he had been giving you advice about your knapsack. Why didn't you kick him out ? I could not wait any longer, for you know how displeased papa is at chattering in bedrooms late at night. Yes, Aunt Dora has told me the whole story, and it is very sad. It seems to have been all misunderstanding, and thus something that does seem hard and unjust was done.

Aunt Dora says that Birdie was at school for the first year or two after papa's second marriage, and was a good deal with an aunt of her own, who died. She was a very beautiful creature, full of poetry and delight in all the ideas that were thought dangerous at home. She was passionately fond of everything beautiful, music and pictures and poetry, and this aunt had cultivated her enthusiasm, whereas dear mamma thought it dangerous, and tried to sober her down, and shut out everything exciting, till she grew quite hungry for beauty. Oh yes, I can understand how dull and dreary it seemed to her. And she had not our lake and mountains, though in truth I never knew how to look at them till Mr. Fanshawe came and seemed to give me eyes as I had never had before. She was allowed only such poetry as Cowper's, and no novels at all; no newspaper but the *Record*. She had been brought forward, and made much of, when visiting in country houses with this aunt, though she was not then out. And dear mamma's dislike of society and dread of worldliness made a great change to her. Aunt Dora was sorry, and thought it a pity to make so sudden a difference; but dear mamma had strict notions of right, and would not yield to worldly tastes for a moment. Then the old vicar died, and Mr. Bernard came, fresh from Oxford, then throbbing with the revival of Church life, and he began to infuse a new spirit into the whole place. Mamma liked him, and Birdie threw herself into all the new forms of parish work which he introduced, and all would have gone well, Aunt Dora thinks, if he had not taken home a sister to live with him, who had been a governess.

She had been a good deal in Italy, with a gay, thought-
less family, and her refuge from their ways had been
in the beautiful churches, the splendid services, and
simple devotion she had seen at Milan and other places.
Bertha made great friends with her, and seemed happier
than ever before, as if the restlessness was passing away,
and she was settling down into home life and parish
work, while the truth was that she was talking and
romancing with Miss Bernard at the Vicarage, and
reading her books. Miss Bernard had been thrown
among the Italian patriots, and was full of enthusiasm
about them ; and you know well enough what a horror
papa has of them, as rebels against lawful authority, so
that Birdie lived in an entirely different world at the
Vicarage from what she was in at home, and nobody
suspected it—not even the aunts. By and by there
came an Italian refugee patriot, a Signor Marini, whose
family Miss Bernard had known in Italy, quite a
gentleman, but very poor ; so that he took a lodging
and gave lessons in the neighbourhood. Most people
looked on him only as an Italian master, and there was
no notion of any danger to Bertha from him. Aunt
Dora saw no more after that, for Aunt Bessie's trouble
came, and they had to go to Madeira. The next thing
they heard was that Miss Bernard had gone off, and
had been received into the Roman Catholic Church.
Poor mamma and papa were horrified, and Bertha was
nearly wild with distress and doubt. They thought
Mr. Bernard was at the bottom of it, and would not
let Bertha see or speak to him, or perhaps he might
have settled her mind, and shown her what was her
duty. She wrote to Miss Bernard in secret, and got
letters that unsettled her more and more. Then came
discovery, and a worse storm still. And at last she

was missing, leaving a letter to say that she must choose between her soul and her home, that she was convinced that the Roman was the only true Church, and that she was gone to be married to Signor Marini. Papa followed her to London, and found that she had gone to Miss Bernard, who had managed her being received into the Roman Church, and her marriage to Signor Marini, with whom she was gone to Switzerland. Papa could not overlook the concealment and deceit, though Aunt Dora is sure that the absolute deception was almost all Miss Bernard's, and that Bertha did not know of it. However, she had certainly behaved very badly to dear mamma, who was quite ill with worry and distress. (I think I recollect something about her illness.) And papa was aggravated by the way Miss Bernard talked to him, so that he declared that he would make no advances to Bertha, and would never have anything more to do with her. And is it not dreadful? They have never heard of her again. He thought Mr. Bernard as bad as the rest, and took us all away to High Scale, to grow up out of reach of the same influences. But when the aunts came home, Aunt Dora found that Mr. Bernard had known nothing about it, and that his sister had deceived him as much as everyone else, both about her Romish intentions, and as to the affection between Bertha and M. Marini. He was almost heart-broken about it, and he fully believed that Bertha had been more deluded by his sister, than absolutely and wilfully deceitful and headstrong. Of course he has lived down all the imputations that fell upon him, and Aunt Dora believes that papa quite exonerates him now; but this explains all that puzzled me so much in the coldness towards so good a clergyman. When Aunt Dora came home and understood

I

the matter, she could not bear that poor Birdie
should be so entirely cast off, and she wrote to her;
but the letter came back from the Swiss post-office
where it had been sent, and nothing more has ever
been heard of the poor dear girl.   Is it not dreadful
to have no notion whether she is alive, or whether her
husband is kind to her, or if she is in dreadful poverty,
longing to make it up!   Aunt Dora says she was so
fond of us, and that petting us was her great comfort.
Oh, Miles, can we do nothing ?   We are not children
now, and our sister surely has a claim on us.   I fancy,
too, that I see a sort of clue.   Perhaps I ought not,
but before I knew there was a secret, I had written to
Emily all our odd impressions, and when we were at
Dallington, we went up into her room, and she asked
me questions till it all came out.   You know there is
no resisting her.   Well, she told me that Mr. Fanshawe
met somewhere in Italy with a lady who talked English
perfectly, and asked him whether he had ever met any
of the Winkworth family, seeming quite excited about
it.   This was all she knew, and I tried to get at him
alone and ask him about it, but he seemed to be in a
maze ; I could not get him to understand, and just then
Aunt Dora sent out to say it was time to go home,
and she seemed so vexed at my delay.   Dear Miles,
do think if anything can be done !—Your loving sister,

S. W.

54.—MILES'S VIEW.

Miles Winkworth to Zoe Winkworth.

SCHWEIZERHOF, LUCERNE, *May.*

My dear Zoe—I spoke to Mr. Meyrick about
Bertha before I left home, and heard from him the

whole story.   He put it more harshly than Aunt
Dora; but the account was substantially the same.   I
did not tell you about it, as I thought you had better
hear it from the family point of view.   I can't say I
feel much sympathy with our half-sister.   Without
knowing the part played by this Marini, whoever he
was, it is impossible to judge of the rights of the story.
It is all very well to talk of her preferring her soul to
her family, she preferred her lover, which is quite a
different thing.   I daresay she had hard lines, and was
misunderstood, which isn't pleasant for any one, but I
can quite understand the repulsion caused by her conduct.   There is something hateful in mixing up religious
motives with any sort of deceit, or with any more
obvious attraction.   But, as I said before, we don't
really know her story.   Meyrick exonerated the Vicar;
and perhaps, as they were all so young, Marini was a
scamp, and took them all in together.   And if you
think of it, mamma herself was very young then, and
must have found a grown-up step-daughter rather a
handful.   She was too anxious about us all ever to
think we should do any good with ourselves.

I don't suppose Bertha would be at all to our minds
if we did see her, and probably if there hadn't been a
fuss and a mystery, we should have thought nothing
about her.   I conclude the separation has been as
complete as it appears, or Aunt Dora would have
known more.   And I think this a great mistake, and
not right by my father's eldest daughter, be she what
she may.   Therefore I should be very willing to go
into Italy and make a few inquiries about Marini at
Brescia and Varese.   One could do that without
making one's self known to him; but I have no money
to spare of my own, and I can't use what papa has

given us for the trip for such a purpose. Besides,
there's none too much of it. It is *absolutely impossible*
at present that I can ask him for any more. So I
don't see what I can do just now, but I will keep the
idea in mind.

I didn't see Fanshawe to speak to afterwards. I
noticed that every one was more or less disagreeable.
I'll ask him to tell me about the Italian lady. There's
no reason why you should not talk to your friend about
it—if she cares to hear—the facts are no secret to any
one but ourselves. This is a very pretty place, something like our own lakes on a larger scale, and soon we
go on to Engelberg. I think Algy enjoys himself in
his way, and he does all the proper sights. The lake
is extremely blue, and there is a little chapel some way
up it, with a figure of William Tell on it.   .

Be sure you send on Clyffe's letters, if there are
any. Give my love to the children, and don't let Polly
make a fool of that pointer puppy by petting him ; he'll
be no good as long as he lives, if she does.—Ever your
loving brother,   MILES WINKWORTH.

55.—MILES'S INQUIRIES.

Miles Winkworth to Edgar Fanshawe.

SCHWEIZERHOF, LUCERNE, *May.*

Dear Fanshawe—My sister has heard that you once
met an English lady in Italy who knew my father.
Can you tell me who she was and where you saw her ?
Zoe has set her heart on discovering some traces of
our half-sister, who married an Italian called Marini
many years ago. What was this lady like ?

I suppose you have often seen this place; but if you were Turner or Raphael, or all the new fellows that you admire so much rolled into one, I'd defy you to enjoy a place in company with Algy Bootle. He points out the objects of interest and tells one the height of the mountains, and talks about the effects of scenery on his inmost being, till I can think of nothing but the effects of the sun on my outer being, which makes my head ache horribly, till I am too stupid to know Greek from Latin. However, we must go up Pilatus before we go on to Engelberg. Couldn't you turn up somewhere unexpectedly? how jolly it would be. Of course I grind as hard as I can, but I know I shall be plucked; I'd rather be shot than examined any day. I forget everything I know directly the fellows in their white ties look at me. So I daresay I shall justify every one's opinion of me next June. I don't think I answered that letter you wrote me when you left Westmoreland. I didn't know exactly what to say, except that I suppose things of that sort never do go right in this world. But if it is only opposition and other people's objections, *I* wouldn't give in in the long run. Only, since I have heard all this family history, I see why my father and mother were so strict with the girls.

Nobody's friendship does one any good in such matters, but I am yours always,

MILES WINKWORTH.

Zoe says I shall be a great duffer if I don't enjoy the scenery after knowing you.

56.—EDGAR'S LADY.

Edgar to Miles.

EBURY STREET, *May.*

Dear Miles—I have several times lately been reminded of my meeting with that English lady, and the last time was in the study at Dallington, where you may remember a pretty group of heads. One of these struck me at once from its likeness to your sister Zoe,—the same pure Greek outline,—and to the very handsome, but much older face of the lady I met at Brescia. I happened that night to be writing to Carlo Monti, at whose mother's house I met her, and I asked him a question or two about her. Oddly enough I had his answer this morning, and can therefore answer your questions fully. Madame Marini—Carlo tells me this was her name—did not live at Brescia, but was staying there for a short time with relations of her husband's, with whom she came one evening to my aunt's villa. Her home, Carlo believes, was at or near Varese. Her husband was a patriot of the most restless kind, one of Garibaldi's friends, and certain to be an officer in the irregular corps he is organising now. My recollection of Madame Marini is that she was glad to meet an Englishman, and asked me a good many questions about England, especially about Wiltshire and about your family. My acquaintance with you, which was slight enough then, seemed to interest her very much, but at the same time I remember that she seemed sad, and that it was evidently an effort to pronounce your name. I forget how our talk came to an end, but I think some friend of hers interrupted us, and I remember her saying that she hoped we might

meet again.   We never did, however, for I left
Brescia the next day.   My aunt's house at Brescia, as
you may have heard, has since been broken up by her
death, and her family has scattered itself; but I still
think it would not be difficult to trace Madame Marini.
Her husband is certainly well known in Lombardy,
and will be better known now as one of Garibaldi's
officers.

When I am among mountains I like to be alone, or
with a fellow like Monti, who never mentions or thinks
of his inmost being, but collects wild flowers.   Do you
despise a white umbrella?   No doubt you do, but you
might find it a comfort in headaches.   Too much
baking does not, I think, fertilise the brain.

Thank you for your good wishes.   They may not
change the course of the world, but they are pleasant
and valuable all the same.   If I can do anything more
in the way of inquiries about Madame Marini, you
must let me know; and in any case I hope you will
write and tell me how you are getting on.—Yours
very truly,   EDGAR FANSHAWE.

PART IV.

OLD LACE.

Is't lost ?   Is't gone ?
Speak ! is it out of the way !—OTHELLO.

57.—RAISING MONEY.

Zoe to Emily.

THE MIZ MAZE, *May.*

MY DEAREST EMILY—I have been out of heart lately, or I should have thanked you sooner for all you tell me. If we had but known it sooner, for actually Miles has made up his mind to try to search our poor sister out; that is, if he has the means to do it, for he cannot take papa's money for such a purpose. Now, Emily, I want your help. You know how we have laughed at you, the heiress, having such a misplaced talent for bargaining, and this is the time to exercise it! Here is a list of such of my jewellery as can be parted with, not having been dear mamma's, nor given to me by any one that I care for. Besides, there is that old lace, I think it was Bertha's, and that she left it behind. I believe it is all the fashion, and ought to fetch a good price. Anna Grant had the bad taste once to hint that if I ever grew tired of it and wished to dispose of it, she should jump at it. I felt myself affronted then, but I should be thankful now if you can get enough from her to provide for Miles's journey on to Brescia and back to Switzerland. Hide me in the transaction as much as you can, and manage it well, like the clever girl you are. And, one thing more, always direct to me as Miss Sophia Winkworth. If Aunt Dora gets a letter to Miss Winkworth about

which she is doubtful, she keeps it to open before me,
a process which is sometimes rather trying, and a
bank-note or cheque might be astonishing to her.   We
were getting on much better together after she told me
about poor Bertha, but since the Dallington day some
chill has come between us.   Did she think our running
after one another in holes and corners missyish and
silly, or was she shocked at my turn in the garden
with Mr. Fanshawe ?

Poor dear Aunt Bessie ! So that is the way people
live on after they have lost the light of their life.   I
thought her too soft and placid to have a history, except of her inconvenient spine !   I suppose if the man
had lived, she would have been a good-humoured, bus-
tling, commonplace clergyman's wife by this time, just
like all the rest of them !   Has Aunt Dora never done
anything but wait on her and the parish ?   I fancy
so ; Aunt Dora seems to me one of the heart-whole
working bees, who are very nice, and very proper, but
cannot go deep enough to sympathise.

How I wish Mr. Fanshawe was with Miles instead
of Algy Bootle.   It is of no use to think of it just as
the Academy exhibition is opening ; but he would have
been able to make it all easy, and he has really seen
Bertha.   But of course he cannot go now.   I wonder
how his picture looks.   Tell me all about it, and how
many people stop before it.   I hope they like our barn
door.   I do ; but that may only be because it brings
back the delightful day when he sketched it, and told
us all about the crops of maize in Italy.—Ever your
loving   ⋅⁏ S. W.

58.—A READY PURCHASER.

Emily to Zoe.

HATCHETT'S HOTEL, *May.*

Dearest—Indeed I will do my very best to help
you. There is something very fine in the idea, and I
am delighted to aid in any small way. Those Grants
are not worthy to touch that lace with the tip of their
fingers, but the thing can be done most readily through
them. I wrote at once to Mrs. Grant as safer than
the girls, and without naming names, told her what a
chance there was for her, giving her full description,
length, and breadth, and all, and telling her she should
have it for £25 in hand. *Le voilà.* I grudge it
horribly, but it can't be helped. Moreover, as I pro-
gnosticated that you would be such an innocent as to
send Miles Mrs. Grant's cheque in its pristine form, I
whipped into a cab, with Poole to do propriety, went
off to Drummond's, and put it into an available shape.
I mourn the loss, but kindred blood is more than
Brussels point, and loving hearts outweigh a coral pin.
I always hated that coral set, it made you look so
prim ; so I advertised that and the malachite fetters in
the *Queen*, but the only offers I have had in exchange have been a Persian kitten, an ivory prayer-
book, and half a million old postage stamps. I would
advance the price and keep the things, only I suppose
that would be unpardonable. You can't think how
pleased I am to have a share in what will certainly be
a family reconciliation. I expect Miles will find your
Bertha living on the fifth floor of a ruined palace on a
mouthful of polenta a day. Did you know that they
have actually got a sketch of her at Dallington, in a group

of heads kept for the sake of Mr. Thorburn's brother,
who was engaged to your aunt? It seems so strange
to find that the old generation has had its romance
and outlived it. We shall seem pussy and prosy in
our turn thirty years hence, all the more as I shan't
have any romance, but be Mother Emily in a big white
lawn cap and apron. I have such a lovely plan and
elevation for my chapel school, and as soon as I go
home I mean to go to Black Joe's Pit and choose a
site for St. Joseph's, and take some toys and books to
the children.

I have not seen Edgar for more than a moment,
and could not ask him any questions.—Your affectionate
E. W.

59.—TWIN BROTHERS.

Clyffe to Miles.

MONTREAL, *April.*

My dear old Boy—I only wish I had been at home,
and I would have found a way to make Miss Emily
hear reason. Nothing shall ever persuade me that the
tiresome little sprite didn't make a difference between
you and me, and I know which she thought the most
of. But she's fairly spoilt. It used to be such fun
to hear such a bit of a creature run on and lay down
the law, that we all gave in to her, and though she
doesn't think she values herself on her money, she gets
used to being thought much of. And so by the time
she came out, she was as disdainful and cold as possible,
and as unpopular as ever such a pretty girl with a lot
of money could be. A fellow does like to feel that a
girl knows he's there, when he talks to her; but she—
she looked down out of the clouds at one, as if she was

superhuman. And so she thinks she's above caring for *you*. I hope she'll soon find out her mistake, and cry her eyes out when it's too late. Couldn't you go up there and try a turn with one of the Grants, and make her a bit jealous ? I'm sure I've been in love a dozen times at least, and got over it. And why you should break your heart for Emily, who always looks at one as if she didn't see one, or as if one were transparent, and her thoughts were fixed upon the landscape beyond, I can't think. Now, you'll be in a rage, and want to throw something at my head, and I'm only writing all this stuff because it's too bad to be away from you just now. I'd give all the girls in Canada for one good talk together; but I shall write to father and tell him that he must let you come out for a trip as soon as ever you've got your degree, and then we'll go and see Niagara and do the States and everything. A young lady told me the other day that she had no idea Englishmen were so agreeable and had so much to say. I told her she had no idea of the conversational powers of Englishmen till she had seen my twin brother.

As for our sister Bertha, I do recollect her, and I think somehow that I have always known that she made an unlucky marriage, but I thought she was dead. I agree with you that there never should be family mysteries, and whatever she did, I daresay it was taken much more seriously than it deserved. Everything is at home. I hope Lisa will keep up the frivolity of the family till I get back again. I know quite well that there never will be anything but heavy dinner parties at Stokesworthy, till she comes out. I delight in the aunts, as you know, and of course, dear old ladies, they are prepared to think their nephews and nieces perfection. Why, how dull they

must have been before we went back. I have had a
letter from Zoe full of all sorts of fads about her duty
towards them, and their misunderstandings of her nonsense; let her kiss them and laugh at them. That's
what old ladies like. After a bit you should get them
to ask Emily to stay with them. Mrs. Warburton
would make her go, and then you would appear before
her in quite a new light. I don't believe she is as
indifferent to you as she tries to appear, so don't be in
too great a hurry to take no for an answer. I may
mention in passing that I have the reputation among
all *new* acquaintances of being a perfect *screw*. It's a
long time since I had a letter from father. I suppose
he has had plenty to do at Stokesworthy. Don't be
miserable, there's a dear old boy, for my sake.—Your
loving brother,   CLYFFE WINKWORTH.

60.—THE TUTOR TAKEN IN TOW.

Miles to Clyffe.

MEYRINGEN, *May* 16.

Dear Clyffe—Zoe has just forwarded your letter to
me. You need not put yourself into such a fever about
it all. Of course I should have got on better if you
had been here; but nothing that you could have said
or done would have altered the facts. She showed me
at Dallington too plainly that her dislike to my proposal had destroyed even her old liking for me, for
she would not give me the tips of her fingers, talked
only to Zoe, telling her of some church she had seen
in London, and stopped me when I was just thinking
what question I could ask her about it, by saying that
she knew the subject wouldn't interest me. And then

she pointedly asked me if there was any hunting at Stokesworthy, as if *that* was the only subject I could care for. I said, " Yes, it had a great advantage over High Scale in that respect, and I looked forward to next winter very much." " So I thought," she said. I said, " Yes, it suits me exactly ; I was made for the sort of life." " It must be quite a relief to you to get rid of our lakes and mountains," she said, with a spiteful little smile. And I looked right at her, and said : " Yes, there was some comfort in getting reasonable sized cornfields without rocks sticking up in the middle of them."

" Oh, Miles," cried Zoe, " there was the dear rock in the field at home, with the young oaks on the top of it, and the heather all in and out, and the boulder-stone where we made the great slide——" How could she ! Girls have no sense. I hate the thought of all those plans now. I hate these rocks here because they remind me of them, though we had nothing to oppress one's senses like these great snow peaks, and make one long to get out of the way. No one ought to fret after a girl who shows she despises him. I don't. I've quite made up my mind to it ; but everything else is so worrying just now, I can't see my way through it. If I do manage to take my degree, I can't think how I shall settle down at Stokesworthy. Father would get across with me every day. And yet I'm sure I don't want to live anywhere else. And there is no end to the foolish things girls will do. I told you all about Bertha. Well, Zoe wanted me to go and find her. I told her I couldn't afford it just now, and what does she do, but get Emily to sell the old lace to the Grants, and to help her dispose of her jewels. Just imagine those two girls selling their ornaments ! What would

father say ?   And how angry he will be with me when
he knows what they did it for !   I had half a mind to
send the money back again, but I thought, after all, I
had better set the matter at rest; and so I have made
up my mind to go down to Varese and Brescia, and
make some inquiries.   Fanshawe has encountered an
English lady in those parts who knew the Winkworths.

After all, it may be waste of trouble, for it has
occurred to me that perhaps Mr. Bernard may know
where she is all the time.   I wish I had asked him
before I started, for of course I can't put the idea into
Zoe's head after what passed formerly, as we know so
little the part he really played in the matter.   However, I suppose one ought to like the chance of a sight of
Italy, and times are rather lively there with this French
war against the Austrians.   I can't help hoping that the
poor fellows will get their liberty, if all is true that one
hears on the subject, and that Fanshawe has told me.

I didn't know what line Algy would take about it,
so I told him straight out that I was going down to
Varese to inquire about my sister Madame Marini,
as I wished to know her address.   Would he like to
come too ?

"But Sir Walter ?" said he.   "Have we his permission to extend the tour ?"

"No," I said.

"But our funds are calculated for a certain time
and place," he said.   So I told him I had other money,
and that I should make it right with my father myself
(*shall* I ?), but that he might do as he pleased.   So,
after a great deal of bother, he said he thought it was
his duty to come too, as Sir Walter didn't intend us
to separate.   I believe his curiosity is extreme on the
subject.   Then he has made acquaintance with an

Austrian countess who speaks a little English, and she has imbued him with a notion that the Italians are fiends incarnate, so there's a great excitement in coming to close quarters with them.   Of course there's no chance of our seeing anything of the war, as I should not think this independent movement of Garibaldi's would come to much, and I shall only just stay long enough to make my inquiries, and then we are going back to Geneva.   I find Algy's foreign languages (modern ones at least) don't come up to the scratch, so I have been learning up some Italian sentences, out of a dialogue book in five languages, which he has, and I hope I shan't forget them.   Algy was so certain that all Germans were Protestants, that it took a whole monastery at Engelberg to persuade him of his mistake.   So we are to take refuge in Geneva if we get out of Italy without being caught either by Garibaldi or the Pope.   Algy always insists on carrying the passports, for which the knapsack has a special pocket.   It is too convenient by half, and he always straps himself up into it whenever we take a walk ; he *says* to get himself into training, but I believe he thinks it looks well, and suits the British tourist.   It is an awful weight, but of course he didn't grow up among our fells for nothing, and he does his mountains very fairly.   Not that we have done anything very desperate, for if I do, I get so sleepy over the reading that I can do no good with it.

Well, I shall write again from Geneva, and tell you what our adventures have been, not that we are likely to have any.   Mind, you always hear the worst of my troubles, but I shall come out of them somehow, no doubt, and it's always good to get a letter from you.—
Ever yours,   M. WINKWORTH.

61.—THE LEATHERN BOTTEL.

Passages from A. Bootle's Journal.

MEYRINGEN, *May.*

Miles and I were out walking to-day, when he suddenly turned round. "I say, Algy, did your mother ever come across my eldest sister, do you know?"

"The one that ran away with the music-master?" I was going to say, but stopped, for Miles is quite ridiculously irritable if any one mentions his relatives without what he considers due respect.

"I mean Madame Marini," said Miles.

"I did not know her name," I replied. "I don't know if she ever saw her, but I have heard her talked of."

"Oh," said Miles, and asked no more.

"Is she likely to be paying a visit soon to her ancestral home?" said I.

"Not that I know of," he said, shortly.

"I have always thought the relationship must be a trial," said I, sympathetically; but Miles is not a person who responds to sympathy. He said,

"A light one, as I have never set eyes on my brother-in-law. Besides, though he had no business to run away with my sister, he may be a decent fellow for anything I know to the contrary."

"My dear Miles—a music-master!"

"I expect he belongs to a much more swell family than we do, if you come to that," said Miles.

"Than you, Miles? The oldest baronetcy in Wiltshire!"

"Nonsense," said Miles. "It's my belief that if you want to get left out of all the fun there is in life

—and what is better than fun besides—you'd better be heir to the oldest baronetcy in your county." And he slashed at the hedge with his walking-stick.

" The powers that be are of divine appointment," I began.

" Did I ever say they weren't ?" said Miles.   " My good fellow, you ain't a parson yet, so shut up till you are.   You don't know anything about it, as you have been spared the infliction."

" The Bootles," I said, proudly, " are of an ancient family also, though without a title.   The name, as perhaps you are aware, was originally Bottell; and the article of common use known by that name is said to have taken its appellation from my ancestor William de Bottell, who first used it.   It is to him that the well-known words apply :

> " 'I hope his soul in heaven may dwell
> Who first invented the Leather Bottell.' "

" Most interesting," said Miles, and walked on in front, with what looked like a broad grin upon his face. Could he have been laughing at my ancestors ?   I called after him :

" He was not a mere craftsman, Miles.   I do not wish to imply that he made the Leather Bottell himself."

" No, old fellow," said Miles, grinning; "no one who knew you would dream that any of your ancestors could have done such a thing."

It is evident, then, that I *have* impressed even this scoffer Miles with my personality.   I am more than satisfied.

62.—ZOE'S EXPEDIENT.

Zoe to Miles.

THE MIZ MAZE, *May.*

My darling Miles—Here is something to begin
with ; I hope to get more. Was not it a happy thought
to use that old lace which really ought to have been
Bertha's, and was left behind by her? Who would
have thought it would have fetched so much ? It was
all Emily's doing, and she is a capital manager. She
will dispose of some trumpery jewellery too that nobody here has ever seen, and I never cared for. I
wish I did. I had rather be sacrificing something
when you are acting.

Dear old fellow, I am sure this will do you good.
It is a comfort to see through all your grumbling that
you agree with me in the main point about finding our
sister. I only wish there was time to get advice from
Mr. Fanshawe. If only we had known it in time, you
could have talked to him at Dallington, and he might
even have gone with you, and made all delightful.
Dear old fellow, I wish you could look up and admire.
I am sure being in the midst of so much beauty must
do you good.—Your loving   ZOE.

63.—MILES TO THE RESCUE.

Miles to Zoe.

MEYRINGEN, *May* 17.

My dear Zoe—How could you think of selling that
lace ? It was no more yours to sell than it was Aunt
Dora's in her time, or will be any one else's. Of

course I can pay you back the money at midsummer, but that won't get the lace back, which is worth at least four times what you got for it. And as for the jewels, I can't see how a young lady can find any proper way of disposing of such things, it is quite out of the question either for you or for Emily. The £25 is quite enough, and I won't have any more. I strongly advise you if you are in any difficulty to tell Aunt Dora the truth; but if you are afraid to do this you can say that I know all about it, and will explain it to my father when I come home, or sooner if he wishes it. And on *no account* do either you or Emily go into shops asking the value of your ornaments. She is in London, isn't she? and she cannot possibly know what places are fit for her to go to. And only suppose she was recognised by an acquaintance. The idea drives me perfectly frantic! Now take particular notice of what I mean to do. We start to-morrow and go over the St. Gothard by Lago Maggiore to *Varese,* which I hear from Fanshawe is the place where his English lady lived. It is full, he says, of villa residences. I shall inquire if the name of Marini is known at the Post Office, and perhaps at the Bank. I shall find out where they live, and what the family consists of, if possible, and what position Marini holds. If I succeed, I shall go straight off to Geneva; if not, I shall go on to Brescia, and see if I can find anything out there. If both these places fail, we have no other clue. In any case you may expect to hear from me in nine or ten days at the very farthest from Geneva. Send letters there (Poste Restante). I cannot of course give an Italian address, but when I get to Geneva I will write at once.

I have had a good deal of trouble with Algy, who

is "afraid Sir Walter will think him to blame," but
told him I would take it entirely on myself, and he
might stay behind if he liked. However, he is coming
to take care of me! He was all wrong about the
Protestant canton, though where there is an English
service I can't see what difference it makes to one;
but we promised father, and so I have ascertained for
myself that Geneva is as Calvinistic as possible.
Besides, they say it is very fresh and open, with a
great big lake, where one can get bathing and boating,
so I think I shall like it better than this narrow valley.
I did not mean to write severely about Bertha; on the
contrary, I didn't say half what I feel on the subject.
We are doing very well, and Algy is no fool when he
gets to work at his business, but very patient and
clear, so if. I can give my mind to him I think he will
pull me through. It is not easy to see one's last
lingering hopes disappointed, but it is no doubt better
in the end. I shall never annoy Emily again by the
slightest allusion to the past, and I think I could have
taken her refusal without obliging her to treat me as
she did at Dallington. It is all over now, and the
sharper the pain the shorter, so don't imagine I am
going to be broken-hearted. But what good you think
scenery can do a fellow when he is out of spirits, I
can't think. I should like it very much under other
circumstances. One can only do one's best, and try to
believe that it's all right. Only, my dear, I'm very
sorry if I was a savage bear, as Polly says, and found
fault with you; but mind you don't get drawn into
saying or acting anything untrue, nor into letting
Emily conceal things from her mother.—Your loving
brother   MILES WINKWORTH.

64.—WHERE'S THE LACE?

Fanny to Annie.

MIZ MAZE, *May.*

My dear Annie—I write by desire of Miss Elthwayte, who is too much put about and fussed to write herself, to ask you to get old Mr. and Mrs. Long to let you look over all the boxes and drawers that was left at High Scale. She cannot find nowhere that lace that Miss Winkworth used to wear on her blue silk. She could have taken her oath before a Justice that she put it into the big black box, and put it away in Miss Winkworth's cabinet when we got here, but now she cannot find it nowhere, high nor low, and she does hope you will find it and post it to her before Miss Winkworth misses it. It is old thick stuff, a terrible bad colour, and nothing to look at, but it is very old, and my late lady sets great store by it, for it had been in the family hundreds of years. It is made up in a bertha and is in blue paper, so you cannot miss it. Poor Miss Elthwayte says it is as much as her situation is worth to find it before it is missed, and it may be soon, for Miss Winkworth will be lightening her mourning.

Mr. Winkworth and Mr. Algy are gone to foreign parts together. If your young lady could see Mr. Winkworth she would have pity on him. And so no more from your affectionate friend   FANNY.

From Mrs. Bootle to Sir Walter Winkworth.

High Scale Vicarage,
May 1859.

Dear Sir Walter—I take up my pen to discharge a sacred though painful duty. Sacred it is to the memory of our departed saint.

To begin at the beginning, you will, I know, be surprised and sorry when you remark the black edge of this letter. Mr. Bootle has lately lost a relative of whom he had heard nothing for many years, and who remembered him handsomely in his will. Now, as I always say, one good turn deserves another, and so I told Mr. Bootle I should deem it highly ungrateful if I did not have a black gown made at Hurst and Dugdale's in Kendal. You know what Mr. Bootle is, and will not be surprised that he said, "Maria, my dear, you know best of course, but could not Susan Fell come and work here as usual, and save you the trouble of a journey to Kendal?"

"Mr. Bootle," I replied, "you surprise me. I could not in conscience touch the money of your late relative, did I not show him proper respect." As, however, Mr. Bootle did not seem to understand the matter, I merely desired him to mention at the school that, owing to family bereavements, I should not take the sewing class, and sending him to visit one or two of our parishioners in my place, I started. By-the-bye, it *is* so tiresome that when he visits instead of me, he never *can* remember to leave the right tracts; the drunkards don't get the intemperate ones, and that elect woman

Mrs. Scroggs was so offended because he gave her "Are you Converted?"

Now, it is well to observe the chain of providential circumstances which lead to great results. Happening then to pay this visit to Kendal, and having my steps so marvellously directed to Hurst and Dugdale's, where my simple wants have rarely taken me before, Miss Dugdale casually remarked, while taking my measure, that she was executing a very handsome order for that stuck-up and worldly-minded Miss Grant—would I step up and see it? "Miss Dugdale," I replied, "I will. Painful as the sight must be to a simple Christian like myself,—if I may humbly say so,—yet it is well to know to what extent the vanity and worldliness of the unregenerate heart can go in the fashion of those garments, which, as we know, should only recall our shame." And ashamed I truly felt when I saw a dress,—a ball-dress I think Miss Dugdale said,—and on it, if you can believe me—yes, I know it's painful —was that beautiful old family lace our poor dear Lady Winkworth once showed me,—Brussels point, I believe it is, and very valuable,—not that I know anything about such things, of course. There it was, arranged in a berthe fit for a princess. This is painful enough; I feel for you indeed, dear Sir Walter, and sincerely sympathise, but worse remains to be told.

"Miss Dugdale," I said, "I doubt that lace is stolen!" And that was my firm conviction, knowing how easy it is for a maid to take away such a small matter as lace when the mortal body it once adorned is a prey to the worm. I therefore made it a point of duty, due to our lengthened friendship, to drive over next day to call on the Grants and tell them my suspicions. And I assure you you might

have knocked me down with a feather when they said
they had merely bought it through Miss Warburton.
I asked, idly enough, chiefly for the sake of saying
something, the date of the advertisement. Another providential and undesigned coincidence! And happening
on my way back to have to call for some fresh tracts
(capital ones, comparing life to a railway—I enclose a
few—" Have you taken your Ticket?" " Change Trains
Here!" "The Awakening Whistle," &c.), I chanced to
notice the *Queen* of the very date the Grants had
named, and reflecting how unlike Hurst and Dugdale's
cut poor Susan Fell's is, I thought it would be quite a
boon to her if I presented her with a copy, explaining,
of course, she must only make a modified use of the
fashions contained in it—fashions, Sir Walter, which
I will not shock your delicacy by mentioning. Judge
of my amazement, and I may add distress, when I
saw almost at once the advertisement I enclose. Poor
Zoe! it will doubtless be most painful to her to be
thus detected by an indulgent parent in a course of
deceit at her tender age; for can I doubt, seeing her
lace thus disposed of by her chief friend, that it is her
doing, and for what object? Knowing that you will
be grateful to the friendly hand that opens your eyes,
and with heartfelt sympathy, I beg to sign myself—
Your Christian (though unworthy) friend,

MARIA BOOTLE.

P.S.—Mr. Bootle would desire his compliments,
but I have not thought it well to confide this matter
to him.

66.—SIR WALTER'S GRATITUDE.

Sir Walter to Mrs. Bootle.

THE MIZ MAZE, *May* 1859.

Dear Mrs. Bootle—I am greatly obliged to you for your letter, though its contents have both startled and pained me. Zoe happens to be spending the day with her aunts, but I shall question her at the first opportunity with regard to the strange transactions which you have made known to me. She does indeed seem to have acted most unaccountably, but I endeavour to suspend judgment on the case till I have heard her explanation. We must, of course, take immediate steps for the recovery of the lace.

I have good accounts of our travellers, and it is a great satisfaction to me to know that Miles has such a companion as your estimable son, and is pursuing his studies under the most favourable auspices.

Permit me to condole with you on your family loss ; and with best regards to Mr. Bootle, believe me, Yours very sincerely,   WALTER M. WINKWORTH.

Many thanks for the little books you were so good as to send.

67.—ZOE IN DISTRESS.

Zoe to Emily.

MIZ MAZE, *May.*

O Emily, dearest, this is a dreadful state of things ! First, there were little alarms over a new black silk which Aunt Dora suggested might be trimmed with the Brussels point. Had I ever worn it ? I said yes, and looked sheepish, and felt like a monster of deceit

when I put her off with affecting a passion for
Honiton.

And then comes to papa such a letter as I should
hardly have thought even Mrs. Bootle could write.
Fancy her going to Dugdale's at Carlisle! It could
only be for the purpose of beholding something against
which to uplift her testimony, for I never suspected
Miss Dugdale of *her* dresses. However, there she
espied the unhappy lace displayed on some gorgeous
robe, which she hunted down to the Grants. Then
she must needs go and warn them that it must be
stolen goods, and the poor creatures could only explain
that they got it through you. Next, she "happens"
to take up the *Queen,* and with the scent of a blood-
hound, pounces on the coral and malachite, cuts out the
advertisement, and glories in sending it to papa, with all
her investigations about the lace. Never before had
she the chance of making so much mischief between us.

I knew something was coming when he called me
into the study. He gave me the letter to read, and
asked me if I could contradict it. I said, "No;" and
after that there was nothing for it but to hold my
tongue, and say I could not explain why I had done
it. I longed to tell him all, but then he would have
been able to stop Miles, and all the hope of finding
Bertha be over; besides, it would have been sacrificing Miles. He asked if I had fallen into any money
difficulties, and I said, "No." I almost wish I had
begun then to say I could tell him nothing, for when
he said that comparatively he should be satisfied to
know that I had raised money for my brother's sake,
it seemed cruel not to tell him; but then he would
have fancied Miles extravagant.

I felt so wicked and obstinate in denying all explanation, and leaving them all to think what they please of me. I find really that it was a much more serious thing than I fancied to part with the lace, for it is a regular heirloom, and came into the family with the old Lady Dorothy, who was maid of honour to Queen Anne. I had no right to part with it, and I managed to say that I was sorry to have done so, but that it was for no bad reason, and I hoped he would forgive and trust me.

He is terribly hurt about it all, and I don't think he half believes or trusts me. He even seems to think I am not a safe companion for the little girls. How could the woman dare to come between us? But I must not write or think about her!

I am like a prisoner at large, and he is always going down to discuss me with Aunt Dora. Aunt Bessie cries whenever she sees me, but neither asks me any questions. I wish Aunt Dora would; I should not tell her, but I think she would believe me to have an honest purpose if I had it out with her. Now I am not sure what they think, or of what they suspect me, and I dare not begin to ask, lest I should betray it all. Is not it miserable? And yet I think I tried to do right.—Your loving, but poor, unhappy,   S. W.

68.—EMILY'S ENCOURAGEMENT.

Emily to Zoe.

TRIERMAIN, *May.*

My poor Dear—How horrid! What a satire on us poor *nouvelles riches* that I never conceived the idea of heirloom-lace that might not be disposed of as one's own. I will do my best with Mrs. Grant. " Shylock, there's thrice thy money offered thee!" not literally, but figuratively. And after all, what is lace to the recovery of a daughter and healing a wound? Depend upon it, Sir Walter will be ready to go down on his knees (metaphorically) to thank and bless you and brave old Miles for what you have done.

You have regularly sent the knight-errant out on a quest. How he would gruffly contemn the notion. I hope he will not let Algy hinder him.

Keep up a good heart; we will recover the lace and satisfy Sir Walter, and don't you worry your poor little conscience. I have been over to St. Joseph's and chosen my site. The children stood about and stared. They snatched the toys; I hardly think they had ever seen one before.—Your loving   EMILY.

69.—THE ABIGAIL'S MIND RELIEVED.

Fanny to Annie.

THE MIZ MAZE, *May.*

My dear Annie—I must write one line to say that Miss Winkworth told Miss Elthwayte not to trouble about the lace; she had sent it away herself.

She went so very red, and Miss Elthwayte thinks she had done it to raise money for something. Her pa and her aunts have found fault with her for it. I wonder now what she done it for. Most like to send something to her brothers. I'll never believe nothing else, though there are them as says she was carrying on with Mr. Fanshaw, and he havn't got nothing of his own. But Miss Winkworth is that good as I know she'd never do nothing for her young man on the sly. "She baint no serpent," says I; I

make sure that 'tis them brothers. Mr. Ratclyffe he
is a pleasanter young gentleman and livelier than Mr.
Winkworth, but he baint so steady; and it is like he
had his little expenses as he would not tell his pa of.
And Miss Winkworth is a good sister, no doubt, and
she spoke so handsome about the blame being hers,
that Miss Elthwayte said she could have cried. I
can't say no more, for the bells is ringing.—Dear
Annie, I am, yours,   FANNY.

70.—ZOE'S SILENCE.

Miss Winkworth to Mrs. Home.

May.

My dear Mary—You always have inflicted on you
the history of all our worries, and here is one for you.
Of course you remember the beautiful Brussels point
always enjoyed by the reigning eldest daughter of the
house. It struck me that now Zoe is going into
slighter mourning it would look well on her black
silk, and I advised her to have it put on. She coloured
and made no definite answer, so I thought either she
associated it with her mother, or that it might be torn,
and that she did not like to say so, or else that she
resented interference, so I said no more. So little do
we understand these girls!

Yesterday, Walter came in great perturbation to
show me a letter from that Mrs. Bootle, who had
recognised the lace at a dressmaker's at Carlisle, and
traced it to a lady who told her that Miss Warburton
had offered to secure it for her for ready money. Mrs.
Bootle also enclosed an advertisement from the *Queen*,
a paper that enables girls to dispose of their jewels
and other keepsakes anonymously. We could not but

own that the ornaments offered for sale were Zoe's.
Most extraordinary and annoying, is it not ?   I could
not have believed that she would part with the lace
or the coral set which her godfather gave her.

There has certainly been something odd and reserved about her ever since that day at Dallington
when she met Miss Warburton.   Can it be a romanti-
cally foolish charity ?   The Thorburns seemed to think
Miss Warburton had tendencies of that kind, and one
knows how stories speak of laying down diamond rings
and jewels as offerings, just so as to make foolish girls
think it grand to give away what is not their own.

I cannot bear to think of any other motive for it, and
I have told her father that probably she did not at all
understand the value of the lace to the family, indeed her
mother's unworldliness would prevent her from dwelling
on it.   Walter, however, is very much disturbed at the
secrecy of the affair, and, recurring to the former shock,
is ready to believe anything.   His notion is that Miles
is in some scrape, and has made her assist him.   He
says Miles has never been open with him about his
expenditure ; and then he breaks down, poor fellow,
and asks what has he done to forfeit his children's
confidence.   I wish they could know what pain they
have inflicted on him ; but I suppose they think his
dignity unapproachable.

5 P.M.—Walter has been here again.   He cannot
extract anything from Zoe but that she did part with
the lace, and that she had never understood that it was
not her own to do with as she pleased.   She declined
to give any reason, and when he pressed her to say
whether she had been trying to raise money for Miles
she would make no answer.   He even told her that,
wrong as her brother might be, it would be a relief to

find that this was the case; but she only looked white
and fixed, but said she could not explain.   It is a
wretched business, and has thoroughly upset Walter,
who is full of vague suspicions, such as he would never
have entertained but for Bertha's doings.   Still, I cannot believe that Zoe can be deceiving us.   Why are
girls so inscrutable to their elders?—Your loving

D. W.

71.—Miss Madgewick in a Fog.

Miz Maze, *May.*

My dear Emily—What did you all do with your-
selves that day at Dallington? for it seems to me that
nobody here has been quite the same since.

Perhaps the aunts and the Thorburns, added to the
original elements, have produced some odd and unac-
countable results (you see I am fresh from a chemistry
lesson to Mary—effect of new elements in decomposing
an original combination, etc., hence this simile).   But
be the cause what it may, something mysterious has
certainly come over the house, and yet it is not easy
to say what it consists in.   Ever since that lunch at
Dallington there has been a sort of stiffness between
Zoe and Miss Winkworth.   They all seemed more or
less depressed that evening, I thought, except the
children; but, considering all things, that was explic-
able enough.   Sir Walter was in his most frigid and
majestic mood, and Zoe seemed nervous and preoccupied, which was no more than I expected.   But
there is clearly something wrong beyond the grievance
of your cousin happening to be at Dallington.   Miss
Winkworth has grown colder and graver, not only to
Zoe, but to us all, and, I fancy, particularly so to me;

and as for Sir Walter, icy is too warm a word for his
manner just now to every one but Lisa. Could Mr.
Fanshawe have said something definite the other day?
and do they fancy that Zoe knew of his being there,
and that I was aiding and abetting?

But things have been much worse this last week.
I can't understand Zoe at all, or, indeed, any of them.
She looked this morning as if she had been up all
night, and the tears are always coming into her eyes.
But she keeps her own counsel, so that I cannot say a
word to help her. Perhaps you may be able to draw
out some explanation. I am really getting quite
uneasy about her, and so evidently are the aunts.
They watch her in an anxious, distressed way that, I
can see, drives her half frantic. Miss Bessie at last
went so far as to ask me whether I had any idea what
Zoe had on her mind——whether I thought there was
anything between her and Mr. Fanshawe; to which I
could only answer that I had no reason to believe so,
that it was evident to everybody else that he cared for
her, but that, so far as I knew, when we left High
Scale she had not discovered it. Then Sir Walter, as
we were walking home from church on Sunday, astonished me by suddenly asking in his magisterial manner,
whether I had ever had cause to suppose that Zoe
was exceptionally careless about money. Did she
keep her dressmaker's bills within reasonable limits?
Was she in the habit of exceeding her allowance? I
was so much surprised that I could not answer for a
moment. It was such an extraordinary sort of question
for him to ask me. And he went on to say (by way of a
sort of excuse, I suppose) that Zoe must not be allowed
to fancy that she could afford to throw about her money
as lavishly as Miss Warburton. I told him that foolish

extravagance was the last thing of which I could accuse Zoe, and I must say I felt very indignant.   What *did* he mean ? and what have they all got into their heads about her ?   Something is certainly very wrong between her and Sir Walter.   I am only too well aware that our feelings on the subject of Mrs. Bootle amount almost to a monomania; but, do you know, I can *not* get rid of a dark suspicion that she has something to do with this, unlikely though it seems.   It is an odd coincidence that Sir Walter has undoubtedly looked blacker, and the plot, in general, thickened, since Tuesday, when Lisa drove into Salisbury with her father, and announced on coming home that he had found a letter from Mrs. Bootle by the second post.

Altogether it is a doleful state of things.   I wish Ratclyffe was at home.   He was like a sea-breeze in the house, and just now the Miz Maze is infested by a fog that is growing of a pea-soup-like density.   We never had anything quite like this at High Scale, though the atmosphere used now and then to be somewhat oppressive.

Do write to Zoe, and see if you can do anything to clear it.   What you are pleased to call my powers of divination are entirely at fault.—Your affectionate but thoroughly bewildered   MADGE.

PART V.

THE CAPTIVE KNIGHTS.

" I am sick of captive thrall."

72.—In Captive Thrall.

Miles Winkworth, imprisoned in Varese, to
Sir Walter Winkworth.

May 24.

My dear Father—I hope that when this letter, which I address to you, is read by the authorities here they will see good reason to put an end to our troublesome detention, and I hope, therefore, you will not be under any great anxiety when you receive it as to our safety, and that I shall soon be able to follow it up with fuller explanations.

Having reason to think that my sister, Madame Marini, was living in this neighbourhood, Algernon Bootle and myself left Meyringen, where we were staying at your desire, and where I was reading with him for my degree, and came here over the Grimsel and Furca to Andermatt, and so over the St. Gotthard Pass into Italy.

When we arrived here we found the town in much excitement, preparing to receive the Cacciatori delle Alpi, under General Garibaldi. I considered that as we were British subjects, and had no concern with either of the contending parties, nor any connection with the Austrian Government, this fact could make no difference to our purpose, so we proceeded to make inquiries for Signor Marini at the Post Office and other places. There was a great crowd and excitement at the landing-stage, and unfortunately we left the knapsack containing our passports behind in the boat, and have not been able to recover it. Whether, being ignorant of Italian, we expressed our friendly inquiries awkwardly, or whether they mistook us for Austrians from our English appearance, we were taken in custody by some of the Italian soldiers, and given to understand that our inquiries for an officer of the Cacciatori delle Alpi were suspicious, and we have since been detained without the opportunity of speaking to any official who could understand us. We hope, therefore, that either by means of this letter, which Algernon Bootle is translating into French that it may be more easily understood, or by your answer to it, the authorities in possession of the town will understand that I am your eldest son, and that my tutor is the son of the Rev. Joshua Bootle, Rector of High Scale, Westmoreland, England, and that our inquiries were of a purely personal nature, and had no concern with any foreign politics whatever, with which we have nothing at all to do.——I am, my dear father, your affectionate and dutiful son,   MILES WINKWORTH.

To Sir Walter Winkworth, Bart.,
        The Miz Maze, Stokesworthy,
                Wiltshire, England.

Miles's Diary.

VARESE, *May 25.*

There is nothing at all to do in this horrid hole, so as *my* knapsack was not left behind, and I have got pen and ink, I may as well try and write a diary as well as Algy, and it may amuse Clyffe to have it by and by, for of course somebody will read my letter to my father, and let us out.

It was great fun, I thought, to come in for such an excitement as the entrance of the Garibaldians: all the bells ringing, and everybody shouting and wild with joy. It is something to have seen, and I felt quite kindly towards all the poor fellows, and began to ask every one I could about Marini, but they all took it amiss, and at the door of the Post Office we were surrounded by some soldiers, who, as far as we could make out, asked us why we were inquiring for Colonel Marini. I said at first that was our own affair, and Algy was foolish enough to say in French, which unluckily some one understood, that they had better take care and not annoy us, as we were friends of the Emperor of Austria. Then they howled at us and shouted like demons. I said, "Inglese, Inglese," as loud as I could, and I would have explained about Marini, but I couldn't remember the Italian for brother-in-law. They pointed at our faces. Of course Algy is very pink and white and sandy-haired, and I suppose even I am much fairer than Italians, to say nothing of being a good deal bigger. So at last I thought we'd try and fight our way out, and I knocked one fellow down, and Algy hit out with a will, but he would go on about the Emperor of Austria, and I soon saw that it was no good resisting, as there were a couple of dozen of them, and I hoped we should get taken before a magistrate who would hear reason. All this while it was lightening, and thundering, and pouring with rain, so we were wet through, and they dragged us off and shut us up in this horrid dirty place, which is as damp and stuffy as ever it can be. I don't grudge the Italians their liberty, but I hope they'll learn to

have a little more respect for other people's. I asked
for the parish priest; I thought we could make him
understand, but I think he must favour the Austrians,
for the fellow that looks after us was more uncivil than
ever, and wouldn't fetch him.

·I think I must have caught cold in the thunder-
storm, for I do feel uncommonly seedy.

May 26.—I couldn't sleep all night, and to-day
I can hardly sit up, my head is so dizzy. Algy talks
about malaria fever, which is a nice idea. No one
takes any notice of my letter. The water they give us
has a horrid taste, and I hate all these dirty Italian
ways of cooking. If one could climb up and get that
window open——

27.—I turned so faint in trying to get at it that
I had to give it up and lie down, but I'm better this
morning. I dare say it's half fancy, and only the close
room. It's so unlikely that I should be ill when Algy
isn't. He was dreadfully frightened when I fainted,
and said he could never look Sir Walter in the face,
and he ought not to have come without his knowledge.
Perhaps we ought not, but it was all my doing, and
there's no use in telling one how fellows die of these
fevers, and in saying things that make one home-sick.
Of course we shall soon get out, and one breath of
fresh air would set me right again. He says I mustn't
write any more now, and I don't think I can. I *hope*
father got the letter. Perhaps he'll soon be here to
look for us.

June 3.—I have been so ill that I hardly know
how we have got on; but I am quite myself now. I
want to beg my dear father to listen to what Zoe has
to say about Bertha, it is not good for her to keep it
all to herself. Don't let any one blame Algy, whatever

happens, he is very kind; and if I don't get better, my
love to every one. Tell Emily to think as kindly as
she can. No one will ever love her better. You'll all
forgive me for being so dull and savage lately. There'll
be Clyffe,—oh, dear, dear Clyffe, if I could only see him
again! The others will have *him*, but he will miss me.
I want just to see him.

June 5.—Algy says it is Sunday. He has read
some of the service. So you are all praying for the
prisoners and captives. I think I can say "His will
be done." She would be frightened now if she had
cared about me; and this place might make Clyffe
ill too.

73.—TRUE TO HIS PRINCIPLES.

Algernon's Diary.

AOSTA, *May 21.*

Miles has brought us both here on what I cannot
characterise as anything but a wild-goose chase of his
own. He rebelled against Meyringen, its wood-carvings
and its waterfalls, and indeed I myself, though possess-
ing a mind better stored than his, began to find the
narrowness of the Hasli Thal monotonous, in spite of
its untainted Protestantism. Accordingly, yielding to
his urgent representations, we came over the Pass into
Italy; and we may, I suppose, claim the glory of being
the first tourists who have done so this season.

We travelled over the Grimsel and down to this
place with a most fascinating person, in whom I am
able to trace all the attractions of the ancient aristocracy
of the Hapsburgs. The Countess Ida von Rosenhals—
such was her graceful and euphonious name—is a
comparatively young woman, but it is evident that she

has a large experience in the life of Courts and political
circles. When we found that we were travelling along
the same road, and that she wished for our escort, I
first proposed that we should enjoy the pleasure and
advantage of her conversation — she spoke English
fluently—turn and turn about ; but Miles said gruffly,
"You may have all my share, and welcome, of that
German chatterbox." In this irreverent way he spoke
of such a vision of beauty, grace, and culture as had
never before greeted my eyes ; and thus he missed
much most valuable information about the country to
which we were going, which I retail here, that I may
have it at hand when I publish an account of my
Continental travels, as my mother is so anxious for me
to do.

The Countess Ida von Rosenhals informs me that
the popular view about the discontent of Italy with
the Austrian Government is entirely erroneous. In
Sicily and Naples, she says, where the people are all
brigands, it is natural that they should have been
discontented with any one who tried to keep order
among them, as the unfortunate King of Naples had
done, and sacrificed his crown in the attempt. But in
the north of Italy, she informs me, though there is a
party of so-called patriots, they are thought entirely
beneath the contempt of the Austrian authorities.
Some of her friends have tried to persuade her not to
return to Italy, but to remain at Vienna, where she had
been on a visit to the Court ; but so certain is she that
the Austrian Government is able to keep down the
Italians with a high hand, that she insisted on
returning. "I simply say," she said, with the high-
bred grace of an aristocrat, "that I am a personal
friend of the Emperor of Austria, and any opposition

to my wishes goes under at once." When I told Miles this, I feel grieved to say his only remark was, "Humbug!" To such an extent can prejudice colour the most candid mind, as I would charitably hope Miles's to be. I at once made up my mind, however, that in case of getting into any difficulty in Italy, I would at once describe myself as a friend of the Countess Ida von Rosenhals, an *intimate friend* of the Emperor of Austria.

Miles is not so vivacious a travelling companion as I could have hoped he would prove. He marches on for miles and miles in silence, and when we reach the inns he abuses the cookery, and refuses to eat. He drinks great draughts of water, which he says do him as much good as disgusting foreign messes. In vain I recommend him to do at Rome as Rome does; he is stubborn in his own way, and cannot understand my excellent appetite.

Varese, May 23.—How little I thought the last time that I wrote in this diary that my next entry would be that of a prisoner immured in a dark and odoriferous room! Yet such we are, for how long I cannot say; and Miles is a cause of anxiety to me besides, for though he is now asleep on the miserable straw bed they have provided us with, his face is flushed, he is perpetually starting and talking in his sleep, and I am afraid he must have caught a severe cold, for he shivered like anything last night, though I found it only too hot and stuffy.

We arrived by boat at Como on our way hither, and an unfortunate oversight of mine was the beginning of our troubles. Being somewhat tired with a long walk and the sultriness of the weather, when we got into the boat I unfastened my knapsack and laid it

down beside me. In this knapsack were our passports; for as I am a better linguist than Miles — it
would indeed be hard to find a worse one—I always
carry the passports, and do what my good father calls,
with his accustomed humour, the *parlevooing* over them.
When we arrived at our destination, I saw a crowd
standing on the shore, and anxious to see what was
the cause of it, I forgot my precious knapsack, and
sprang out of the boat without it. When Miles perceived my loss and said : " I say, where's your knapsack ?" the boat was already speeding away up the
lake. Well for me that I carried my diary in my
waistcoat pocket to put down stray notes as they
struck me, otherwise I should be even without this
poor resource for passing away the time.

When we were on the boat nothing told us of our
coming adventure. A little dark Italian, it is true,
came up and said, *Amici d' Italia?* to which, remembering the Countess Ida von Rosenhals, I replied in
my best Italian, *Amici d' una amica dell' Imperatore
d' Ostricia.* I felt that this would show that our
sympathies were with the governing classes, and the
man looked glum and retired. Miles asked me what
I had said, and objected strongly when I told him.
He even went so far as to say that the lady was a
relative of Miss Carolina Wilhelmina Amelia Skeggs.
(*N.B.*—To inquire when I get back who this lady may
be. I do not find her name familiar to me, and I do
not wish to betray to Miles that this is the case.)

We took a carriage to drive to Varese, and were
followed by another carriage, in which was seated the
little Italian who had catechised me. When we
stopped to rest the horses, he came and spoke to our
driver, evidently about us. I remarked to Miles that

my speech about the Emperor of Austria had evidently
made him understand that we were persons of consideration.   Miles, who was very sulky, said : " Bosh,
they are looking at us much more as if we were
pickpockets.   Ask him if he knows where Colonel
Marini lives at Varese, and tell him we are going
there ; perhaps that may suggest to him that we are
not conspirators."   I asked him if he knew any one of
the name of Marini at Varese, at which he scowled
and said, *Accidente !*   I wished to ask what accident had befallen him, but my Italian dictionary
had been left behind in my knapsack, and I thought
it was better to keep silence than to expose my
ignorance.   We had told him to draw up at the best
inn described in Murray ; but when we entered
Varese the driver passed the inn and drove us up to
the court-house, where a crowd of Italian soldiers were
standing ; these were, as we afterwards discovered, the
Cacciatori delle Alpi.   We said we wanted to go to
our hotel, but they shook their heads and swarmed
round us, looking anything but friendly.   Miles said,
" We had better go straight to the post-office and
inquire for Marini there ;" and though they did not
stop us when we pointed to the post-office just over
the way, they insisted on escorting us there.   I tried
talking German, as they would not or could not
understand my Italian, and remarked both in German
and Italian that I was a friend of a friend of the
Emperor of Austria.   Whereat Miles got furious, such
is his antipathy to any mention of the beautiful
Countess, and said : " Shut up, do, Algy ; don't you see
that they get more vicious every moment you talk
about the Austrians ? "   He then tried talking about
Marini, as far as he knew how, but the subject seemed

M

to please them no better.   At the post-office they
demanded our passports, and evidently did not believe
us when we said we had accidentally left them in the
boat.   We tried at last to fight our way out of the
crowd, as they would none of them understand a word
we had to say; it came on to rain hard in the middle,
and they collared us and brought us on here.   They
made Miles take off his knapsack and rummaged
through it for papers, which they did not find.   Then
they searched our pockets, and found a photograph in
Miles's pocket, which they studied with great care,
and finally gave him back, saying, *Bella giovane!*   I
suppose it was his sister's, but he looked furiously
angry all the time they held it.   At last they left us,
and some old hag has just been in, and brought us
some sour bread and coffee made of figs.   We have
had no dinner, but Miles cannot touch a morsel.

May 24.—Miles fainted just after I wrote this, and
has been very ill all night.   I have been trying to get
a doctor for him, but the old beldame says that the
only doctor at Varese is gone with Garibaldi.   Miles
is better this morning, but in the night he alarmed me
greatly, for he became quite delirious, asked me why
I had taken away his photograph, and assured me that
Zoe had another, so that he did not at all see what
harm he had done by taking this one.   This morning,
finding him better, I thought I should amuse him by
telling him what nonsense he had talked in the night,
but he flushed and apparently did not like it at all.
" I had bad dreams," he said, " and was talking in my
sleep."

" I was afraid," I said, " that you were going to be
ill with a malaria fever, or something of that kind."

" I'm all right this morning," said Miles, " except a

cold, and not being up to much. You needn't listen
to what I may say in my sleep; do you suppose it
would show a bad conscience if I accused myself of
murdering Clyffe?"

"Miles, you were not asleep," I said; "your eyes
were open, and you sat up in bed; you were as
delirious as you could be. I wish I knew it was not
malaria fever."

"Malaria fiddlestick!" said Miles. "Give me some
writing-paper and ink, and I'll write to my father;
that will get us out of this best."

I got him some materials, and he has been writing
more or less all day; but he looks most wretchedly ill.
If he were to die here in this stifling hole! My
conscience at any rate is clear, for I warned him
against this rash act, though how rash it was to be, I
did not know.

May 25.—Miles is much worse to-day. He was
again delirious last night, and to-day he lies in a kind
of stupor. The old hag brought a doctor of some kind
who wanted to bleed him, but I recollected my mother's
prejudice against bleeding, and refused to allow the
deed to be done. The doctor went away shrugging his
shoulders and opening out the palms of his hands to
express that he washed his hands of all responsibility.

May 29.—The days pass with but little change.
Miles is delirious at night, and faints if he tries to
move in the day. He is most patient and considerate;
I would give anything to see him cross or sulky, such
is the perversity of human nature. He talks sometimes, but I imagine he does not care very much about
getting better. He lies hour after hour looking at that
photograph—it is not Zoe, but Miss Warburton; once
I heard him say in his wanderings, "If I die, my spirit

will guard you as you would not let me do in life, my
darling !" This made me feel more anxious than ever,
for I always considered Miles to be a person without
any touch of sentiment. He is evidently most deeply
religious too, poor fellow! I wish my mother, who
always considered both him and Zoe to be in a
dangerous condition as to their souls, could see his
calm and cheery acceptance of our present condition,
joined, in his case, to sickness which may be to death,
and the brave way in which he speaks of the possible
end. I feel, even now, that he is a greater support to
me than I am to him. Who would have expected
this ?

June 1.—The days go on; surely something must
happen soon. I endeavour to prepare myself for the
worst. After all, I say to myself, I am an Englishman
and a Protestant, and when we are let out of this
stifling hole I will make such a protest, on behalf of
my country and my creed, as will make our· miscreant
captors realise what they have done. Let the· British
Lion once roar, and these craven Italians will shake in
their shoes ! But suppose it should be part of their
policy to immure us lest we should anticipate and betray
their treasonable designs ! Suppose they bring us out
and confront us with a battery of cannon, threatening
us with instant death unless we will belie our English
blood and our Protestant principles ! Why, then, we
must prepare ourselves to die like Englishmen and
Protestants !

But I should like to get out of this place alive.
As for Miles, if he does not get out soon, he will not
get out alive, I fear. He is very low about himself,
and talked to-day as if he knew it could not last much
longer. Ought I to have him bled ? Surely not; he

is far too weak to bear any further weakening.   But
God grant that some relief may come soon!

74.—" BOTTIGLIA AND VINCHIORTE."

Miss Winkworth to Mrs. Home.

May.

Dearest Mary—Oh why are young people so self-
willed, or rather, why cannot old people win their confidence?   We are in much anxiety, though at least my
dear Zoe is cleared of all but wrong-headed generosity.

Walter is staying at Dallington for a Conservative
meeting, and this morning at breakfast-time, Mary
rushed wildly in, begging that I would come up instantly, Zoe was in "such a way, that they could not
tell what to do with her."   On the road, she told me
that Zoe had been looking at the *Times,* when she gave
a little scream, turned pale, and flew out of the room.
Miss Madgewick found her insisting on having a horse
saddled for her to ride to Dallington (as her father had
taken the carriage).   The butler reminded her that her
own horse was lame, and that her father did not think
either of the others safe for her, whereupon she fell into
a passion of tears, ran upstairs, and bolted herself into
her room.   To all entreaties from Miss Madgewick, she
only answered that she must have the horse made ready
instantly.   She had taken the paper with her, so that
they could not make out what was the matter, though
Mary had implored her to say it was nothing about
Miles.   I think Mary inclined to believe that he had
been caught in an avalanche.

However, when I spoke, Zoe opened the door, saying, "Aunt Dora, you will help me.   I must go to

papa. No time must be lost." Then she pointed to a
paragraph, saying that the Garibaldian insurgents have
occupied Varese, and at the moment of their entrance
had arrested two Austrian spies, calling themselves
Bottiglia and Vinchiorte, professing to be English, but
unable to produce their passports. I saw nothing
alarming in this, but Zoe exclaimed: "Oh yes! I know
it is they. My poor Miles! I had a letter from him!
They were going: that very day." I was confounded,
for I believed them at Meyringen. "Aunt Dora, you
don't know," she said. "Miles was going to see after
Bertha. He thought it his duty, and I persuaded him.
Now, don't you see I must go to papa? He may do
something before it is too late."

But at that instant a note was brought. Her father
had sent home the carriage, having gone on to spend a
couple of nights at Lord Daylesford's, and meant to be
met at the station on Friday. It seemed to be utter
despair to the poor girl. She wanted to telegraph, but
the names seem to me too uncertain, and perhaps
another day's paper may show them to be really
Austrian. However, she has written, and laid the
whole before her father. This was of course the cause
of the selling the lace, though I wonder that Miles was
so short of money as to require it for this additional
expedition. Poor children, one has to call it wrong-
headed and self-willed, and yet I cannot help loving
them for it, and I am, above all, glad that all concealment is over, and Zoe is quite open with me. She
says Miles acted from a sense of duty, thinking it right
to know whether his sister is in any distress; and she
works herself up into a perfect agony at having persuaded him to do what may have involved him in this
trouble. I really cannot suppose there is actual danger.

She is so miserable that the dread of her father is almost swallowed up by her anxiety. She really is a very dear girl. I know if Walter is hard on her I shall take her part; and as to Bessie, it is all, " Dear, dear children, how good of them !"—Your loving

D. W.

75.—TERROR AT THE MIZ MAZE.

Zoe to Emily.

THE MIZ MAZE, May.

Dearest Emily—I am almost too sick at heart to write to you, but still, as it is of no use to attempt to sleep, I will try to think myself talking to you. I have your photograph before me on the table, and try to see your look of cheer. Of course you know what I mean, and have seen that terrible paragraph that seems graven in upon my brain, even while I don't half believe it. If it were really true that Miles was in prison, could the sun shine as usual ? Papa was away when the paper came, and I believe I was like one crazy. It is like a bad dream now to recollect my trying to go over to Dallington to tell him all, and their all rising up to hinder me, and then hearing he was not there. But then Aunt Dora seemed something to trust to, and I told her all, and the relief of having it out was unspeakable. She was very kind; and she was so fond of Birdie, that she quite entered into our feeling, though of course, as an elder, she thought us wrong; and so I was, I know—but not Miles. Indeed, I was able to show her a letter I had had from him two or three days before, really angry about the lace, and seeming to think you and I had gone hawking and bartering my poor keepsakes about the world.

We even got a little laugh out of his notion. You
can't think how nice she was, almost as if she had
been a girl and one of us. And she could laugh, for
she does not believe this fearful thing. She says " Mr.
Bootle would never do anything rash." Not that she
likes him, but she believes in him, and has not found
out what a solemn imposition he is on himself as well
as the rest of the world. She has never seen what
Miles and Clyffe can do with him. She agreed that I
had better send the cutting to papa; but I think she
did so chiefly that I might confess—as, indeed, dear
Miles had bidden me do. His letter was from Meyringen, and they were really going! I shall be able
to show it to papa, who will be satisfied about him at
least. Aunt Dora begged that we would not tell the
children, though I see poor Mary is sadly puzzled.
Meantime there is only one thing I can do for my
darling.—Your loving   ZOE.

76.—ZOE'S CONFESSION.

Zoe to Sir Walter.

THE MIZ MAZE, *May.*

My dear Papa—I am afraid you will be still more
displeased with me after reading this letter, but I could
not explain what had passed till I had had Miles's consent. The money for the lace was sent to him, but
not for any foolish debt, or any such expense. But a
strong feeling had come upon us both that we ought
to take some means of learning whether our sister
Bertha is living or in any distress. We thought you
might be bound by some promise; but Miles, as her
brother, could hardly be wrong in ascertaining where

and how she was.   She was so kind to us little ones that we could not help loving her and longing to know about her.   Miles could not use your money provided for a special purpose, and I tried to raise the amount by disposing of the lace and coral.   I did not then see, as I do now, that I had no right to do so.   But the worst is to come.   It was to Varese that Miles was going, because Mr. Fanshawe said he had there met an English lady married to an Italian who asked about all of us.   And look at the paragraph I enclose.   It must mean Miles and Algernon Bootle!   You will know what ought to be done to save him.

I am afraid of losing the post, or I would write this over again, for you will be vexed at this great tear blot.

Please, please forgive me, dear papa.   It all is so very dreadful; and I feel as if I could care for nothing that happened to me if only Miles were safe.——Your dutiful and affectionate daughter,

SOPHIA WINKWORTH.

77.—SIR WALTER IN DISPLEASURE.

Sir Walter to Zoe.

DAYLESFORD COURT, *May.*

My dear Zoe—I will not attempt to describe the surprise and concern that your letter has caused me. I can scarcely credit the notion that Miles and Algernon Bootle have been arrested.   I have too much confidence in the latter to believe that he would foolishly run into danger, much less sanction your brother's doing so while in his charge.   As, however, in this matter both Miles and you have shown a curious independence, it is of course possible that some headstrong act of his may have involved himself and Bootle in danger, without the latter's consent.

I have written to the Foreign Office to make inquiries, and, upon consultation with Lord Daylesford, have further decided to go to town myself to-morrow morning. I shall probably return home by an evening train, but should I be unexpectedly detained in London, I will telegraph to you in the course of the day.

And now, with regard to your own conduct. It is of course some satisfaction to me to have the mysterious sale of the lace accounted for, but I have read your explanation with profound astonishment, and I cannot but view with displeasure the steps that you and Miles have taken. It was natural that when your recollections of your sister had been revived, you should have felt anxious on the subject of her present condition; but you ought to have laid your anxieties before me, and I should then have explained to you my motives for keeping aloof from the daughter who was once as dear to me as you are.

It grieves me more than I can say to trace in your conduct something of the same underhand disposition which caused her ruin. I *had* hoped that my children would have been, above all things, true, straightforward, high-minded, incapable of the smallest secrecy or deceit; and when I think of the pains which your mother lavished on your training, I feel thankful that she is spared the knowledge of how completely you have run counter to it.

I shall speak with you regarding your sister Bertha when I return, and I must then ask you to throw light upon the strange circumstance of your brother's being so short of money as to depend on *you* for the means of prosecuting his inquiries about her. He ought to have had plenty of his allowance in hand.

Trusting to find you ready to be open with me for the future,—I am, your affectionate father,

WALTER M. WINKWORTH.

78.—LISA IN PERPLEXITY.

Lisa to Frank.

MIZ MAZE, *Monday.*

My dear Frank—We are all in such a commotion here, and Zoe is in disgrace with papa I can see, and she won't tell me what about. It is some fuss about *lace*, I know from little things I hear said, and Emily has something to do with it again. Zoe is always getting letters from her, and never tells me anything that is in them.

Wednesday.—Since I began this the house has all been upside down, and it began with something Zoe saw in the newspaper when papa was away for a night. I am sure she thinks something has happened to Miles in Switzerland, and Aunt Dora is always coming and having private talks with somebody, and there is a bother about everything one wants to do. I do wonder what it is all about. What can Emily, having stolen Zoe's lace, have to do with Miles having gone to Italy? (It seems very odd Emily should steal lace, but what else *could* she do that made everybody angry?) and I *know* it has to do with Zoe's lace. It is just like a story, only in the books little girls get told all the exciting things, and here we don't; we get sent out of the room, and are told to hold our tongues. It is very tiresome. Polly is very tiresome too. She is dreadfully frightened about something, always locking our door and saying her prayers, but she will not talk a bit about it; she says we should be told if we were to know. Papa is gone off to London, and he gets letters from Mrs. Bootle. It is very exciting.—Your loving sister   LISA.

79.—EMILY RECOGNISES SIR BORS.

Emily to Edgar Fanshawe.

TRIERMAIN, *May.*

My dear Edgar—Look at this dreadful paragraph and fly to their help. It can't be anybody else, and half of it is my doing. Don't laugh at my incoherence. I told you about Signora Marini, whom you met, being the banished half-sister of the Winkworths. Well, Miles, in his dumb chivalry, has gone in search of her, little guessing that Italy would be all up in arms. These names are just what Italians would make of theirs. It is just the time they were going, and I am sure that horrid Algy Bootle has run him into a scrape. There's no guessing what those awful rebels may do to him. Oh yes, I know they are your own dear patriots, but patriots can be very horrid when they think they have a spy. You know the ways of them, and you are the only creature that can help. I shall break my heart if anything happens to that generous fellow, who would just go and die in his mute way, unconscious of his own heroism, for the sake of saving that miserable Algy. I know they were going to Varese, right into the thick of it.

Go and find Marini or anybody—Garibaldi, if nothing else will do—and get them out of it, if you ever cared for Zoe, or wish me to have another happy moment.—Your affectionate cousin,

EMILY B. WARBURTON.

80.—EMILY'S CHAMPION.

Emily to Zoe.

TRIERMAIN,
HIGH SCALE, *May.*

Dearest Zoe—It is fearful; but I see a hope. I had seen that paragraph and sent it to Edgar, who telegraphs to me that he is setting out for Italy, like the good fellow that he is, "ready, aye ready for the field." He will be able to manage the Italians; he has lots of friends among them; you know he has been about everywhere with his father. I do not believe that after the first frenzy, the Garibaldians would hurt any one who could prove himself English. If I did not think Edgar would succeed, I don't know how I could endure life and silence. You have an aunt to talk to; I have no one, and my only comfort is that the Bootles have not taken the alarm; but I have to keep up before mamma, and not tear open every paper the instant it comes in. Only, you dear little goose, don't worry yourself. You always were so horribly introspective, just as if you had a multiplying glass inside you, and went on making dozens of Zoes, each worse than the last, till you don't know what she is like. I am sure the evil is sufficient for the day. Never mind what you or anybody else ought to have done. I am sure we are all wretched enough without that. Heroism is very disagreeable while it is going on.—Your most loving   EMILY.

81.—IN THE SERVANTS' HALL.

Fanny to Annie.

MIZ MAZE, *May.*

My dear Annie—I take up my pen to tell you of
the dreadful affliction as have befallen this unfortunate
family, for them in high station is not more exempt
than others.   But perhaps you have heard particulars
from Mrs. Bootle's Ruth, if she can get out.   Mr.
Winkworth and Mr. Algy is in the hands of the
Spanish Inquisition at Rome.   It was in the newspaper; Miss Winkworth saw it while her pa was away,
and she ran like a wild thing for her horse to ride
after her pa to rescue them.   Miss Magic was forced
to send to her aunt to pacify her, and send over to Sir
Walter.   He is gone to London to get the Queen to
interfere, but there is ever so much fear it will be too
late, and that the unfortunate young gentlemen will
have fallen a sacrifice.   I declare none of us could do
nothing all the morning, and I got out my *Fox's Book
of Martyrs*, and showed Lucy, the under housemaid, all
the interesting pictures, till we both cried so that
neither of us could touch a mossle at dinner.   And
Mrs. Parsons scolded us, and told us we was silly lasses,
which was quite uncalled for and very unfeeling.   And
Mr. Brown, the butler, says they do not burn folks
now, and that it is Garibaldi as has them; but Peter,
the footman, says he wears a red shirt, and is just such
another as the Pope, and that he saw a picture of the
Inquisition where they had high caps and yellow gowns
all over black imps to be burnt in.   To think of Mr.
Winkworth coming to that.   Poor young gentleman!
Mr. Ratclyffe will never get over it, though he will be

the barrowknight. And Miss Winkworth, poor young lady, goes about so as it is a pity to see her. Mr. Algy is so pious, he will be sure to speak out like them in Fox's book; but it is awful to think of them two fine young men cut down by Popery in their prime.

I wonder does your young lady shed a tear for her cruelty now? So no more from your affectionate friend   FANNY.

82.—MATERNAL ALARMS.

Mrs. Bootle to Sir Walter Winkworth.

HIGH SCALE RECTORY,
May 1859.

Dear Sir Walter—Mr. Bootle says I had better write at once and send you this cutting from the *Carlisle Patriot.* And, dear me! who would have thought it actually had a special correspondent in the army of Garibaldi? Do you think he takes it in? If so, the postage must come expensive. I find it so. Have you heard from Miles? We have had no letters, and don't know what to think. There has been time to hear over and over again since they ought to have reached Varese. Mr. Bootle is much alarmed; but, as I tell him, who can say what the Pope does with all the letters in Italy? I am sure when I was a girl, Sir James Graham read all our letters—and very unpleasant too—all on account of the Chartists. So who knows but the Pope has all dear Algy's letters and the lovely tracts I sent, served up at breakfast. And perhaps it will do him some good. I would go anywhere myself for Algy's sake. But which would be best—the Austrians or the French? Or should I fall at the feet of Garibaldi, or the Pope himself even ? I shouldn't much mind who, if it did Algy any good. Only I should take very little luggage, for fear it might be stolen. Oh, Sir Walter, only think if, when his life comes to be written, it has to be said he was once among the Jesuits! They *do* say Garibaldi isn't a Jesuit, but I wouldn't trust an Italian. Mr. Bootle has just come in, and says I should do no good if I did go, but I should like to hear what you say, though certainly Mr. Bootle has more opinions of his own than I ever knew him have before.—I remain, dear Sir Walter, very truly yours,   MARIA BOOTLE.

P.S.—Has the "Pulpit and Pew Defence Associa-. tion" any influence abroad? Mr. Bootle is a local secretary, and I am an "Original Associate." If they *could* do anything, and you mention me officially, be sure you add "Original Ass." after my name.

83.—THE FOREIGN OFFICE.

Sir Walter to Mrs. Bootle.

CARLTON CLUB, PALL MALL, *May.*

Dear Mrs. Bootle—Your letter was forwarded to me just as I was leaving Daylesford Court this morning. I had already seen the newspaper paragraph which you kindly enclosed, and, though I did not attach much weight to it, I thought it better to come up and make inquiries at the Foreign Office.

I have seen the Under-Secretary, and I find that no official tidings of the arrest of any English subjects in Italy has been received, but he has promised me that investigation shall be made into the matter without delay.   He seemed to be of opinion that the English are much in favour with Garibaldi and his troops, and that, even if two of our tourists had been captured by mistake, they would be released immediately on the discovery of their nationality.   This impression has been confirmed by the old friend with whom I have just been dining here, and he is well acquainted with the Continent, and has followed much more closely than I have the variations of political feeling in Italy.   I will let you know directly I hear any certain tidings of our travellers, and in the meantime I agree with Mr. Bootle that it would be most inexpedient for *you* to go in search of them.   I think you need be under no apprehension of their falling into the hands of Jesuits. Garibaldi is, I hear, a determined foe of priests and monks, though rather, I imagine, from revolt against " the powers that be" than from any enlightenment in his religious views.

With best regards to Mr. Bootle.—Yours very truly,   WALTER M. WINKWORTH.

84.—ZOE IN DESPAIR.

Zoe to Emily.

MIZ MAZE, *May.*

You dear Girl—to have thought of the very best and only chance ; and how good of Mr. Fanshawe— just like him !

It bears me up when the horror of it comes over me.   He will forgive us if it turns out not to be true after all, as every one is saying here, and I try to believe.   Papa, however, is gone to London to try to find something out.   He has written to me, as I know

N

he must be greatly grieved and displeased at the concealment and what he calls my underhand ways.   He
is glad dear mamma does not see this conduct of mine.
Ah ! she would have understood, and it would never
have happened if she had been here.

Suppose this is all a mistake of ours, then perhaps
Mr. Fanshawe might find Miles and take him to Bertha,
and it would all come right.   I sometimes hope it may
be so.   Any way, there is no thanking you and him
enough.—Your more than ever loving   ZOE.

85.—EMILY MORALISING.

Emily to Zoe.

TRIERMAIN, *May*.

My beloved Child—You are such a one for worrying
yourself when every one else is doing the same office
by you.   Underhand ?   What do they mean by that ?
You have deceived no one.   Is everybody bound to
tell everybody everything, and blazon abroad whatever they do ?   Well, that's lucid.   You may get a
laugh out of it, if you can laugh at nothing else.   But
surely there must be a time when passive, unquestioning
faith in any fallible being gets outgrown ; and then, are
we never to think or act for ourselves ?   Suppose I
told poor mamma all my projects, she would simply
forbid me to think of them.   Yet I am not going to be
disobedient to her, but to develop them bit by bit as
she can bear.   Cousin Charles Fanshawe told me that
was the only way to manage between my two duties.
" The young outrunneth the old, and thus all things
become new."   Not that I have much heart while the

suspense lasts; and they won't sell me my site in one
parish, because they think I shall set up some opposition to some dissenting interest there. And in the
other, where the ground is my own, the clergyman is
dead against me; I can't make out why, for he never
does anything. What's the use of trying? But that
is not right I know. I must go at them again, with
Cousin Charles to back me, though he laughs at me for
canonizing Black Joe. E. W.

86.—SUSPENSE.

Miss Winkworth to Mrs. Home.

THE DOWER HOUSE, *May.*

My dear Mary—I have nothing as yet to tell you.
Walter wrote a severe letter of elaborate Christian
forgiveness which cut poor Zoe to the heart, and then
he went on to the Foreign Office, and has procured
that letters of inquiry should be sent to the Consuls
and Vice-Consuls at Milan, Florence, Turin, etc. But
I do not think either he or the officials had any real
belief that Vinchiorte and Bottiglia represent the two
lads; though, as the days go on without bringing any
letters from them, it becomes alarming; and the
Bootles have taken fright and inflict letters upon him.
Zoe grows whiter and sadder every day. She keeps
up before her father, knowing that it only makes him
angry to see her fretting; but nothing seems to suit
her so well as to curl herself up on Bessie's footstool
and talk over Miles, just as if he was dead. And
really he must be a very good and excellent fellow. I
wish I knew he was safe.

May 30.—Answers from the Consul folk, very civil,

but not very consoling. Before they can set any inquiries on foot they want more questions answered than we can reply to, and they say everything is in great confusion. Nothing is ascertained but that the passports were viséd at the frontier, so that the young men must really be in Italy. One of the Vice-Consuls has no doubt that they are among the Englishmen who have gone off in a fit of enthusiasm to join Garibaldi's army. You may suppose how indignant Walter is. "They will say he is gone to join the Red Republicans next. If I thought it of a son of mine !"

June 2.—Despairing, as he says, of those consular fellows doing any good, Walter has actually thought of applying to Marini, if he can be traced. He asked Mr. Bernard for information, but in vain. The sister who had kept up the communication died in a French convent, and he has no papers of hers. Then Walter recollected that his wife had had the keeping of some letters that might serve as a clue to Marini's native place, and he made up his mind to open her desk, which he had never borne to look through before. Nothing was there which could serve the purpose, but there came to light the beginning of a letter to Bertha, candidly acknowledging that in the harshness of youth and inexperience, there had been few allowances made, and asking pardon ; but it was not finished, and it was dated on the very day of poor Sophia's last seizure. She never spoke intelligibly again, though Walter now believes that something she reiterated, but could not make him understand, had reference to Bertha and pardon. Poor Sophia, how wretched for her ! But she knew the way to the All-hearing, All-pardoning. I hoped it would have softened Walter towards Zoe ; I think it will in time, but he is one whom pain hardens, and it is a shock that his wife should have admitted herself to have been mistaken.

I told Zoe without asking his leave, and it seems to be a great comfort to her. She is very gentle and patient, and it is beautiful to see her sweet temper with noisy Lisa, and with her father, whose trouble shows itself in hot criticisms on the cookery or anger at finding untidy overshoes and umbrellas in the hall. I should never have been half so good.—Your affectionate

D. W.

87.—SOFTENING.

Zoe to Emily.

THE MIZ MAZE, *May.*

No news, not a scrap, my dear, and nothing but muddling from the official folk. They have all grown so kind to me that it seems the more as if they believed it. Mrs. Bootle does. It is one thing to be thankful for that I am out of reach of her. Poor woman, she is not past improving the occasion, and she has not my comfort in knowing there is one trusty friend gone after them. However, one thing has been a real joy that nothing can cloud. Aunt Dora told me that among dear mamma's papers papa has just found a letter, half-finished, to Birdie, a beautiful letter craving forgiveness and reconciliation, and trusting they might yet meet where all these——, and there it stopped. Aunt Dora said poor papa was quite overcome, and that night he kissed me as he had not done since he came home. It was all a formal forgiveness, common-place kiss before; now it was a real one. And some-how it went to my heart as it had never done before

that I had set up my own opinion and abused his
confidence, and deceived.   I don't feel as if I deserved
to have any hope, but perhaps there may yet be mercy
on us.   If I could only bear it all instead of my dear
boy.—Your loving   ZOE.

88.—CLYFFE'S JUSTIFICATION OF MILES.

Ratclyffe to his Father.

MONTREAL, *June.*

My dearest Father—Your letter has made me feel
indeed ashamed of myself.   Miles extravagant!   Miles
wanting in openness!   It is *my* debts that he has
been paying all this time, and *my* secret that he has
been keeping.   He wanted to tell you, and I couldn't
bear to vex you just as I was going away.   You see
when we were at school we always kept our money
in common, and Miles used to pull me up when I
wanted too much, and say we hadn't got it.   Just as
we did our work.   I never knew how much he did of
it really.   But as I was always rather above him, and
got on much better in class, I thought I had all the
brains, as far as I thought about it.   Then when
the head-master told us that he had advised you to
separate us, that we might find out which was which,
Miles said that it was because I did his work for him ;
but I've found out since how much I depended on him,
though if I had been at home now I don't believe that
he would have made such a mess of it with Miss Warburton!   Then, I went to old Henderson's, and he to
Oxford, and you increased our allowances and made
them different.   Then Miles said that he'd been thinking it over, and he supposed that he should have a

great deal more money than I by and by, and that we couldn't go on for ever with one purse, so he thought we'd better try to manage separately.

Of course we still saw a good deal of each other, Henderson's being near Oxford, and we used to meet on the river, and he got on pretty well. He worked very hard, and sometimes I helped him; but though he has a bad memory, and takes an endless time over things, he is more accurate than I am, and I hardly knew how to read without him. However, if that had been all, perhaps he was the worst off; but a private tutor's is not like a college or a school, and you *must* associate with whatever fellows you find there, and they were not the sort of fellows to keep one steady. I was very friendly with some of them, and, in short, they were very extravagant, and so was I. I couldn't keep the money in my pocket without Miles; I can't think how it went. And then, when I passed and was going to leave, there were no end of bills to pay. So when I told Miles, he was dreadfully vexed, and wanted me at first to write to you. But we were afraid just then of its coming to mother's ears, and we knew how grieved she would be to think that we had been extravagant; so when Miles said that he thought he could manage it, I was only too thankful. I don't think I ever considered that I ought not to take his money, or realised that he would be hard up, till now. And he ought to have told you at once about it. He is always miserable when you find fault with him, and he has been so unhappy about Emily, that I don't see how he can get through his "greats." She has made a great mistake, for he is as romantic as she is, if he could only get it out, and a thousand times more conscientious.

I know that when you told me I had always given

you satisfaction, I ought not to have listened in silence ; but I knew these debts were of a sort for which you have no mercy,—cigars and wine, and my tailor,—and, I am sorry to say, there were bets also.   Everything is paid now, and we—I mean I—shall never, I promise you, be so foolish again.   I have kept my word to Miles ever since ; but I'm not half myself without him, and there is no sort of stupid thing against his own interests that he won't do if I am not there to look after him.   It is a great mistake, the laws ought to be altered for twins, so that they could share everything always.

I wrote this yesterday, and on reading it over I see that that last remark looks as if he ought to make it, not I.   But there's no difference, and, dear father, remember that however the most foolish of your sons may disappoint you, he cannot leave off hoping that you will put the best construction on his many follies. At least, he is always your loving (if undutiful)

CLYFFE.

89.—CLYFFE'S DREAM.

Ratclyffe to Miles.

MONTREAL, *June.*

Dear Miles—Why on earth didn't you tell father all about it the moment he had such an absurd idea as that *you* had got into debt ?   I have written everything to him, but the thought that you have been in a sort of disgrace, when you had troubles enough, has driven me wild.   I suppose that is the reason of a crazy idea I have got into my head that you are in some difficulty. I dreamed last night that you had fallen into a crevasse in Switzerland, and that Algy couldn't pull you out.

When I woke up I felt just like the fellows in the
" Corsican Brothers." Don't you remember when we
went to see it in London, and people stared at us as
we went out in the crowd. We laughed then at the
idea of having instincts about each other; but I felt
this morning just as if you were in some danger or
trouble, and I can't get over it. I declare if there
was such a thing as a telegraph to Europe, I believe I should have telegraphed to find out if you
were all right. Well, you will get a good laugh at me
at any rate; but father's letter has made me miserable.
Ought I to beg your pardon? I don't think I deserve
to get it. But it is your own fault after all, for if
you had not fretted so much about that ridiculous girl,
father would never have suspected you of being in a
scrape. I never had such an awful dream; I can hear
your voice now calling, " Clyffe! Clyffe!" out of that
crevasse in such piteous tones, and Algy tried to lift
you up, and I couldn't see where you were or get at
you. To be sure I had a late supper, which I suppose
accounts for it. But don't go after Algy if he thinks
he is a better mountaineer than all the guides put together. Let him break his neck if he likes, but don't
break yours in going after him.—Your loving brother,

CLYFFE WINKWORTH.

Don't tell any one about this.

90.—AGITATION AT TRIERMAIN.

Emily to Zoe.

(Unsteadily written.)

TRIERMAIN, *June.*

Dearest Zoe—Here is news at last—good news!
I enclose Edgar's letter, though he advises me not. I

can't see or write steadily enough to copy the bits.
The Bootles dined here yesterday, and Mrs. B. said
such remarkable things about her dear son's edifying
conduct under persecution as a champion for the faith,
that it was quite too much for me.   Then she would
have it that I was hysterical, and she frightened
mamma.   So I am not supposed to be up this morning, which is lucky, for I don't know how I behaved
myself when this letter came, and it was as well to
have the bed-clothes to stifle odd noises in.

My sweetest Life, now all will be right again, and
instead of blaming you and Miles, your father will
break out in blessings, like "King Lear" or *Dombey
and Son*.   My dear, I beg your pardon, I don't seem
to be able to keep my pen in order, and this must go
to-day.   Isn't Edgar a duck ?   Mamma is gone down
to the Bootles with the news.   Depend upon it, they
are out by this time, and your sister found.—Your
affectionate   EMILY.

91.—ITALY IN A FRENZY.

Edgar to Emily.

BRESCIA, *June, Sunday Night.*

My dear Emily—I hope you are not angry or
anxious at my silence, but it seemed that active
obedience was the best reply to your letter.   The
date of this may surprise you, who would of course
have hurried direct to Varese.   Knowing, however,
that the Garibaldians had left that place and occupied
Como, I thought that the best way of finding Signor
Marini was to go to Como over the Splügen, which I
did, only to find that they had gone on to Bergamo,

which on their approach was evacuated by the Austrians
in a great hurry. "Der Teufel," as they call him,
seems to inspire a wholesome terror in these excellent
fellows. Here I am rambling heartlessly on, while
you are ready to tear the good news out of my letter.
I have seen Marini. Miles and Bootle are safe, though
closely imprisoned at Varese. In two hours I shall
start for Varese. I shall find Madame Marini there,
and as soon as I have seen her and Miles I shall write
to Sir Walter.

Out of respect to your anxiety I have broken the
thread of my story, and I shall go on writing it for
my own satisfaction, though hardly expecting you to
read it.

I followed in Garibaldi's track to Bergamo, through
country that I know well, across the lake to Lecco,
and on by Pontida, sometimes walking, sometimes
getting a lift in a timorella. I found a mixture of
enthusiasm and desolation everywhere with a good
deal of suspicion; but my face was my fortune, or
rather my tongue, and I lounged along in my own
character, so evidently without any motive but idle
curiosity, mixed with love for Italy, that the most
energetic official could really find no excuse for inter-
fering with me. I had one or two adventures which
I will tell you when we meet. The whole country
was of course ringing with the battle at Magenta, and
Melegnano seems to have been almost as decisive. I
wish I could have seen one of them. I should have
liked them better than Milan as it is now, in wild,
mad devotion to the Emperor, whose intentions reasonable people don't much believe in. Among the latter,
I hear, is Garibaldi. He is a fine fellow, and I hope
you will be large-minded enough not to call him an

"awful rebel" any more.   It seems that Algernon
Bootle blundered himself and Miles into the scrape—
but more of that presently.   I reached Bergamo—one
of the most beautiful towns in Italy, in my opinion—
only to find that Garibaldi had marched on towards
Brescia.   This was yesterday.   I could find no way
of getting on from Bergamo till this morning, for the
country was covered with Austrian hussars hoping, I
suppose, to intercept the Cacciatori.   To-day, however, after I had waited many hours at the station,
being told that no train would leave, and that, if it
did, it would not take a stray traveller like me, I fell
in with an engine-driver who used to work as a lad
for my aunt at Brescia, and who remembered me.
This good fellow was going to start with some trucks
for Brescia, and the end of it was that I travelled with
him as stoker.   We expected to be stopped by the
Austrians, but saw nothing of them, and I finally arrived
rather black at Brescia.

I found the town in a tremendous hubbub.   I wish
my dear Italians could control their feelings a little.
I hardly knew before what they could do in the way
of screaming.   One of the first people I saw was my
old friend Marco Valenti, rushing across the Piazza
del Duomo with a number of fellows after him, chiefly
armed with garden tools.   I turned round and ran
along with him to the bastion, wondering what all this
was about.   It seems that a few Austrian hussars had
ridden into the town by mistake, thinking their friends
were still here, but they soon faced about and rode off
at full speed, with Garibaldi and some of his men after
them.   The Brescians, thinking the Austrians were
coming back, determined to put their word in; and,
literally, I think every creature in Brescia, if only

armed with a pair of scissors, flew out to fight the
Austrians. In the middle of all this I discovered from
Valenti that Colonel Marini was to be found at the
Palazzo del Municipio, so I went to a *café* and washed
my face, that he might not take me for a brigand, and
then went to find him. Two officers in green tunics,
and another, a captain of the Guides, in gray, were
walking up and down before the palace. I went up
to them and asked for Colonel Marini; the tallest of
the green ones replied very civilly that he was the
man. He is a fine-looking man, about fifty, and
getting rather gray. I walked away with him, told
him at once who I was, and asked him about Miles
and Bootle, telling him who Miles was, which seemed
to astonish him considerably. He was rather stiff at
first, and said there was every reason to believe that
the two gentlemen were Austrians. One of them did
nothing but talk about the Emperor of Austria, and
say he was a friend of his. This of course must have
been the unfortunate Bootle. I explained that the
tutor probably thought this a good dodge for frightening
the Cacciatori into letting them go, at which Colonel
Marini smiled. I then told him how I had met
Madame Marini at my aunt's villa two years ago, and
had talked with her about her family, and ventured to
hope that she might remember me. He said it was
very probable, for she had talked of me a good deal at
the time; he added that she was now living in Varese,
and had had an attack of fever lately, from which he
hoped she was recovering. He was a little dry and
dignified about his wife's family, but on consideration
became more kindly, and agreed that her brother must
not be left in prison an hour longer than necessary.
He suggested the possibility of getting leave from the

General, and starting with me himself this evening for
Varese, an idea which I heartily encouraged.   He
asked me to dine with him, but I declined, as I wished
to look up some old friends.   There was nothing to be
done till Garibaldi came back from pursuing his hussars,
as the order for liberating the two prisoners must of
course come from him.   He came back in the afternoon.
It was a glorious day, and Brescia, having thrown aside
spade, fork, and scissors, has been rejoicing ever since
with the whole power of her lungs.   The streets even
now are full of people singing, shouting, and dancing;
the houses are festooned with flowers and blazing with
lights, and the church bells are not yet tired of ringing.
I went at eight o'clock to the Café Fiorentino, where
Marini had told me to meet him, and there found
everybody in a more tremendous bustle than ever; the
General had had orders from headquarters, they said,
and I began to think that my colonel would have no
time or thoughts to bestow on me.   As I was asking
questions, however, he strode in,—he is a long-legged
fellow,—took me into a corner, and told me that they
were ordered to march at once to the Chiese and occupy
Sonato, that they would start in an hour, that he was
writing my news to his wife, but feared he would not have
time to finish the letter, that he had got the order of
release from Garibaldi, and had given it to a young lieutenant of Guides, who with four men was to be my escort
to Varese.   Then he gave me his good wishes and a
hearty shake of the hand, hoped politely that he might
yet have the pleasure of offering hospitality to his
brother-in-law, as well as to me, and then dashed off
to join some of his comrades, having told me to meet
the lieutenant at the railway station at two o'clock in
the morning.   On the whole, Colonel Marini impressed

me favourably.   He loves the Italians, and even the
French, much better than the English, but I think he
cares for Madame Marini most of all, and of course
I have to thank her for the ready help he has given
me.

After parting with him I felt inclined to pay a
visit to the old villa, which is empty now, as Filippo
Monti and his wife are at Milan worshipping the King.
The servants welcomed me, and I am now writing to
you at midnight in the old saloon, whose yellow satin
and marble floor you know by description.   The windows are all open on the loggia and the broad terrace
with its white, gleaming balustrade; a low yellow
moon is throwing strange shadows from the cypresses,
across which the fire-flies are flashing.   Down below
is the town with all its wild lights and noises; now
and then comes a sudden lull, and then I hear the
nightingales singing in the trees of the garden.   *Buona
notte.*   I am half sorry now that I came up to the
villa.—Ever yours affectionately,

EDGAR FANSHAWE.

Please yourself about showing this letter to your
friend, but I think you had better simply tell her the
chief news it contains.

PART VI.

THE RESCUE.

o

"And when we cam' to the lower prison,
    Where Willie o' Kinmont he did lie;
'O sleep ye, wake ye, Kinmont Willie,
    Upon the morn that thou's to die?'"

92.—BERTHA IN HER ITALIAN HOME.

Diary of Bertha Marini.

CASTELFORTE, *December* 1858.

DIARY is written in large letters on the back of this book; but, certainly, if its name represents its mission, it has completely failed to carry it out. The last entry was made so long ago that, the date being wanting, I recollect nothing as to the time at which it was written. I am afraid that, like other efforts of my life, my journal has been rather spasmodic than methodical. And yet every now and then I don't know what I should do without it. But for it I might forget my own language. My husband has no love of England or the English. Who can wonder? "Yours is a grand country, *carina*," he will say, "but I prefer admiring it at a distance. As for its language—— !" He little knows how, among the flow of sweet harmonious Italian vowels, I sometimes long for a mouthful of hard strong English consonants, as much as I find myself yearning after a sight of the Wiltshire downs, with the clouds flying wild and free above them. The spirit of contradiction, no doubt, for here it is a hundred times more beautiful. Instead of downs we have mountains—Monte Rosa herself the queen of the great chain which walls us in to the north—lakes for ponds, the rich plain of Lombardy for fields. There have been days in my life of which the loveliness will

haunt me for ever. I remember last spring, for
instance, when Luigi drove me in the early morning to
the·castle of Angéra, the mulberry trees knee-deep in
rye and maize, the beautiful patches of red clover
starred with white daisies or bronzed by some yellow
flower, the people in their pink dresses, pretty little
brown barefooted children, patient oxen dragging.
And another day—but all the while my heart is hungry
for England, ugly, unkind, cold England! If only I
could see it once again; if I could, just once, look at
my father's face, and know what the twins and the
baby have grown into, and hear Aunt Dora's quick,
decided voice, and Aunt Bessie's kind little doubtful sentences, when she tried to make out that, after
all, nobody was much to blame! I feel sure that
Aunt Bessie has been making excuses for me all these
years. But that they should keep this dead silence,
that they should treat me as a creature too vile for
words, that the letters I have written to my father
should be returned unread! I did wrongly, I own;
but I did nothing to deserve the fate of an outcast.
My husband's family is as good as our own; he is a
brave, honourable man, my Luigi! So far as marrying
him, I have never for one instant repented the step I
took. However, of course, it is easy enough to know
who has been at the bottom of my father's unforgiving-
ness; he loved me too dearly for Lady Winkworth not
to do all in her power to separate us; to her I was
always a reminder of that first wife, the darling of his
heart, for so my mother was. Oh, father, how could
you let any one come between you and her dear
memory? How, especially, could you let *her*—so
cold, so stiff, so jealous! . . .

It is very strange that I should have written those

words; perhaps I ought to unwrite, or at any rate soften
them, and indeed I should like to do so, if I honestly
could.   For she is dead—actually dead.

I had just laid down my pen—for thoughts had
come in such an overpowering rush that I could not
any longer keep pace with them in my writing—when
my husband came in, bringing with him an old copy
of the *Times*.   Situated as we are, it is exceedingly
difficult ever to get hold of an English newspaper; but
just now Luigi and other of his friends are, above all
things, anxious to know what is said in England about
that fermenting which is going on in the heart of Italy.
They feel that a great hour is coming for her, and they
want to know who will sympathise; so that if any
chance brings a newspaper within their reach they
don't let it slip.   And my husband knowing—a little
—how I long and yearn for English papers and English
books and English news, manages so that when the
political information has been extracted, the prize is
passed on to me.   He is always amused by the eager-
ness with which I seize it.   But to-day in the midst
of his jest he stopped short.

"What is it, Berta?   Has anything happened?"
and he came behind me and read where I pointed, for
I could not speak.   "Ah, it is she, and dead!   Well,
I am glad it is no one you loved better."

I do not know.   Sometimes I think that death
never seems so terrible as when he claims the object of
our unkindest thoughts and judgments.   I said hastily,
"May she find mercy!"   It was the first time that
ever I had prayed for Lady Winkworth, and she was
dead!   And I determined to ask Padre Girolamo to
say three masses for her soul.   She was a heretic, to
be sure, but Padre Girolamo will ask no questions so

long as I pay him. And I will sell my gold locket for
that, if it is needed.

If Luigi had thought that I wanted comforting he
would have stayed. But he went away, and I have
been thinking and dreaming and going over the old
times, and wondering whether now my father will be
his old self once more. He will feel it, I am sure;
she had got so much power over him, and perhaps—
yes, I suppose she did love him in her own way, cold
and comfortless as it seems to me, even in looking back
and trying to be just. At any rate, she could persuade
him anything, anything! persuade him that his dead
wife's daughter—that is what I find it so hard to forgive—deceived him throughout. If it had been blame
on myself! But it was casting reflections on my dear
mother. They used to irritate me beyond endurance;
and dear Ellen Bernard was my only friend. With her
I was sure of sympathy. Then came Luigi, despised,
of course, just because they did not understand him.
Imagine Lady Winkworth understanding *anything* out
of her own groove, poor woman! I remember her
telling me that the very name of patriot always made
her shudder and think of assassinations, and that no
respectable person would dream of setting themselves
up against the powers that be. As for me, I was
young enough to think it the very grandest thing in
the world. When Luigi talked to me of his Italy—
Italy the great and beautiful, now in such miserable
thraldom and degradation—and his brown eyes kindled,
and his voice thrilled with his heart's burden of shame
and longing; when he, as it were, stood on one side
holding up all that was noble and beautiful and chival-
rous, and she on the other with her poor petty
restrictions, and her chilling manners, and her want of
trust, how could I resist him?

I really can't wonder at myself, though it is true that I see that I was not very wise. None of my love for my husband, but a good deal of my enthusiasm for Italy, has come to an end. There has been so much talk and so little done, and I don't think now that *all* patriots are disinterested. They say that this man Garibaldi, to whom they are all looking, *is*, and that the country is on the eve of a great deliverance. It may be so, but I must say Italians do provoke me with their indifference and want of energy. They talk a great deal, but nothing seems done. When I advise the women about keeping their houses and their children cleaner, or give them hints as to better management, they smile and say it is all excellent, and do nothing. It is a great disappointment, for I meant my life in this curious country village to have been of use to those about me, and, so far as all that is concerned, I believe I might just as well have stayed at home.

Our village is perched upon a hill, some miles from Varese. The road, which is rough and very steep, climbs upwards past vine terraces, and when it becomes a street is paved in the most primitive manner with round slippery stones. The church, its tower plastered with pink, stands, of course, in the centre of the town; but some of the streets are mere tunnels, piercing under and through the houses. Our house is the last in the place, and the largest. I try very hard, but I fear with small success, to make my garden look English; when this fails I console myself with the view, which stretches as far as the lake and takes in a great expanse of smiling and beautiful country. It lies before me now, steeped in sunshine. At the bottom of our garden a small gate leads into a lane, and you have but to cross it to be in the farm. The entrance

arch is curled at the top, and picturesquely painted
and frescoed; on the left is the house where our silkworms are born and nursed—a different sort of farm,
indeed, from those which lie under our Wiltshire downs!
How my thoughts go back to Wiltshire! I suppose it
is this news. . . .

Varese, May 28.——Glancing back at what I wrote
a few months ago, I see that I was unjust to the
Italians, who have this time proved themselves in
earnest. Great events have taken place, and we are
on the eve of greater. France is with us, Austria has
already suffered defeat, and the name of Garibaldi is in
every man's mouth. As for me, I am as enthusiastic
as the rest, and that is saying a good deal. But I
must go back a little.

When the war broke out and Garibaldi was permitted to enrol his Cacciatori delle Alpi, my husband
was one of the first to volunteer and to obtain a command. He was anxious that I should at once leave
our home and take shelter at Varese, but I only did
this about a fortnight ago, when there was a rumour
that the Cacciatori were on their way to the little town.
It is impossible to give an idea of the excitement of
this time of waiting; all sorts of rumours were afloat,
the street arcades were so thickly crowded with people
that one could hardly pass, and hasty defences were
improvised, for it was a question which would reach
Varese first—our own troops or the Austrians.

On the night of the 21st, what with rumours and
excitement and the turmoil in the streets, I did not
close my eyes, though I was in a small villa standing
a little back from the road, where the long grass was
starred with large narcissus, and where the nightingales
sang all day and night,—if one only had the heart to

listen to them. I got up very early, and looking out
at the beautiful mountains and at the Sacro Monte,
with the Tre Croci behind, I felt that I must climb
somewhere, and that from the pilgrimage hill I should
get a view, at any rate, of the country round.

I went alone; there was no one I cared should be
with me. I was not sure that I should pray, but my
heart was very full when I thought of Luigi. I got
a little country cart to drive me up to the cluster of
houses which nestle just outside the tall archway which
is the entrance to the Mount, and then I sent it back,
meaning to walk down to Varese after I had climbed
the hill.

Our Sacro Monte is a steep conical hill, set at
intervals with chapels in which some scene of our
Blessed Lord's life is represented by life-size coloured
terra-cotta figures. You do not enter, but there is a
broad iron grating, with steps leading to it, where one
can kneel and pray. There are always a few peasants
faithfully carrying out their pilgrimage, and making
their way by slow degrees towards the top of the hill,
stopping to kneel at each chapel. I was in too im-
patient a mood to linger as long as they did, and yet
many of these patient women carried hearts as anxious
as my own. . . . The heat was tremendous; a faintly
throbbing mist seemed to hang over the beautiful Lombardy plains, and by and by the mountains, which had
lain clear and distinct in the morning light, began to
lose their sharp outlines, and to hide themselves in this
veil of blue mist. In the west it took the form of
largely rounded clouds, as yet only faintly visible. An
old woman, who sat on a stone ready to give the thirsty
pilgrims a draught of milk from the goat which nibbled
the herbage by her side, pointed towards them: "The

signora would do well to hasten her pilgrimage," she
said.   I thanked her, but I did not fear the storm.

Later, however, as I turned a corner, and the height
of the Sacro Monte lay before me, I was vaguely ap-
palled by the grandeur of the sky.   The sunshine still
flooded the broad road, all paved with round rough
stones.   In nooks below delicate white flowers as fair as
lilies sprang out of the grass ; but the town which
crowned the hill, the bare white houses running steeply
down, gaunt, jagged, seamed, baked with long centuries
of sunshine, lay white and glaring under a strangely
menacing canopy of cloud.   I have never seen a more
sharply accentuated contrast.   I went on, for I hate
turning back, but I did not stay in the town when I
reached it.   Distant rolls of thunder were growing un-
mistakably louder ; as I hurried along the stony road
the rain came down in glittering sheets, for the sun
was still shining in part, and the air seemed full of
flashing lights.   I shall never forget the extraordinary
beauty of the clouds, the triumphant brightness of the
storm as one turned angle after angle, and saw it in
some new form sweeping exultingly round the mountains on this side or that ; and then, unmoved by all
the hurly-burly, the strange peace and quiet of those
wayside chapels, with their solemn figures and their
awful teaching.

I was not far from the last when a woman met me,
hurrying up breathless.   Before she met me she called
out,

" Good news, good news ! they are come !"

" Who, then ?"

" Our Garibaldi with his Cacciatori !"

" Come !" I cried, amazed.

But she would not stop, she only called back to me:

"Or coming. I go to fetch my husband," and hurried on, while I, wild with the thought that Luigi might arrive when I was not there to welcome him, ran as fast as I could down the hill, quite heedless of lightning or rain. People were pouring out from the houses which lie just below the arched gateway by the first chapel,—men, women, children, old and young, rich and poor; horses were saddling, *vivas* sounding. Garibaldi's name was in all mouths, and we all flocked down the hill with but one thought, how soon we could get to Varese, for nobody knew more than the woman had told me,—and, indeed, it was only she who had brought the news,—and nobody was certain whether the troops were in or only on the road.

Presently we heard a clattering behind us.

"Eh, it is the Count's carriage!" said an old man, looking back.

I had forgotten that the Contessa Fenze had a villa below the Prima Capella, and she, for her part, was doubtless shocked at seeing me running down with the people; but she stopped her carriage and insisted upon my getting in, and then I boldly asked permission for old Angelo Borgo, who is more than eighty, to be taken on the box, and she consented.

She was really kind and anxious about my condition, for I was very wet, and I had not long been in the carriage before I began to shiver. But it was impossible to think of such things on such a day.

The crowd thickened so much that, as we got near the town, we had to drive very slowly; and when we had passed the last field in which the white mulberry trees stood, as it were, knee-deep in the long grass, we could only go at a walk. I put my head out of the window, and spoke to a man who was near.

" Are they in ? "

" They are but one half-hour off, signora.   Ah, the happy day ! "

They are all like that—like children.   I saw men crying openly, not in the least ashamed of their tears.

In the town we found it was impossible for the carriage to proceed, and we were obliged to get out. Poor little Madame Fenze, who was very helpless, was dreadfully alarmed, and very thankful that I was there to take care of her.   I confess, however, not from fear, but because I was anxious to push on farther, that I was a good deal relieved to see a friendly face in the person of a certain Signor Rossi.   He at once took possession of us, and got us into a window above the arcades in the principal street, where we were sheltered from the rain which still fell in torrents, and were sure to see our soldiers well.   The enthusiasm and excitement in the street were overpowering; one could think of nothing else.   Signor Rossi told us that about an hour ago an incident had added fuel to the flame. It seems that two young men, who there is little doubt are Austrian spies, were bold enough to venture into Varese on this day of all days in the year !   It was lucky for them that the people did not tear them in pieces.   Signor Rossi thinks they would have had little chance if he had not passed at the time.   Now they are safe in prison.

Our troops did not arrive so soon as was expected ; it was late evening before distant shouts, caught up and repeated by the waiting crowds, told us that they were at hand.   All the church bells broke into peals of welcome,—and our Varese bells are famous,—houses were flung open, feasts spread ; the joyful tumult was something which I can never forget,—the men shout-

ing, the women, with their shining head-dresses of
silver pins, waving the gay handkerchiefs which they
had dragged from their shoulders. We, too, waved
with all our might, and Luigi, looking up, saw us, and
made a sign to me which I did not need, for I had
already recognised Garibaldi. His face is too well
known to need description; I can only say that it was
more lion-like and heroic than I had imagined.

After the great crowd had in some measure dis-
persed, we left Madame Fenze, rather against her will,
alone, and Signor Rossi kindly took me home. Luigi
did not arrive for an hour,—the men had to be fed
and their clothes dried,—and he could only remain
with me a few minutes, for an attack was expected
the next morning, and the General had to employ all
the night in strengthening his position. There was
no time for anything, and the next day the Austrians
attempted to shell the place. A shell fell very near
this house, and I suspect I should have been greatly
alarmed if I had not been very ill; but the chill of
the wetting, after the great heat on the Sacro Monte,
brought on an attack of fever, and at the very time
when I longed to be of use to Luigi, I was tossing in
my bed and miserably ill.

To-day I begin to feel myself again, and can listen
to all Rosa's excited stories of what has happened.
The Austrians seem to have been splendidly repulsed,
and my husband, unwilling as he was to leave me, of
course had to go with the Cacciatori. We think they
are at Como. Rosa is very full of the spies, who, it
seems, actually used my husband's name. . . .

June 14.—The strangest event has happened. I
ask myself if it is possible that I am going to see one
of my own people. Two years ago I accidentally met

an English artist, a Mr. Fanshawe, and found that he
knew my father and the children. This morning Luigi
writes that he has come across this same Mr. Fanshawe at Brescia, he having travelled night and day
from England in search of Miles, my half-brother;
dear little sturdy, fair, curly-headed Miles !

Luigi's letter stops abruptly,—I suppose he was
called off on duty; but the suspense is almost more
than I can bear. How can Miles be in Italy? Has
he ever thought of me, I wonder? No; how should
he? Still——

93.—RELEASE.

Edgar to Sir Walter.

VARESE, *June* 16.

Dear Sir Walter Winkworth—Your son asks me
to send you the enclosed letter and diary, which will
give you the history of his detention here.[1] I am glad
to say it is now at an end. He wrote the letter a
fortnight ago, but the officer in charge here did not
think it his duty to allow it to be posted. He was
waiting for some fresh orders from General Garibaldi
with regard to the prisoners, which, in the hurry and
confusion of the campaign, were never sent to him. I
reached this place yesterday from Brescia, where I
went in search of Signor Marini. I found him there,
and he procured an order for the liberation of your son
and Mr. Bootle, and sent me on here with an escort.
I arrived last evening, and have removed Miles from
the prison to the villa where his sister, Madame Marini,
is now living. He is now in her care. I do not think
they have been very badly treated, but the confinement

---

[1] See Letters 72 and 73.

in a close damp room, bad food, and distress of mind, have pulled Miles down very much. He has had an attack of fever, which is still upon him, and I fear he will not be fit for a journey for some time, and Mr. Bootle agrees with me. Mr. Bootle does not appear to have suffered much from the imprisonment, and Miles speaks well of his care of him in the fever.

I am glad to be able to set your mind at rest so far about Miles, and will only add that I shall stay here for the present, at least till we hear from you. Anything more that is in my power I shall be ready and glad to do. Miles begs me to give his love to you.—Believe me, yours truly,

EDGAR FANSHAWE.

P.S.—The fever returns at night and exhausts him, so Mr. Bootle says, very much, though he is quite conscious at present.

94.—NEWS AT LAST.

Sir Walter to the Rev. J. A. Bootle, at High Scale.

THE MIZ MAZE,
STOKESWORTHY, June 20.

Dear Mr. Bootle—News has reached us at last, though not of the best kind. Your son is safe, and apparently well, and he and Miles are both at the house of my daughter Madame Marini at Varese; but they *were* made prisoners by some of Garibaldi's rascally soldiers, and confinement in a close damp cell so affected my dear son's health, that he is very ill with fever. I am going out to him at once, so you will pardon a short letter.

No doubt you will soon hear from your son, but as

you may wish to write immediately, I enclose his full
address.—Faithfully yours,

WALTER M. WINKWORTH.

95.—A PROUD MOTHER.

Mrs. Bootle to her Son.

HIGH SCALE RECTORY, *June.*

My dearest Algy—I must write at once to say how
proud and happy both myself and your father are to
feel, not only that our dear boy is safe, but that we
have a son so true to the principles of the Protestant
faith.   I declare I feel just like the man who said:
" Happy is the king who has a son so willing to die a
martyr, and a judge so ready to prevent him."   For a
blessed Protestant martyr you have been, my beloved
boy, as much as Hooper, George Wishart, Latimer, or
even poor Peter Martyr, who, I take it, must have been
the greatest of all, and whose wife, poor soul, Mr. Bootle
assures me, has the misfortune of being mixed up with
the remains of a Popish saint at Oxford, and very unpleasant too !   We are giving thanks, your father and
I, every instant, that you were saved from a fate so
dreadful as a martyr's death.   Mrs. Warburton has
called in to tell us of that Mr. Fanshawe's letter ; and
from what she says, I feel sure, my boy, that you saved
your young friend Miles's soul from all the perils of
the Pope's emissaries.   How fortunate indeed that Sir
Walter had secured for his son so safe a companion as
my Algy, otherwise the perils of his soul might have
been greater than those which have attacked his body !
I dined yesterday at Triermain, and when, to keep up
all our spirits, I told them how I felt sure you would

stand up gloriously and triumphantly amid Red Republicans and Popish priests, and convert them all, that saucy little Emily began giggling, until I rebuked her for levity, when she said something which ended in a sob and a burst of tears. So I advised her mother to keep her in bed, as it was certainly a fit of hysterics. Your father desires his love, and will write shortly. He talked of returning thanks in church; but I said: "Mr. Bootle, return thanks if you please at the family altar, which is a sacred Protestant institution, in the bosom of your wife and servants, but do not defile High Scale church by introducing a Tractarian custom, which I can only class with invocation and the sale of indulgences." Now and then your father surprises me. —Your devoted mother, MARIA BOOTLE.

96.—RELIEF AT STOKESWORTHY.

Miss Madgewick to Emily.

MIZ MAZE, *June.*

My dear Emily—Zoe begs me to give you our latest news, as she is not likely to be able to write herself to-day. We are in a state of great commotion and excitement here. Sir Walter starts to-morrow for Varese. He got a letter from your cousin this morning, enclosing one from Miles, with a diary, written in prison, both of which ought to have come a fortnight ago, but were kept back by the prison authorities. Zoe has just taken them down to her aunts. I need not repeat all that your cousin says to Sir Walter, as I know he will have sent you full details. It is such an immense relief to us all to get this news. That weary waiting and expecting a letter by every post has been

P

terribly trying to them, and it is especially bad for
Zoe. Sir Walter was on the point of setting off for
Varese yesterday, only Miss Winkworth persuaded him
to wait one more day for a letter. The news of poor
Miles's illness decided him upon going at once. Zoe
and Mary have been crying over the diary, and from
what they tell me, the poor fellow seems to have been
very seriously ill. No wonder! considering the amount
of air and exercise he has been used to all the days of
his life; but I hope he will soon be himself again, now
that he is safe with his sister.

You see, I am in the secret now, which seems to
be no secret to the neighbourhood in general. Miss
Winkworth told me all about Madame Marini, saying
that there had been too much playing at cross purposes
already, in which I most heartily agree with her; and
she also cleared up the domestic mystery over which I
have been puzzling myself lately, little guessing that
you were in the thick of it! I am afraid I cannot say
more for the wisdom of the scheme than Miss Winkworth herself. It was rather, I may say, *very* mad;
and if you had consulted me, I think I should have
foreseen that to let that lace go anywhere within a
radius of ten miles of Mrs. Bootle would be fatal; not
to mention all the other considerations. Zoe told me
what Miles said about the matter. Murray holds
" that the masculine gender is more worthy than the
feminine," and the male mind does, now and then,
prove itself the strongest in practical common-sense, I
am afraid. How these private interests have put all
excitement about public affairs into the background.
The Marinis are a great deal oftener in my mind than
Garibaldi! It is like Sir Walter to have held to his
word all these years! Poor Lady Winkworth would

never have allowed it of her own free will, though the
aunts no doubt think it more her fault than his. I
long to hear more of Madame Marini.

No time for more now. You shall hear directly
there is anything fresh from Varese.—Your affectionate
MADGE.

97.—PARDON TO CLYFFE.

Sir Walter to Ratclyffe.

MIZ MAZE, June.

My dear Ratclyffe—I am just starting to go to
Miles, who is at Varese, suffering from the effects of
fever, though already better. I will write further to
you as soon as I reach him. No time now except to
say that I have received your frank confession, and
feel sure I may trust you for the future, spite of what
you tell me. I am grieved to have doubted your
brother for a moment.—Ever your affectionate father,
W. M. WINKWORTH.

98.—WHO IS SISTER BERTHA?

Lisa to Frank.

My dear Frank—Only think, papa is gone to
Italy to see about Miles, who has been in prison, and
is very ill. He is being nursed by a Sister Bertha. I
wonder who she is. A nun, I suppose. They call
themselves mothers and sisters, you know; but Sister
Bertha is not such a pretty name as Sister Clarice had
in that book Mrs. Bootle gave Zoe on her birthday.
I wonder if Miles likes being nursed by a nun, and
whether she tries to make him believe in the Pope.

That would be horrid.   This Sister Bertha has got a husband, a General in somebody's army.   I thought nuns did not have husbands, but I suppose she was like Sintram's mother, and did it for some noble reason.

Miles and Algy were both in prison.   There were some rebels who took them captives, and they were shut up till Mr. Fanshawe came.   I think he paid their ransom.—I am, your affectionate sister,   LISA.

99.—JOY AT HIGH SCALE.

Annie to Fanny.

TRIERMAIN, HIGH SCALE.

My dear Fanny—I make no doubt as you have heerd that the pore young gentlemen has been delivered. Mr. Bootle gave thanks for it in church, and there was not a dry eye.   I hears as how they had taken pore Mr. Winkworth from his bed in a loathsome dungeon, and Mr. Algey was a holding him up in his arms to be shot by the gorillas, that they might die together as Protestants and martirs, when in comes Mr. Fanshawe with a parding from Garey Baldey in his hand, and dares them to shoot him through his own body.

They do say as Miss Warburton will never hold out agin Mr. Winkworth now, and Mrs. Bootle as good as told Mrs. Skewton we should have Miss Winkworth back again.

So I lay down my pen.—Your affexionate friend,
ANNIE BROWN.

100.—"THE SCAMP OF AN ARTIST."

Miss Winkworth to Mrs. Home.

June 21.

My dear Mary—We are in some degree relieved. The paragraph was only too true. The two poor young lads have been all this time prisoners at Varese, and Miles has been, and, I fear, still is, very ill with fever; but he is with his sister, and his father is setting out to go to him. And how do you think he was discovered? Miss Warburton saw the paragraph and sent it at once to her cousin, " the scamp of an artist." I must say it was an act of great friendship on his part to throw up all his occupations and make his way to Marini at the headquarters of the Garibaldian army. Zoe heard from her friend by the morning post, enclosing Mr. Fanshawe's letter, before he had reached Varese. Walter was the least in the world inclined to pooh-pooh it, and think that whatever Mr. Fanshawe did must be of the wild-goose kind, and he growled at " the fellow Marini" being brought in. " There you see, as I always said, he is nothing but a rebel and democrat." " We never used to think Sir William Wallace a rebel," put in Bessie, softly. " I should like to know what else that Garibaldi is, with all these lawless ruffians?" returns Walter.

We are, of course, much relieved, though still anxious. And Walter is in a great hurry to set out, dreading the effect of all these Garibaldian surroundings on his son, "though at least Bootle is with him," quoth he, whereat Zoe very nearly burst out laughing. She excused herself for it afterwards by telling us, as she had never done before, what a joke this same

Algernon's complacency and awkwardness was among them all. "It is Mr. Fanshawe whom papa might trust to, if he only would," said she. I said, while allowing the observation, something in a tone of warning about young men who would not settle to any steady profession. She asked me what I meant, so I said I thought he had refused a good situation in a bank to lead this sort of artist life. Bohemian is the fashionable word for it. "Oh, Aunt Dora !" said Zoe, "I thought you would have seen how noble it was of him !" And then she told me that he had two uncles at Rome, one a very rich banker, and one a Monsignore. When his father died they wanted to adopt him, and he might have lived a prosperous, art-loving, do-nothing life, but the condition was that he should become a Roman Catholic, and this he refused to do, choosing English poverty, and living chiefly by his art rather than give up his conscience. Zoe grew quite hot and eager over it, telling us that, though his father had been a wandering, idle man in bad health, there was a good old English grandmother, who had gone about with him, and to whom this son owed all his first impressions. He had often told Emily Warburton about *la Nonna*, as he called her. And he was sent to an English public school,—Winchester, I believe,—and spent some of his holidays with those Fanshawe cousins, to whom Emily looks up so much. Certainly, as he has no prospects, it is a pity that Zoe has heard and seen so much of him, for I see she has made a hero of him in her heart, and gratitude will add to the fuel. However, I trust the spark has not yet been kindled, for her father would never consent ; and, so far, it seems to be mere hero-worship, quite unconscious.—Your affectionate

D. W.

101.—OPENING PRISON DOORS.

Edgar to Clyffe Winkworth.

VARESE, *June* 16.

Dear Winkworth—Your brother wishes me to write to you, as he thinks you will be anxious at not hearing from him for so long, and he fears some rumour of his late scrape may have reached you. Very likely you may by this time have seen the paragraph in the papers which sent me off to look for him, and may have drawn the same conclusion that we did in England.   He came here in hopes of finding your sister Madame Marini.   Unfortunately he and Bootle reached the town on the very day that it was occupied by the Cacciatori delle Alpi, who took it into their heads that they were Austrian spies, and locked them up in prison, where they have been till yesterday, when I had the satisfaction of fetching them out.   It seemed likely that the best way of hunting them up was to find Signor Marini, your sister's husband, who is a Garibaldian officer.   I therefore followed him to Brescia, and fortunately succeeded in making him feel answerable for their safety.   You know the Italians are relations of mine, and, though that may be a misfortune from some points of view, I have been rather glad of it lately.   Colonel Marini sent me here with an order of release, which he got very easily from his General, and also a small escort, making my journey quicker and safer than it might otherwise have been.   This country is in a most disturbed state, and I had some difficulty in reaching Brescia.

We arrived yesterday at this town, which is now settling down after its patriot enthusiasm of two or three weeks ago. Lieutenant Canzio, a friendly fellow, who commanded my escort, went straight to the prison to arrange matters with the officer in charge there, while I found my way without much difficulty to the villa where Madáme Marini is now living, these wild times having driven her from Castelforte, her home in the country. Miles may have mentioned to you that I met Madame Marini at Brescia some time ago without any idea of her relationship to you. I therefore thought I might venture to call on her, as I had understood from Colonel Marini that she remembered me. I believe your recollection of her, like Miles's, is very faint. I was charmingly received by a very beautiful woman, with a great likeness to your sister, but darker and with the air of her adopted country. She had already received an unfinished letter from her husband, saying that he had seen me, and hinting at the object of my journey, which of course interested her deeply. First, however, I had to explain to her where and how I had left Colonel Marini. After that a few words were enough to tell her everything. She knew all about the supposed spies, and would have gone with me to the prison, but she is weak from a recent attack of fever. As soon as I had made everything clear to her I hurried off to Miles. My friend Canzio was waiting for me at the prison gate, and the first thing he put into my hands was a letter from Miles addressed to your father, which ought to have been posted a fortnight ago, but these foolish fellows chose to keep it back. I have sent it on, with a diary that Miles has been keeping, and a few lines from myself to relieve Sir Walter's anxiety.

I went into the prison with Lieutenant Canzio and Captain Serra, a lumpish fellow, in whose charge the prisoners have been all this time.   It was both painful and amusing to see the care they had taken of your brother and of Algernon Bootle, whose harmlessness was surely plain enough.   I cannot say I liked the prison.   It is much nastier than any English one I ever saw—damp, and with bad smells prevailing; the walls and passages were mouldy.   After a great deal of unchaining and unbolting, the turnkey opened a door, and I walked into Miles's cell. 'He and Bootle were together.   The cell was small, with one barred window very high up; two straw beds, a rough table, and a bench were the only furniture ; and these supposed Austrians were in some ways treated worse than felons, for the gaolers were unwilling to give them any comforts, even when paid for it.   Mr. Bootle was sitting doubled up disconsolately.   Miles was lying on his bed.   I am sorry to say he is sadly pulled down by the imprisonment.   He has been rather seriously ill of fever, and is now suffering from extreme weakness. He started up at the sound of my voice, and tried to walk across the room to meet me, but he was not strong enough, or the sudden relief was too much for him, for he fainted away, and I only just caught him in time.   When he came round the first word he said was your name.   "Does Clyffe know about me ?" and he has been talking about you at intervals ever since.

I was furious with the prison people and with Captain Serra and his discipline, but it was no use storming at them, so, with Canzio's help and Bootle's, who seems to have behaved very well, and nursed Miles kindly, I got him to a carriage that was waiting, and took them straight to Madame Marini.   I do not think the poor boy is likely to forget his sister again. He ought not, but he will write to you himself on that subject by and by. You must not be too anxious about his illness. I think he was below par when he came here, having exposed himself too much to the hot sun in Switzerland ; and, as you may already know, he started on his travels rather low and out of spirits. He has, however, gained his object. Miles generally does that in the end, I think.

There are of course a great many particulars about his imprisonment which he will tell you himself. I hope it will not be long before he is able to write to you. Freedom and fresh air, and Madame Marini—if I may say so—have already brought a shade of colour into his face ; but of course he is pining for England, and likes talking to me, as I seem the nearest point to that dear old country. I have told Sir Walter Wink-worth that I shall stay here till we hear from him. Miles sends his love to you. I think his being here is a great happiness to your sister.—Yours very truly,

EDGAR FANSHAWE.

102.—OLD THREADS PIECED.

Bertha Marini's Diary.

VARESE, *June* 17.

I wonder whether writing it down and seeing it in black and white would make it seem more real ? At times I find it so difficult to realise that I get quite sick with the fear that it is all a dream, and that I shall wake up and find myself at Castelforte again, where nobody at this time of year thinks of anything but the silkworms. I was afraid to look just now when the door opened ; only suppose if it had been nobody but Rosa, rubbing her sleepy eyes after a

night spent in watching and feeding those small
creatures! But it is all true, true, true! It was
Miles, my own dear, little, curly-headed Miles, who
had come, like the brave fellow he is, to get some
news of me, and whom these stupid people had actually
imprisoned as an Austrian spy. And now he is in
this house; and is it wonderful that I cannot believe
it? I felt sure that I was altogether forgotten by them
all, and I am ashamed now to think how proud and
angry my heart kept itself; I would make no
advances, though I was the one who should have made
them; I tried no softening; I shut myself up in a bitter
exile, and here are these two children—for it seems
that my little Zoe had set her heart upon it as much
as Miles, more, he says—remembering me all these
years, keeping me in their warm hearts, and now
carrying out this romantic plan of theirs which had
nearly ended so disastrously. And they are *her*
children, that is the wonder!

But now let me try to put down as connectedly as I
can the bare outline of what has happened.

Luigi's letter. That set one thinking, as may be
imagined; thinking and wondering and perplexing
one's self with a hundred wild ideas. But the next
evening I was sitting on the terrace, and feeling as if
I could no longer endure the uncertainty, and must
follow Luigi to Brescia in spite of his wishes, when
Paolo came out and told me that a gentleman wished
to speak to me. In fact, the gentleman was close
behind, and the moment I saw Mr. Fanshawe my heart
leapt up.

"Madame Marini ——" he was beginning, but I
think he saw something in my face which made all
apologies unnecessary, for he went on at once with a
directness for which I shall always bless him.

" I have come from Brescia, where I have seen your husband——"

Fever shakes one's nerves. There instantly leapt into my heart the fear that Luigi might be wounded, and that Mr. Fanshawe had come to break it to me, and I interrupted him :

" He is ill !"

" No, no," said he, smiling. " Pray don't look upon me as a bringer of bad news. Colonel Marini is in excellent health, and the Cacciatori are winning victories in such a rapid fashion that they take them as a matter of course. I am come on other business, connected with your brother Miles."

Of course, then it all rushed back upon me ; just for the moment the other fear had driven it out.

" It really is true ? Do you mean that Miles is in Italy ?"

He looked surprised. " Did not Colonel Marini's letter explain that he was here, in Varese ?"

" In Varese ?"

I started up, but the faintness which I hoped had left me came back so strongly that I was obliged to sit down again hastily, while he gave me some particulars. Miles in prison, in Varese itself, and I, his own sister, close at hand and knowing nothing ! Mr. Fanshawe began some sort of explanation, as to how he had first come to me in order to find out whether I wished him brought to the villa, and if so, how soon I could be ready to receive him. Of course it was what I should have expected, but if he could have known how each word fell like a blow, I think he would have been sorry for me. As it was, he suddenly interrupted himself.

" 1 don't believe I need say any more, but fetch

him and let him speak for himself," he said, jumping
up.

"I shall go with you," I said, as quietly as I could,
for my knees trembled so much when I stood that I
was dreadfully afraid my strength might altogether
fail. And Mr. Fanshawe only shook his head with
a smile.

"Thank you!" he said, with as much warmth as if
I had said something quite unexpected, "but after the
illness of which Colonel Marini spoke, I feel quite
certain, if you will allow me to say so, that for you to
go to the prison at this time of the evening would be
sheer madness. I have an excellent ally in Lieutenant
Canzio, who is armed with full powers, and I hope by
the time you have given directions for Miles's reception,
to bring him back in triumph."

He shook my hand very heartily, and was gone.
It did not take long to give my orders; then I stood at
the window listening for wheels, and thinking of—ah,
what did not come back to me! The night was
exquisitely clear and soft; I could see the pale outline
of Monte Generoso lying softly against the sky, fire-
flies flashed delicately here and there out of the
darkness, the green frogs were croaking in the fountain,
scent of orange blossom stole across the terrace; I saw
and heard all, and yet I was no longer in Italy, but in
England. Only think, I had not seen one of them for
nearly twenty years, and here was Miles close at hand!
I wondered whether he would be like my father, or—
his mother; whether he would distrust me, and be cold
as she was. It may have been only manner, but I
thought it would break my heart if Miles were cold.
At any rate I was determined that he should not go
away without having learned to like me a little bit.

Mr. Fanshawe did not look or speak as if he were greatly prejudiced, and that comforted me. But I went over and over our coming meeting, little thinking how different it would be from anything that I expected.

I heard the wheels after an endless time of waiting, and I tried to hasten to the door, but the trembling came on again, and I only reached it in time to see Mr. Fanshawe and another gentleman almost lifting some one from the carriage. Was this Miles ? Paolo held a lamp, I could see a white pinched face, and my heart stood still when Mr. Fanshawe put up his hand and said quietly, " Where ?" He meant that I was not to speak, and I was able to take the lamp from Paolo, tell him in a whisper to go for Dr. Zamperini, and lead the way to the room next my own. There they made him rest on the sofa, and I was standing a little back in the shadow, not daring to come too near, when I heard him say, in a low voice :

" Is that my sister ?"

I could not help it ; I pushed Mr. Fanshawe on one side and put my arms round Miles—my brother.

" Yes, yes," I cried ; " I am Bertha. Have you really remembered me all these years, and done this for me ?"

He said very feebly, " I am glad, but—it was Zoe," and Mr. Fanshawe put his hand on my arm and drew me back.

" He is exceedingly weak," he said, gravely. " Bootle tells me that he has had a most serious attack of fever, of course aggravated by that wretched prison. I am sure you will see that excitement is the worst thing in the world for him."

It was hard, but Mr. Fanshawe was right, and

moreover he was kindness itself. I wanted him to stay, but he said Lieutenant Canzio had gone off to secure lodgings for himself and Mr. Bootle, Miles's companion, and now that he left Miles in good hands he felt happy. He just waited to hear the doctor's report—which comforted me inexpressibly—and to have some food, and then went off, promising to come early in the morning.

Already it seems a week ago, and yet it was only the day before yesterday. Yesterday Miles seemed to have improved wonderfully, but last night there was a return of fever. Dr. Zamperini, however, is most cheering; he says he only wants good nursing, and I have become so prudent! Even my husband's aunt, Madame Lecchi, who is installed here in order that Mr. Fanshawe and Mr. Bootle might move to the villa from their lodgings, only shakes her head occasionally.

Miles *is* like my father. I see it now much more strongly than at first. Perhaps it is rather in small ways than anything more definite. From the little he has said he seems to me to worship his father, but to have a little fear of him. I don't know if I am right; I believe I am on the lookout for signs and indications, until, perhaps, I dream them. At any rate, my wild hope that my father was a party to this search of Miles's is altogether dashed to the ground.

Mr. Fanshawe's kindness has been the greatest possible comfort. He has confided to me—what I had already begun to suspect—his love for Zoe. He is very despairing about it, poor fellow! and though I long to encourage him, I don't dare; I have not the right. All that he has told me about her has endeared her to me more than I can say; her sweet girlish frank simplicity, her honesty, her warm affections, and the absolute truthfulness on which he dwells so lovingly. She is better than ever I was; I see this more and more as I look back and compare myself with her. And, remembering my own doing, how can I by a word suggest anything which might seem like a repetition of my own headstrong conduct? I can't. I told him so, and I think he understood, for he wrung my hands and thanked me.

But I find it impossible not to believe that my father would appreciate Mr. Fanshawe, if he only knew him. There is so much that wants nothing but that —just knowing. *Tout comprendre c'est tout pardonner.* Perhaps even if I had known Lady Winkworth better, things would have turned out more happily, at any rate I shall try to think so.

June 19.—Miles gets better slowly, but still he *is* better. And *à propos* of the advantages of knowing better, I am beginning to find his friend, Mr. Bootle, a little less odious. At first I really disliked him so much that I would not write anything about him. For a young man there seemed such an extraordinary pomposity and self-conceit about him that he was a continual astonishment. I had never seen any one like him. From the very little Miles let drop, and from what Signor Rosa, who soon came to see me, brimful of curiosity, had to tell, it was very easy to understand that it was Mr. Bootle who brought them into the scrape, and yet to hear him talk, you would suppose he had been a sort of guardian angel to poor Miles. He proses away until I am completely exhausted, and I cannot understand how my father can have such a good opinion of his sense. However, Mr. Fanshawe assures me that he is decidedly improved by all that has happened, and I do notice that every now and then he pulls himself up. I hear this is quite a new feature, and so I try to be patient, the more that I can't help feeling that though he may have had his share in causing poor Miles's illness, I am the real cause of it all.

I have just been sitting with Miles. He is on the sofa in his room, decidedly better, but as weak as a child. He has been talking of the home people and things till it seemed as if my heart must break, and it was all I could do to appear calm. Excitement would be so bad for Miles. But—the pictures which some chance word of his brought up! "My father and I were walking in the lane behind the farm—you know the lane?" he would ask. Know it? There is not a stone I do not know. I smell the honeysuckle now, and see the old thorn growing up stiff and sturdy near the gate! I asked if it were still there, and Miles said yes. Mr. Meyrick and he both advised its being taken away, but my father would not hear of it. I wonder —it is not possible—yet I can't help remembering that it used, long, long ago, to be called Bertha's tree. Of course, now—still I am glad the old thorn is not cut down.

Miles talked a great deal of Clyffe; he seemed astonished that I remembered so much about him.

"Why should I forget?" I asked, as quietly as I could.

"Well, you appeared to have given us all up," said Miles, quickly.

I felt as if, once I began to speak, I might say too much, and I bit my lips. Miles went on the next moment with an evident effort. "I say, Bertha, couldn't you write to some of them? They'll be in no end of a fuss about this illness of mine."

I write! But I dared not agitate him. "To whom?" I asked.

"Well, to Zoe."

Ah, he did not say my father, and how could I write to Zoe?

"Would it be right, Miles?"

He hesitated and looked uncomfortable.

"Aunt Dora, then."

"Do you think I might?"

"Of course. It would be the greatest happiness to them all."

When he said that I could have no more doubt. I have come down now to do it; when I took my pen it was to begin that letter, but something seemed to make it impossible until I had thought it all out once more. And first I must write to Luigi. He is well and happy, and proud of Garibaldi and of Italy. Their successes have been wonderful. At another time one could have thought of nothing else, but now, so long as I know that Luigi is well, I have hardly any thoughts to spare. Yet it is selfish, for the poor people in the town suffered sadly from the Austrian shells, and almost every one has friends in the army.

103.—From Exile.

Bertha to Aunt Dora.

VARESE, *June* 19.

Dear Aunt Dora—I don't know whether you will like me to write those words, or whether you will care to read this letter, but I fancy you will not refuse, if only for the sake of Miles, and without thought of me. He is decidedly better, though still weak and unfit for writing, and he is very anxious that you should all be told that he is making good progress. I really think in a day or two we shall try to get him out; fresh air will do more for him than anything. I hope you understand that my husband was in no way responsible for this dreadful imprisonment. It happened on the day that he came into Varese, it is true; but Colonel Marini is attached to Garibaldi's staff, and great events have followed each other so rapidly that there has been no pause or time to investigate matters which at other times would have called for attention. We are most deeply indebted to Mr. Fanshawe for all that he did; his conduct throughout has been the very reverse of Mr. Bootle's. The latter certainly did his best to bring suspicion upon them.

When my husband will return it is impossible to say, for they cannot spare him, and he has some very important work on hand. But I trust it will be before Miles leaves us, I long so much for them to know and appreciate one another.

If you are kind enough to answer this letter, I hope you will tell me a great deal about Aunt Bessie. Miles assures me that my father bears up bravely under what must have been a heavy sorrow. I suppose I must not send him any message, nor a word to Zoe; but, oh, Aunt Dora, if you knew how I long to see them, to see you all, you wouldn't think me quite so heartless as I dare say I appear. It has been a long exile; perhaps I deserved such a punishment, and, on the other hand, I am quite sure I did *not* deserve a husband such as Luigi, but I do crave for the home people. One love need not drive out another, need it? Don't you think you could kiss Zoe for me? It was she who planned this search of Miles's, and you must never blame her for it—never! If you do not consider it right to let her know how much her unknown sister loves her, kiss her still for me without saying a word; that cannot do her any harm.

Good-bye, dear Aunt Dora. Try to think of me as kindly as you can, but never think of my husband except as one of the best and most honourable of men. Believe me, *he* was not to blame, only I; and let me still call myself your affectionate niece,

BERTHA DOROTHEA MARINI.

104.—THE DANGERS OF FOREIGN SOCIETY.

Algernon Bootle to his Parents.

VARESE, *June.*

My dear Father and Mother—You will be thankful to hear that, after much peril and privation, I am at last safe and well in the house of a most hospitable lady, Madame Marini, Sir Walter's daughter, and the object of Miles Winkworth's journey into Italy. I have great pleasure in assuring you both, when I contemplate my past conduct, that I find in it nothing unbecoming to a gentleman, a Christian, an Englishman, and a Protestant. In the face of imminent death, when at any moment we might have been led out to be shot, I kept my presence of mind; and had I fallen, I should have done so in the spirit of a martyr to my creed and my nation.

My imprisonment was, I know not whether to say aggravated or alleviated, by the cares of attending on Miles Winkworth, who was very ill all the time with fever. I am thankful to be able to assure you, my dear mother, that the disbelief you so strongly expressed in foreign doctors before I started on this tour, has stood me in good stead. They brought some one to see Miles who, Fanshawe informs me, was a cow-doctor, as the right man was gone off to Garibaldi, and he wanted to bleed Miles. I sternly refused to allow this to be done, and Zamperini, who has since then been brought to attend him, assures me that, with his English constitution, he would most likely have died if it had been done. He is now, I am glad to say, getting better. Fanshawe is staying here, and as he was greatly instrumental in bringing us out of our dungeon, I must not say too much against him; but I confess that I consider that he is a forward young man, who does not realise his position as a mere artist, but evidently considers himself quite upon an equality with the rest of us. Madame Marini, who, like most Italian ladies, does not seem to observe the dictates of British conventionality, accords to him much more intimacy than she does to me. I feel, however, that this may partially be owing to the natural dignity which I always feel it right to assume among strangers.

There is much danger in foreign society as regards the young and unwary, and I think it was most wise of Sir Walter to send with his son a person of firm and settled principles like myself. It is true that Miles is not so susceptible as many young men, but he might have proved so. We travelled down the St. Gotthard Pass with one of the most lovely and fascinating personages whom it was ever my lot to meet. She assured us that she was a personal friend of the Emperor of Austria, and so worked upon us that we both fully believed that she was one of the brightest, as she certainly must have been one of the most beautiful, ornaments of the Viennese Court. Indeed, the

opinion which I formed of her importance led me to
make considerable use of her name on our way to
Varese. Madame Marini, however, informs us that this
lovely being is so devoted to gambling, that she has
actually gambled away an estate left her by her deceased husband ; and that she is not by birth aristo-
cratic at all, but quite of low rank. Conceive how
terrible it would have been had she succeeded in casting her toils round Miles. I will not allude to myself, as without any undue self-confidence, I may fairly
consider myself too highly gifted with common sense
to be caught by any such siren.—Believe me, my dear
parents, your affectionate and dutiful son,

ALGERNON BOOTLE.

105.—ZOE COMFORTED.

Zoe to Miles.

THE MIZ MAZE, June 21.

My dearest Miles—Here is a letter from Clyffe to
cheer you. Little can he guess where you are. I
cannot tell you how great a comfort it is to be writing
to you once more. This has been a terrible time,
though we did not know the half, and never thought
of your being ill as well as a prisoner. I dare not let
myself out to write about all we felt, for you would
only say, " Bosh !" But I must tell you about Polly.
Dear child, her loyalty forbade her to ask questions
about what was kept from her. I thought she looked
white and wistful, but I durst not speak to her, until
one night I heard a sobbing in Bertha's room, and
there was my poor child huddled up in the moonlight

on the floor, sobbing as if her heart would break, having slipped in there for fear of waking Lisa.

I found she had all sorts of wild ideas about banditti and rebels, and thought that you would be shot, or at least have your ears cut off, if there was not a ransom paid in time, and that I had sold my things to raise it, because I could not tell papa. Oh! would not I take everything she had to help? So I was obliged to explain all, and put her out of her misery. The truth was bad enough, but being a fact, instead of a series of nightmares, she felt the relief, and I had hardly got her into bed before she was asleep.

It seems too wonderful to be true that you are with Birdie. I almost grudge her the nursing of you; and yet that is very selfish, for she must have longed for you all these years.

Aunt Dora has been most good to me all through, and Emily has been the very centre of it all,—feeling one with me as no one else could do. Actually she has been quite ill and hysterical, the dear girl! And how ready of her to send to Mr. Fanshawe before I had even written to her. As to thanking Mr. Fanshawe, that is quite impossible,—one can only feel it in one's heart of hearts; next to the higher thankfulness.

Papa will be with you no doubt as soon as these letters. I wonder if I may send dear love to Birdie from the little sister who used to turn out her box of jewels.—Your loving sister,   ZOE.

Extracts from different Letters of Miles to Clyffe.

VARESE, *June* 23.

Dearest Clyffe—They must let me write to you, if it is only a little bit at a time, for you will like to see my writing, even if it is shaky. I must send three lines to Zoe,—she wrote to say my father was coming, —and Fanshawe shall have the pleasure of doing it up and directing it. You will soon get his letter telling you that I am better, and since then I have got on by degrees; there is nothing for you to mind about. Don't fret about father's mistake; of course I knew you would tell him if I asked you. I'm glad he knows, and that it is all square, though I dare say it vexed him. But his letter upset you, and made you dream about me, I suppose; though it was true enough that I was in danger then. My dear boy, I'd defy you to dream of anything so disgusting as that prison. Let us hope Garibaldi will reform *that!* I think poor Algy was almost the worst off; for he was so dreadfully frightened about me, and though, of course, when I was sensible, I tried to keep him up to the mark, when I was off my head I worried him with fretting after you; and he says I did really cry out one night "so that he thought they would almost hear in England." I remember fancying that you were here, and I couldn't reach you. Then he thought father would blame him for not keeping me back: easier said than done. I do think I should have died if I had been by myself,—he took all the care he could of me,—but the awkwardness of him, and indeed of us both, was beyond everything. Sometimes

I almost laughed when he upset the water—when we
hadn't half enough. Poor fellow, *he* almost cried about
that, because I was so thirsty. Then he *would* talk
about the Emperor of Austria, and one day the fellow
who took care of us said that he was so dangerous
that he must put him in solitary confinement. They
wouldn't listen to him, and by that time I could
recollect nothing but English, and not much of that;
so I could only take hold of Algy's hand, and look as
imploring as I could, and, would you believe it, the
fellow who had abused us like a pickpocket, actually
burst into a flood of tears, and gave in! which shows
that these Italians are made of queer stuff; for he
ought not to have threatened us if it wasn't his duty,
and if it was, he ought to have stuck to it. But he
got me some stuff to take after that, and after Algy
had decided that it wasn't poison, I think it did me
a little good. But, oh, it was wretched, and I got so
weak I hardly knew where I was, even when the fever
wasn't on me. I did give myself quite up. I thought
I should never see you, nor Zoe, nor the children again,
and I thought of every one, even the dogs, at home,
and how I had felt before I went away, as if I didn't
care for any of them—but I did then. And I thought
I shouldn't have minded so much if there had been
any sense in our imprisonment, or if one could have
felt that one was doing any good by it, or if there had
been any sort of principle involved. But if they
would only have listened to me, I would have said
anything civil of Garibaldi to get out; and if they
did believe we were spies, of course they were justified
in detaining us; but I shall always maintain that
they ought to have taken the trouble to hear what we
had to say. Bertha, who is quite as romantic as Zoe,

says that I sacrificed myself for her, which is nonsense; for, of course, I never expected to get caught by the leg in such a ridiculous manner.

June 24.—Algy was in a most perplexed state of mind about what he called the political aspect of the question, and I suggested that he had better appeal to the Pope to complain of the rebels; and I really do think that to find the Pope on his side was quite an affliction to him. You see, this sort of Italian fever is very odd, and sometimes in the morning I felt almost well, but it always came back at night,—it does still if I get tired,—and so at last I had no strength left. And then, one evening I was lying looking at poor Algy, and thinking, in and out, how miserable he looked —never having shaved, nor anything comfortable— and how I had dragged him into the scrape, and I wanted to say something about it; for I had been so angry with him about the Emperor of Austria and his Countess, with whom, by the way, he was *immensely* struck, that I had thought it was all his fault; but I was too sleepy and stupid to speak, and then there was a great noise and tramping, and the room seemed full of people, and there was such a chatter and gabble. I thought I was dreaming, and Algy thought, he says, that we were going to be taken out to be shot, and he hoped he should stand up like a man, and not disgrace the name of an English Protestant. Fanshawe says that he folded his arms and glared at him. But I saw old Edgar, and I tried to get at him, but I couldn't,—and the next thing I recollect was his real voice close by. I held on to him,—I felt as if I should die if I let go, —and he says he thought so too for a moment; but he gave me some brandy, and I came round a bit, and then he said that it was all over now, and my sister

was close by, and he was going to take me to her.   I
was so stupid that I thought he meant Zoe.   Then
they carried me out.   I wished they would have let
me alone; but I began to remember in little bits as we
went along in the carriage, and presently, when it was
all still and quiet again, I saw Bertha, and she cried
and kissed me, but they would hardly let her speak
to me.   Oh, it was all so clean and comfortable and
jolly,—I was afraid all the time that I was asleep
and dreaming; but by the next morning, I was quite
sensible, and Fanshawe told me all about it.   I was
so glad when he came back; he made it seem real.
Then Bertha came in again.   You know I never liked
the idea of her; but she looked so kind and sweet,
and her voice was so nice, I couldn't help liking to
see her.   She asked if I had been quite well when
I came to Varese.   I said, Yes, I believed so; but
Edgar said,—

"I don't know; life has been rather hard on him
since Clyffe went away."

"Clyffe?" she said; "where is Clyffe?"

So Edgar told her how you were with your
regiment.

"Little Clyffe!" she said.   "Yes, they were always
hand in hand."

Then Edgar repeated Zoe's old joke about our having only one tongue between us; for really I could not
tell what to say to her.

"I remember Clyffe could talk the best," she said;
"but he was much the most mischievous!"

Then I said I wanted your wits as well as your
tongue, for you would have managed to find her much
better; and that it all came from my forgetting the
Italian I had learnt so carefully.

Then they laughed, and she said, "Can Clyffe speak Italian?"

I said, No; but that you would have spoken first to my father, and set it right in that way. But they would not let me talk about it. Edgar said something to her in Italian, and she kissed me again, and said that she was glad my hair was still curly, and I must tell her all about Clyffe.

Perhaps you don't know, I said, there are Frank and Polly and Lisa; then she laughed and half cried, —I do think she is very fond of us all. She is very like Zoe, and has the same eager way of talking.

June 25.—If you could see this place! There is the most wonderful view, and a terrace with great pots of orange and lemon trees. I have got quite used to Bertha now, and Edgar and Algy both admire her immensely. I don't think my father can help forgiving her when he comes here; but she can hardly bear to speak of him.

The Italian officers called and apologised to Algy for our detention,—Fanshawe acting as interpreter,— and a funny scene it must have been. I wasn't strong enough then to see them. Now, I am out here on the terrace for half the day. They say that I over-worked myself in the spring, or I should get strong faster; but I get tired directly, if I sit up much, or try to do anything—scribbling to you doesn't count. I wish my father was come, for Bertha's sake at any rate.   M. W.

107.—A Scrap from Miles.

Miles to Zoe.

VARESE, *June* 25.

Dearest Zoe—I must answer your letter, though I
have been writing to Clyffe.   It wasn't *quite* as bad as
the Inquisition.   Bertha is kindness itself, and very
like you.   I wish I had not made *every one* so wretched,
—even poor Clyffe,—but I must tell you all about that
another time.   Fanshawe will not let me write any
more now.   Words can't say what he has done.   I am
much better, and shall soon be all right again.   Love
to all and Polly.—Your loving brother,   M. W.

108.—The Little Niece.

Aunt Dora to Bertha.

June.

My dear, dear Child—For you have been like a first
child to me always, the first little niece that ever I
loved!   Yet it seems strange that after this I should
have to account for our losing sight of one another.   I
did write, my dear, as soon as we came back from
Madeira, and Mr. Bernard sent the letter to his
sister to be addressed, but she returned it, saying she
did not know where you were.   Sometimes we have
talked of a journey to Italy to see if we could
find you, but Bessie has never been equal to much
travelling.   She feels any jar to the spine so much,
that she never even went to High Scale.   She is,
however, better now than she has been for years, and
her spirits have recovered · their tone.   As I dare
say Miles has told you, we have sobered down into
regular old maids, extremely like Ben Jonson's tree,

but very glad to have the young ones to enliven and
excite us.   I hope you will some day know your sisters.
Zoe is a curious compound of frankness and reserve,
impetuosity and self-restraint, and with a beautiful
ideal standard always before her, with which she com-
pares herself, to her own distress.   It is pretty to see
her happiness and relief now, so entirely free from any
unbecoming exultation in having been the means of
restoring you to us.   Indeed, the thought of Miles's
illness and danger seemed to swallow up all the rest
with her.   "I led him into it," she said again and
again.   The two young ones are nice little girls, rather
bewildered, but, I suspect, understanding more than
they choose to show.

My dear, when your father comes to you, I do hope
you will remember his dislike to cigars.   It may make
a great difference to his first impressions.   And do not
let him sit in draughts, for remember he is not as
young as when you saw him last.   And Aunt Bessie
hopes you will persuade your cook not to put oil and
garlic into your polenta, or macaroni, or whatever it
is that you eat.   No doubt you are used to national
dishes, but take care he is not made ill by them.
There, I told you how old-maidish we were, and now
you see it; I write this stuff when I meant to tell you
that our love and prayers have been with you all these
years, and that we always felt there had been trials in
your home life.   I have often tried to realise the life
you are leading, but I do not know anything of Italian
country life later than *I promessi sposi* and *My Last
Duchess*, so you would only laugh at my guesses.   It is
joy to know of you watching over Miles.   Aunt Bessie
sends her dearest love.   So does Zoe.—Your loving
aunt,   DOROTHEA WINKWORTH.

PART VII.

THE BARONET ABROAD.

"Remote, unfriended, melancholy, slow."

109.—WRITING AT A LITTLE TABLE.

Sir Walter to Aunt Dora.

PARIS, *June* 23.

MY DEAR DOROTHEA—I have just arrived here, and have paused to dine at a restaurant close to the station before making my way to the other line, where I am to take the night train for Italy. While my meal is preparing, I take the opportunity to send you a few words that you may know I have got thus far safely, and am obeying your injunction to "take care of myself." I can scarcely help a feeling of *gladness* that my dear Sophia is not waiting in suspense at home while I hasten to the sick-bed of her first-born. She is beyond the reach of these earthly troubles.

You will, I know, do all you can for our poor little Zoe. It is a mournful time for her, though youth is naturally sanguine, and, happily, she has not as yet had hopefulness crushed out of her. I am oppressed with a sense of remorse for having under-rated Miles and condemned him in my own mind as extravagant and wanting in openness towards me, while all the time he was acting a most generous and self-denying part, and shielding his brother from blame. I left Ratclyffe's letter with Zoe for you, for I felt, as I had confided to you my fears about Miles, it was only right that you should see that they were groundless. You will not, I know, think too harshly of my other dear

R

boy.   He has in a great measure atoned for his past
carelessness by the frankness and fulness of his confession.   I wrote one hurried line to him before I
started, but did not make the worst of Miles's illness,
knowing what grief it would be to him.

I fear this letter is almost illegible, for the little
round table at which I am writing is inconveniently
low, and there is a continual jabber going on around
me from the people who are seated at other little
tables all over the room.

Here comes the waiter with my " bif-tek à l'An-
glaise."

Good-bye to you and Bessie.—Ever, my dear Dora,
your affectionate brother,

WALTER M. WINKWORTH..

110.—AUNT DORA'S WISDOM.

Aunt Dora to Sir Walter.

DOWER HOUSE, *June.*

My dear Walter—I hope you are getting on well
on your journey.   I tremble to think of the state in
which you may find our brave boy.   Otherwise I cannot but be glad of the door that the dear children have
opened, even if they did take the key without leave,
and fumble a little in the lock.

These thoughts have been put into my head by a
letter Zoe showed me from Miss Warburton, who, as Zoe
will have told you, has recovered the lace.   The child
has not thought of it herself, but I suspect the cost must
have been very heavy, and you will, no doubt, wish
to know the amount—unless; indeed, the lace should
end by being Miss Warburton's own, which I begin to

think not by any means impossible.   George Thorburn rode over this morning to ask what news we had heard, adding, with rather a funny face, that he understood that little Emily, as he called her, was quite ill, with a strange attack of nerves,—almost hysteria,—though she would not give up, and that her mother was very anxious about her, she is in such an excited state. This may be only her mother's nonsense; but her letter to Zoe gave me somewhat the same idea, though, as I say, there was a thought in it worth the consideration of us elders.   Is it absolutely reasonable to expect that grown-up children should continue to believe us infallible, or to expect them to make everything known to the elders?   No two generations can be cast in precisely the same mould; and, if there be any power or energy in the younger, a time must come when repression into our own groove begins to gall.   There may be a sense of other duties acting on a conscientious mind, and then it takes refuge from disobedience in silence and concealment, not always deserving to be branded as deceit.   Silence is not the same thing as falsehood; and I am very anxious that Zoe should feel that this is acknowledged by us, and that her spirit, always over sensitive and self-conscious, should not be burdened with the sense that deceit is imputed to her. I know the doctrine may be dangerous, but if we could live in sympathy with the young ones the danger and temptation would be averted.   And when we detect them in these independent actions, even if they have been imprudent, yet, if they have really done nothing itself wrong, surely we should try to put ourselves in their places before being severe with them.   Dear Walter, forgive me for seeming to counsel you, but I grieve to see little Zoe droop under bitter self-blame and fears about your meeting with her brother.—Your affectionate   D. W.

P.S.—What will you say to me, dear brother? It was borne in on me so strongly in my waking hours this morning that it would be the best thing for all parties for us to have Miss Warburton here with Zoe, that I went to Bessie, and found her full of the same notion. She had been dreaming of it all night; and so I have actually despatched a note to ask if she will come to us for a few days. It will make the girls so much happier, and I really want to know her better.

111.—Aunt Dora's Invitation.

Aunt Dora to Emily.

DOWER HOUSE, *June.*

My dear Miss Warburton—I wonder whether you will listen favourably to the request I am about to make to you? My dear niece Zoe is sadly tried by all the anxiety and suspense that she has lately gone through, and I am sure that nothing would do her so much good as a visit from you. Would Mrs. Warburton be so kind as to spare you for a few weeks to the old aunts? You would be constantly with Zoe, and it would be a great happiness to her. Anxieties are always better when shared, though indeed we have every reason to hope that my nephew is recovering under his sister's care. We all feel that probably his life may be owing to the readiness with which you thought of Mr. Fanshawe—perhaps the only person capable of conducting the matter so as to obtain his release so easily. You know our county a little, but there is much that you have not seen on our side of it, and Zoe would delight to make some summer expeditions with you, if all goes as well as I trust it will. I have not told her that I am writing, she would be so much disappointed if you could not come; but my sister and I trust that you will be able.—With best regards to Mrs. Warburton, etc.,

DOROTHEA WINKWORTH.

112.—EMILY'S ACCEPTANCE.

Emily to Miss Winkworth.

TRIERMAIN, June.

Dear Miss Winkworth—I cannot say how much I feel your kindness in asking me to come and stay with you and see my dear Zoe. Nothing could give me greater pleasure, and my mother will gladly spare me after next week, if that will suit you.

I do not think I could stay more than a week, as mamma is expecting some visitors. But I am most grateful for this opportunity of being with my dear Zoe. Tell her that Mrs. Bootle has heard from her son, and that Madame Marini has quite eclipsed the Austrian countess.

Mr. Bootle has felt it very much. He mentioned the special mercy in the thanksgiving with a quivering voice, and there was much genuine feeling everywhere in the church.

May I come on Monday the 29th, by the train that reaches Stoke's Gate at 7.5 ?—Believe me, yours gratefully,

E. B. WARBURTON.

113.—HOW LIES THE LAND ?

Emily to Miss Madgewick.

TRIERMAIN, *June.*

My dear Enchantress—Behold a most kind invitation from the aunts, which I cannot help accepting. It is very good in them, and I shall never be righted till I have talked things out with you and Zoe. Friendships want to be rubbed up together after great crises. Of course I shall only stay a few days, so as to be well out of the way before there is any risk of the mankind turning up, and, by Algy's description, Miles is far from ready to move. I must do something, for I can't settle to anything, and Mrs. Bootle exasperates me beyond Christianable bounds. I was really sorry for their trouble, Mrs. Bootle seemed so bowed down ; but now she is quite uplifted at her dear Algy having been persecuted, and she is so persuaded that he will have a blessed effect on the poor misguided lady that I can hardly endure with patience. Moreover, mamma fancies me ill, and wants me to go to the sea-side, the which I hope to escape. I believe the Charles Fanshawes are coming to us, and I hope to set him on upon my solicitor, who, when I asked for my own money for the site of St. Joseph's (which I have at last bid high enough for), gives me to understand that I am a silly young woman, who can't be allowed to pay such an exorbitant price. Moreover, the other clergyman has become restive, and altogether the *couleur de rose* has come out of my plans, and they look all smoke and dinginess. I feel as if Triermain was a moated grange, and could box my own ears for being so like that absurd Mariana.—Your affectionate

E. B. W.

114.—MISS MADGEWICK'S WELCOME.

Miss Madgewick to Emily.

MIZ MAZE.

My dear Emily—You may imagine how surprised and delighted I was when the aunts told me they were going to ask you.   I quite respect my own strength of mind in not telling those poor girls till your answer arrived.   It will do Zoe all the good in the world to see you, and the news has sent Mary's spirits up with one bound to their usual level.   Lisa, I fancy, has never quite taken in the situation ; at least, she sees it chiefly from the picturesque point of view : a brother taken prisoner by the Garibaldians ; and a mysterious Roman Catholic sister married to an Italian patriot (for Miss Winkworth thought the most judicious thing to do was to tell them the outlines of that romance). How much there will be to talk over when you and Zoe have said your say !   There is no need to alarm yourself about Miles coming back just yet.   He is going on quite satisfactorily from the last accounts ; but plainly won't be equal to travelling for another fortnight at least.

It seems that if he had not been handicapped with that miserable Algy Bootle, the poor boy would not have fallen into this slough of despond.   Till lately Sir Walter's infatuation about Mrs. Bootle seemed to me something utterly incomprehensible (unless one came round to your cousin's theory of mesmeric influence) ; but now one has heard of these old troubles of his, one can see how the simple fact of her anti-Puseyism was more to him than all the cardinal virtues put together.

I am very glad that you and "Aunt Dora" are going to know one another. I like her all through. In fact, I could hardly have believed that one could get so really fond of any one whose traditions and way of life have been so unlike one's own. After all, there is a danger of our getting into "grooves" of our own, perhaps while we are fighting against being forced into other people's. I had not the slightest intention of writing more than a note, as we hope to meet so soon, but I have run on. We must talk over your plans, and disperse the coal-dust that has gathered over them. Your solicitor shall feel when he reads the letter which we will draw up together, that,—like Mrs. Micawber,— "though your form is fragile, your grasp of a subject is inferior to none."——Ever your affectionate

ESTHER MADGEWICK.

115.—THE GOOD GENIUS OF VARESE.

Bertha Marini's Diary.

VARESE, *June* 23.

Miles is delightfully better; of course still weak, but able to stroll in the garden and sit out. Happily we have had no great heat, though I don't know that he would have quarrelled with it, for he has the funniest dislike to shade, and declares that our closely wooded walks, in which I delight, are so gloomy as to make him shudder. If I allowed him to do so, I believe he would sit on the terrace in the blazing sun with Mascherino at his feet. Mascherino has made over all his affections to Miles unreservedly. I always thought he liked me until now, but I see it was only toleration, and that his heart was untouched.

Mr. Bootle is certainly a strange person. I imagine he is one of those men who would rather attract notice by any means, however singular, than fail to attract it at all.   His imprisonment will be a joy to him all his life.   Already he has persuaded himself that he was on the point of being shot, and more than once he has informed me that had he fallen, it would have been as a martyr.   A martyr to whom, I wonder ?   I presume to me.   He professes a horror of our Church, but he is always asking questions about it, and more than once I have seen him in the Duomo, when he had no idea that he was noticed.   After Magenta we had a *Te Deum* in the Duomo; it is impossible to attempt to describe the joy of the people.   They had decked themselves in the Italian colours; the very church was wreathed with red and white flowers set in their green leaves; the sun shone out—shone on the pretty bright colours, on the silver pins which glittered round the women's heads, on the happy faces.   I felt ashamed to think how little I had cared about it all, except the knowing that Luigi was well.   Never mind.   If he were here he would not blame me.   He would understand that unless I were at rest about him, I could be happy about nothing—not even over a new brother.

One does not get on very fast with Miles; but there is the comfort of feeling that a step once gained is never lost, and I can't blame him for being slow to understand that I am not indifferent.   He sometimes talks about them all in a sort of apologetic way, as if fearful of boring me ; while I—if he only knew it ?—am afraid of losing a word.   Yesterday, when it was very hot, and we were sitting in the north *sala*, where the cool drip of the fountain sounds pleasant, he asked me if I would care to see some of their photographs.

Care ?   He would have had little peace if I had known there were such treasures in the house.   However, out they came at last.

"Don't tell me who is who, but let me guess, Miles. Ah, here you are yourself !   It is excellent ; at least, I don't know, there is something which is not exactly right ; perhaps it was taken when you were stronger ?"

Miles began to laugh.

"You have just saved your discernment.   That is old Clyffe."

"Clyffe !   Then you must be a ridiculous pair."

"So they say."

The likeness was indeed extraordinary ; but Clyffe looked as if his eyes twinkled with fun, and his spirits had never felt a touch of care, while it had repeatedly struck me that Miles was unnaturally grave.   I had hoped that light-heartedness would come back as he grew stronger, but so far this was not the case, and do what I would, I could not get many smiles from him. I took the remaining photographs from his hand.

"This must be Polly, by the round cheeks and the fair hair.   And this—Miles, this can't be Zoe !"

He did not immediately answer, and I looked up. Poor Miles !   He was crimson ; it was easy to see that I had, all unintentionally, touched some sore place, and there was nothing to be done but to turn to the next, and to say, " No, of course not, here is Zoe, with her steadfast eyes.   But I am sure she is prettier than this ?"

"It's a horrid thing," said Miles, recovering himself. " Zoe without any of herself in it.   The one you just looked at," he added, with an effort taking it up, " is a Miss Warburton, a friend of Zoe's."

"There is something very lovable in her expression."

" Isn't there ?" he said, eagerly.

His interest was so palpable, that it was a little difficult not to smile; but I tried to keep it out of my voice as I said: " Zoe's friend strikes me as being more enthusiastic than Zoe."

" How wonderfully you read her face," he exclaimed. " She *is* enthusiastic—for all that is good. You see she has always such high ideals, that it is impossible for a commonplace fellow——"

He stopped suddenly, and got red again. Then I knew it was better to take it all for granted.

" Dear Miles, if you love her so well——"

" Better than I knew," he muttered.

" Don't be afraid of girlish ideals. She will not be the worse for having had them; but by and by they will grow into something more real, and therefore more true. If that is all !"

Poor fellow ! It was astonishing how grateful he seemed for these few words, spoken very much at random. I believe he takes me for an experienced woman of the world, and so gives my opinions a higher value than they are worth. His shyness vanished in an eager outpouring of all that there was to tell; and if I did not know enough to give more than vague comfort, it was evidently a great relief to be able to talk. I don't wonder, after being shut up with Mr. Algernon Bootle all this time !

As to my poor Miles's chances, perhaps I spoke rather in advance of my convictions, for the sake of seeing his face brighten all over, as it did. But I honestly believe that things will come right; the chief obstacles are the little perversities of a romantic girl, too young to appreciate Miles, and expecting her heart to be taken by storm by the real hero the instant he

leaps into view.   Sound trumpets, open gates, enter—
well, I am inclined to think that, after all, it will be
Miles who will march in to victory, very much, perhaps, to his own amazement, and a little to hers.

My two lovers keep my sympathies fully strung ;
now it is one, now the other.   But I cannot talk easily
to Mr. Fanshawe ; I long to help him, but I am
frightened.   How can I advise him, when my father
has never yet forgiven me ?   Even if—if—Miles were
to bring us together again, as my heart sometimes
whispers will be the case ; even then, it is impossible
that I should have any influence with him ; he would
rather treat me as a warning.   Will Aunt Dora answer
my letter, I wonder ?   Will she tell Zoe that I have
written ?   And did I say enough to make it clear how
proud I am of Luigi ?   Mr. Fanshawe has gone down
to the *spezeria* to pick up what news he can ; perhaps
he will bring back the letters.

June 24.—Yesterday I wondered whether Aunt
Dora would answer ; to-day I am wondering how I so
utterly failed to understand that all this time I—
holding aloof so coldly and proudly—was yet kept
warm in the hearts of those at home.   First these two
children, and now Aunt Dora.   It has put me to
shame, but it has made me very happy.   I felt as if I
must do something, so I went down to the hospital, and
to the prison, and found a poor young Austrian in a
sad plight.   Signor Rossi was a good deal shocked
when I took him there, and between us we got something done.   I shall visit the prison regularly, and
persuade Luigi to ask the General to send orders about
it.   The place is horrible ; I cannot write of what I saw.

There is something else—very different—of which
I can hardly write.   From Zoe's letter to Miles yester-

day, we find that my father is coming, is on his way,
anxious about Miles.   It is easy to see that Miles is
greatly pleased, though he laughs it off.

"What a humbug he'll pronounce me!" he said,
looking up from Zoe's letter.   "I say, Fanshawe, hadn't
I better take to my bed again?"

"I trust that Sir Walter will fully comprehend the
difficulties of my position," said Mr. Bootle, solemnly.
"Miles will allow that I repeatedly urged him to
remain in Switzerland.   If he had done so——"

"He would have been a worse fool than you took
him for," said Miles, coolly.   "Don't you see how
splendidly everything has turned out?"

"Oh, if you call a dungeon and a fever splendid!"
said the other, turning away with an offended air.
Miles caught him by the shoulders, and laughed.

"At any rate, if it hadn't been for them, Algy, I
should never have known what a good fellow you were.
Never mind, don't be crusty, old fellow, my father is
sure to understand that it was all my doing.   But I
should be afraid that he would think he had been
dragged out here on false pretences—if it weren't for
something else."

Miles dropped his voice as he said these last words,
and perhaps only I heard them.

June 25.—The news of Solferino has just reached
us, and Varese is mad with joy.   I can see that
Madame Lecchi thinks me half-hearted, but indeed I
am not.   How can I be, when my husband is fighting
for the cause?   It is only that so many strings are at
work, pulling one different ways, that I cannot give all
my thoughts, all my heart, to Italy.

This morning, while the air was yet fresh, Mr.
Fanshawe asked me if I would show him a pretty restful

garden which lies a little behind our villa. We walked
up the dusty road, bordered by walls where the lizards
were darting in and out of hot crevices, and went in at
a green door, over which is written the word " Quiet."
Passing the house, over which banksia roses were still
flinging themselves in long trailing masses, and every
now and then turning to look back at the purple depths
of our beautiful Monte Generoso, we came to a tall
clump of cypresses, and climbed a little grassy hill
planted with oaks, which should give thick shade, but
that the cockchafers this year have literally devoured
the young leaves. At the top we sat down on the
bank. Before us lay Varese, the tall tower of the
Duomo in its midst, here and there a gay confusion of
flags tossed out of the houses, the deep clang of bells
swinging gladly up towards us; beyond the town a
background of hills, sweeping away into I know not
what intricate and delicate distances, until they lost
themselves in haze. It is impossible to describe the
clearness yet tenderness of colouring with which everything was touched; but not the least attractive point
was on our right, where a little *pergola* had been placed
to support some clambering vines. The fresh green
branches had flung themselves lavishly across the poles,
and through this setting appeared the pink church
tower of a small hamlet, with the rich and open country
lying beyond it, steeped in broad sunshine.

"When I see such a view as this," said Mr. Fanshawe, "all the Italian in me wakes up." He had
taken out a little sketch-book as he spoke, and began
to draw hastily. "It is a bad preparation for Sir
Walter," he added, shaking his head, "and I had better
have stayed at home. Madame Marini, tell me honestly,
would you take me for an Italian?"

"There *is* something——" I began, but he interrupted me.

"I knew it. Yet what on earth am I to do? I got all my clothes in London, except my hat."

"Perhaps it is the hat," I agreed.

"Misery! For again, what am I to do? I know! Happy thought! I will make Bootle change with me. Nothing can be more British or uncomfortable than his garments, from head to foot. Thank you a hundred times for suggesting the hat. I know Sir Walter likes everything to be ship-shape; and I am afraid an artist doesn't appeal to him in any way. It is most unfortunate. Now, Bootle, if he is an ass, is so tremendously ship-shape. Not that Zo—Miss Winkworth would ever put up with him, but somehow he manages to suit Sir Walter, while I——" he shrugged his shoulders despondently.

"You will have given him back Miles, and that must go a great way," I said, trying to think of him, and not of my own hopes and fears.

"Yes, he is very fond of him," he said, putting some delicate strokes into his Duomo. "I don't know, though, whether he has ever quite understood Miles. Lady Winkworth did most thoroughly, and so does his sister. Indeed, in many points he and she are wonderfully alike. There is the same steady hold of anything which they believe to be right, the same straightforward truth and unselfishness."

Ah, father, you have better children than ever I was! No wonder if they contented you!

Mr. Fanshawe had stopped, having no doubt lost himself in dreams of Zoe. However, presently he went on.

"You mustn't imagine that I am going to give up

my hopes.   Nothing could be farther from my thoughts.
On the contrary, I am a good deal elated over them,
because I venture to think that I have found a friend
in—Madame Marini."

"A friend—yes !" I said, quickly ; and I could not
help stretching out my hand to him.   "You must
never doubt my friendship or my husband's.   But
then——"

I was looking towards Como, when in a moment it
all grew blurred and indistinct with the tears which
would force themselves, though I tried hard to keep
them back.   I am sure Mr. Fanshawe understood, for
he said immediately,

"No, I shall never doubt it, and I am prophet
enough to foresee an end of misunderstandings and
separations.   Miles and—his sister—will have got
their desire more thoroughly even than they hoped.
It will be a great happiness to her.   I am ashamed of
having kept you here so long, but I shall find my way
here again.   Now, let us go down through that wilder-
ness of roses, or Bootle will be suggesting some idiotic
folly for Miles's benefit."

All the way he talked as if my father's coming
would set everything straight.   It comforted me infinitely, particularly when he spoke of my husband, and
of the pride I must feel in him, because he seemed
sure that my father would understand that, of course,
I could have no pleasure in any reconciliation which
did not include him.   It seems to me that, as he is
not here, I must be even more jealous for him.

However, I am full of hope.

116.—Miles resting.

Miles to Clyffe—continued.

June 26.

I am getting on fast now, as you may see by the respectability of my writing, though I still like to be lazy. Algy is afraid I shall forget all he taught me, so that he will get no credit as a coach. I am afraid so too. I shall be a worse dunce next term than ever. But I can't read now; even an idle book makes my head ache. Fanshawe was furious with Algy for mentioning the subject.

"He is much too ready to worry himself about it, as it is," he said.

Algy explained that he had wished to be successful in my case, because "the tutor of a gentleman of position generally obtained preferment,"—which was honest, at any rate.

Fanshawe said that people's brains were all the better for lying fallow, as I should find by and by. I hope so. If—— One wakes up slowly after being ill. The other day it occurred to me for the first time to ask Fanshawe how in the world *he* came to start off to look for me. And he said that *she* sent him a newspaper with a paragraph in it that frightened her, as she was in Zoe's secret. She has been very kind, Zoe says. Of course she would be, if Zoe was in any trouble. But Bertha thinks—I was showing her your photograph, and she saw Emily's by chance, and somehow she found me out; she says girls change their mind very often. If I had a chance, I'd do Algy credit then. But after making such a mull of finding Bertha, she'll think me more of a duffer than ever. If

S

I could have delivered Edgar from prison, and been just exactly the right man in the right place, as he was, the thing might be possible !

The said Edgar stopped my writing at this point, and made me come out into the garden. Algy was sight-seeing; so he is now. · I wish he would let the subject of religion alone while we are here. Bertha never alludes to it unless he asks questions, which he often does. She is very good, I am sure; but I don't think she is naturally so clever as Zoe. I suspect her affections were more attracted than her intellect by the Roman Church. She cares for Italy through her husband. She thinks people she loves perfect, and when she was younger, I expect she was a good hater too; but she was so sweet ·to me when I was ill, it was more like having mother. You must write to her and tell her that I am not ungrateful. I'd give anything for her to see you.

I declare there's Algy walking up and down the terrace with Padre Benedetto. I think he is Bertha's confessor. He comes here sometimes, and I am afraid father won't like the look of him. Algy is such a fool, that if anybody flattered him, they might persuade him that the moon was made of green cheese. If he tries to convert that priest he might get the worst of it, and where should we be then ? I must ask Fanshawe privately what he thinks. And Algy was immensely struck with the splendid services at the Duomo after the victories. Of course I could not go, which was a pity.

117.—THE BRITISH LION IN A NET.

Sir Walter to Algernon Bootle.

ALBERGO, MILAN, *June* 24.

Dear Algernon—I write to tell you that I am detained here by a most unfortunate mistake, and to beg you to come to my assistance, as I am anxious of course to get on to Varese as soon as possible.

While my luggage was being inspected at the frontier, I took the opportunity of getting nearly all the cash I had with me changed into Italian money, and a heap of dirty notes and two or three Austrian florins were given me in exchange for my French gold. What, however, was my consternation at Turin, where I had to change trains and take a fresh ticket, to find that the ticket-clerk refused to take one of these notes in payment! I thought at first that I had not offered him one of sufficient value; but when I offered note after note, and still he shook his head and pushed them from him, I felt completely nonplussed. Fortunately I had kept one or two napoleons, and was thus able to get to this place, but positively I can get no farther, and you can imagine how I am chafing at this unfortunate delay.

As far as I can understand the long explanation of the proprietor of this hotel, the notes which I have are not *forged*, but are Austrian, and therefore not acceptable here just now. He advises me to procure some newly-issued notes,—"Banca Nationale," I think he calls them,—and I have just been to a banker here about it, but he would not cash the cheque I offered him, and I could not understand a word he said. I am going to try and hunt up a fellow-countryman.

There may be one or two at some of the other hotels,
but, owing to the war, there are, I hear, very few
tourists in Milan at present, and even if I come across
an Englishman he may not be able to help me. There
are only Italians here, and though I have a good suite
of rooms, I am miserable, thinking of Miles and longing
to get to him.

What a country this is! I shall never forgive
myself for not taking a courier, as he would have been
up to the tricks of those rascally money-changers.

Pray come or send immediately, and, if you *can*,
bring me better news of my boy.—Very faithfully
yours, WALTER M. WINKWORTH.

P.S.—Be good enough to tell Madame Marini what
is keeping me.

118.—WHO SHALL BE MOUSE TO THE LION ?

Miles to Clyffe—continued.

June 27.

Zoe sends me your last letter. Oh! my dear boy,
to think that you should have got hold of that wretched
newspaper! It was my one comfort that you knew
nothing about it. By this time you will be getting
Fanshawe's letter. How I wish one could telegraph
across the Atlantic! I know I had rather be in that
prison again myself than fancy that you were there.
And I am afraid father is really in a difficulty. He
has written to Algy from Milan to say that he is
detained there by having the wrong sort of bank-notes.
People are uncivil, he says. Fanshawe at once suggested that he would go and see after him, for Algy
would run his head into another hornets' nest. I

wanted to go. I could explain everything there before
he gets here; and, though I don't see what could
happen to him at Milan, the very thought of any
detention for him frightens me after our own experiences. Of course I did not let Bertha guess that I
had any such notion. But I wish he was here.

Edgar insisted on going by himself, and I suppose I
couldn't well have managed it; no doubt he will. But
I miss him. I see poor Bertha is in an agony of ex-
pectation. Algy is very lugubrious, and very likely
I shall put things to my father in a wrong point of
view when he comes, and increase his prejudices. If
you were here!

119.—MASCHERINO !

Algernon Bootle's Diary.

VARESE, *June* 24.

After a fortnight passed here in the hospitable
house of the Marinis, I begin to forget the privations of
our miserable (though glorious) imprisonment. At the
same time I have begun to realise the fact that Italian
life and Italian civilisation are far inferior to English.
I will mention here some of the chief points in which
I notice this inferiority.

In the first place, Madame Marini has no sense of
the conventional position of an artist any more than
Miles himself, and does not seem in the least affronted
by Fanshawe's assumption of equality. This is bad, as
after all she is a Winkworth, and very beautiful and
fascinating. She is, I think, far handsomer than Zoe,
and is evidently accustomed to have her own way.
She has a way of stopping you in the middle of a
sentence which I find at times somewhat embarrassing;

but, at the same time, I do not feel that she intends anything which is offensive to the most sensitive feelings, as she generally makes amends soon afterwards by a most gracious smile.

What I dislike most in the house, however, is her dog Mascherino. At best I cannot sympathise with that exaggerated love of brutes, which makes some ladies so devoted to their favourites, but this dog is the worst I ever came near. He growls when I come into the room, and has a way of snuffing at one's heels, and sometimes even snapping at them. Yesterday being wet, I had to remain in the drawing-room when the rest were away in their respective apartments, or in Madame Marini's sitting-room, and this brute gave me the benefit of his wholly-undivided attention. He lay in the middle of the room growling, and at intervals giving an angry bark. I thought it prudent to surround myself with a barricade of chairs to protect my legs; but so blind are the most charming of their sex when their favourites are concerned, that Madame Marini, when she came in, made light of the danger, and Miles and Fanshawe have chaffed me ever since.

June 25.—What shall I do? To-day I received a letter from Sir Walter, requesting me to come to his help at Milan, where he has got into difficulties about some Italian notes which he fears must be forged. This points to some deep-laid plot, I fear, connected with our late imprisonment. It is evident that emissaries from the Pope or from the Austrians, who have taken alarm at our intimacy with the party of Italian patriots, as they call themselves, have thrown difficulties in the way of Sir Walter, who was on his way to our rescue. I told Madame Marini that I did not think I could go unless some well-known member of the Italian party went with me as an escort, and suggested that she should write to Colonel Marini to ask him to get leave to accompany me. She replied that she hoped I would not trouble myself, as Mr. Fanshawe would do all that was required, and had no fear of getting into imaginary difficulties. No, I said; but he was not, like me, just out of one prison, where he had well-nigh forfeited his life for his principles ; so it would not be so hard upon him to run the risk of putting his head into another. Madame Marini said nothing and withdrew. In fact, my argument was unanswerable.

June 26.—I have just had a most interesting conversation with Padre Benedetto, who speaks enough French for me to be able to converse with him. He assures me that there is no ground for my fears as to having incurred the hostility of the Pope, whom he described as a most amiable and well-intentioned man, infected in his youth with liberalism, but now having returned to more rational views. We entered upon the arena of controversy, in which I flatter myself that I proved the master. The Bible, I said, was the religion of Protestants, and we could have nothing to do with those who scorned it. He assured me that he did not scorn it at all, and that his chief objection was to our translation, which he considered to give wrong interpretations. " My friend," he said kindly, " I feel sure that we have much in common, and I should like to remove your misconceptions of my Church." I felt that I had made a beginning towards his conversion, and gladly accepted his proposal to resume the conversation on some other occasion.

June 27.—Fanshawe has arrived with Sir Walter, the latter apologetic with regard to the privations I have undergone in the care of his son, and full of gratitude for my care of Miles.   This is gratifying, and as it should be.

120.—THE MOUSE AT A DISCOUNT.

Edgar to Carlo.

VARESE, *June* 27.

Dear Carlo—When all this business is over I will come to Rome, and we will go together to Albano, and paint, and rail on destiny.   Perhaps I may even start off in a few days, as soon as one has some idea of what is likely to follow Solferino.   People who know about things shake their heads and smile when one suggests that the French Emperor is disinterested ; and there is even a whisper that he will make peace as soon as it suits him.   This looks as if the unity of Italy was still in the distance, and takes away from the romance of all this fighting and marching and devastating.   I am tired of it all, Carlo.   Men are such fools, and deceive themselves so very willingly.   I speak feelingly ; for I have lately been making a fool of myself, though not about Italy.   I can see that you are frowning over this ; my last letter was lively.   I had been releasing captives, and all the rest of it,—restoring relations to each other,—there was a sunny cheerfulness in my account of things generally.   I was living in the very house with people I cared for ; in your pretty way of putting it, I was " evidently recognised as a brother by these charming Winkworths." That is all very true, and when I told you how much I admired Madame Marini, I did not say half enough. One finds out more of her charm every day.   She is, without exception, the most sympathetic woman I ever met ; without any consciousness of herself or of her own beauty, she is sometimes absorbed in attending to Miles,—who now, I am glad to say, values her rare tenderness, and follows her about like a child with his melancholy eyes,—and sometimes, when he is not there, her gentle friendliness is all for me. Poor Bootle puzzled her disagreeably at first, but she cannot be unjust; and since we have told her the good points of him, her manner to him has been perfect,—not that it was ever anything else. She fascinates him, though he is afraid of her. I am not afraid of her, and one evening in the garden at sunset, with Monte Generoso shadowed out in the distance upon a golden sky,—you · know the sight well enough; and, by the by, it ought to keep one silent in its presence, but you will not be surprised to hear that it only loosened my garrulous tongue,—I told her all my history, and she listened with a kindness that I can never forget. She did not wish to encourage me much, but she did in spite of herself,—the mere fact of her sympathy was enough for that,—and so, for a day or two, living in this happy intimacy with her and Miles, I allowed myself all the ridiculous hopes of a blind idiot, forgetting everything that had gone before, and all the immense obstacles between their sister and me. Remember, *amico*, no one knows this but yourself. I am only telling you my thoughts, which is an old custom; and now, Paradise has shut its gates again, at least the greatest obstacle of all has stopped up the way. A glance at him is enough to wake the sleepiest man from the most enchanting dream. The Despotism of Fact—"l'Ananké des choses"—here he is. I have brought him here myself, would you believe it? and they are all joyful at his coming, and I have slunk away to my room, not feeling even as much right as

Bootle in this family meeting. What am I to them,
after all, or they to me ? These people of one family
belong to each other, and as to a foolish fellow who
calls himself their friend, and has even almost fancied
himself necessary to them, he finds out his mistake
without much showing, and shakes himself and walks
off into his own outside loneliness.

You want the true history of all this, do you,—its
meaning in prose ? You shall have it, then, without
a superfluous word.

A day or two ago came a letter to Bootle from Sir
Walter Winkworth, who had reached Milan on his
way to Miles. He was in a difficulty,—some rascal
on the frontier having changed all his money for him
into notes, but *Austrian* notes, which by this time no
one in North Italy will look at. The good man was
alone, speaking little French and less Italian ; and
thus he could not even make the people at Milan
understand what had happened to him. They were
kind and respectful, but would have nothing to say to
his notes. He wrote to Bootle for help. This threw
Bootle into a state of nervous frenzy ; for, to do him
justice, he has lost his self-confidence lately. I found
him and Miles. consulting over the letter. I afterwards thought it was both weak and presumptuous of
me to suggest : could I help ? but I did it for Miles's
sake, and in answer to Madame Marini's eager eyes,—
here I am going off into speculation again. In short,
they packed me off that very hour to Milan. I found
Sir Walter at the ——, marching wildly up and down
the best rooms in the hotel. He had grown quite
thin since I saw him in England, and his whiskers
were white, which I did not remember ; but I very
well remembered his manner, which was stiff and cold

enough to put me in my right place at once.   I had
arrived with a little effusion, you understand, from my
intimate friendship with his children.   His presence,
however, did away with all that.   I apologised for
coming instead of Bootle with some excuse or other,
gave him the last news of Miles, talked over his difficulty, and, without further delay, took him to dear
old Signor Lecco, who received us in his private room,
and in the friendliest manner took a cheque from him
on his London bankers, and gave him the money he
wanted.   Oddly enough, in coming out of the bank,
we ran against Filippo.   My dear Carlo, if you could
have seen Sir Walter's face, while your brother and I
were talking, and when Filippo, with that beautiful
bow of his, turned to him and asked him to come with
me to dinner!   His face lengthened so much when he
understood this invitation, that I saw it must be declined; but I told Filippo that I would try to pay
them a little visit in the evening.   This did not come
off however, for I found that I could not leave Sir
Walter.   He talked to me incessantly, asking every
question about his son and Bootle that could occur to
the mind of an English magistrate, but never mentioning his daughter.   I was, of course, obliged to do so
in answering him.   He was most entertaining on Italian
politics, being strongly Austrian, with the lowest opinion
of Italians, and their arrangements generally.   Once,
I think, it occurred to him that I might have feelings,
and he checked himself slightly.   I suppose, on the
whole, he was very friendly to me.   I tried to show
him the lions of Milan, but, naturally, they were thrown
away, and he thought the " Cena " amazingly over-
rated.   We started by Vetturino very early in the
morning; the day was splendid, the country in great

beauty.   We talked mostly about crops as we drove
along, and he received a few ideas about silkworms.
All the questions he asked were excellently put.   He
is a man of practical intelligence, just, no doubt, and
reasonable,—only too reasonable for me.   I don't know
whether Madame Marini cares much for her silkworms.   I fancy not.   Her father thinks them con-
temptible beasts, and no arguments of hers, I think,
will alter his opinion.   Poor old fellow ! after all, his
longing for a sight of his son kept breaking out in
every second sentence, and I believe he has a warm
heart for those who belong to him, so that I do not
doubt his thorough reconciliation with Madame Marini ;
but there are limits, Carlo, and those who are outside
must be outside still.

This conviction came to me so strongly at the
house-door, that I hardly waited to show him and
Miles to each other, but came away, as I told you, to
my room.   And I think you will see me in Rome
before many more suns have set behind Monte Rosa.
So prepare a welcome for your friend,

EDGAR FANSHAWE.

121.—MILES MAKING CONVERSATION.

Miles to Clyffe—continued.

July 1.

Well, after we had got the meeting over I missed
Fanshawe.   I had hardly seen him for a moment.   I
thought I would leave father and Bertha together and
go and look for him.   One of the servants told me
that he was in his room ; and then it struck me to
wonder how he and father had got on in their *tête-à-tête.*

He sleeps up at the top of the house in a room with such a view over the plain towards the mountains; but I had never been there before, and it was a long way up. However, there was Edgar sitting at the table, looking very forlorn, but he jumped up quickly enough, and exclaimed at the sight of me. I seemed to know all in a minute what he was thinking of, but I couldn't tell what to say ; besides that, I hadn't much breath left, and he began to scold me for coming up all the stairs.

" I couldn't find you," I said.

" I did not think I was wanted," he said—" now."

" If you ever thought I shouldn't want you under any circumstances, I'd never speak to you again !" I said. " What do you think we're all made of ?"

And he gave me such an odd, melancholy sort of look that I rowed him well, and said that was what it was to be half an Italian, to expect people to be always ready to say what they mean ; he would never understand us.

" You mean what you say," he said, and then it struck me what an awful duffer I was to say such a thing when of course he was worrying himself because he thought that he didn't suit my father; and I knew it would only hurt him to talk about gratitude for all he had done. I should have hated it so myself. I declare he looked as if he could have cried, but he laughed instead, and I said : " Wasn't father very much out of his element ? " which gave him something to laugh for, and somehow he came downstairs with me, and father got up and made him a most tremendous speech about having omitted the necessary acknowledgments of all he had done when in such a state of anxiety, but that now he could never express his gratitude enough to him for saving my life. " Miles," he said, " I hope *you* have not been so behindhand."

"He knows," I said; but he couldn't have looked more uncomfortable if he had been "a Wiltshire moon-raker" too.

Every one looked uncomfortable. Bertha seemed frightened and in a fuss about some coffee she had got for father, and Algy was queer and guilty-looking somehow.

So I asked about everybody at home, one after the other, in order to make conversation, till we got down to Ranger and Smut, and Mascherino came in, and father thought his name was *Maraschino*, which en-livened us a little. All this time Madame Lecchi sat and knitted, and father was much distressed at talking English before her, but I don't think she minds it, and we couldn't well help it.

But we were a queer party, and I *was* tired before the end of the day. Reconciliations take it out of one. This morning it is funny to see father with Bertha. He looks at her as if he were astonished, and he asked me in a doubtful sort of way if I did not think my sister remarkably handsome. And I can see him tak-ing to her by degrees, but not a bit as if she were his daughter, but some new acquaintance whom he found extremely charming. She has taken him for a drive, and left me to rest myself and tell you all about it. Edgar, who is more cheerful to-day, has been drawing all our profiles "to show the likeness." Much he'd care for my profile, or father's, or yours, if they didn't give him an excuse for slipping Zoe's in between.

I don't know quite what you'll say about it. I shouldn't have liked the idea if I had heard of it at a distance; but I believe we shall have to make up our minds to it some day, and if ever he ventures to ask for Zoe I shall stand by him.

July 3.—I have had a talk with father now. He has been very kind about our affairs; he even begged my pardon for mistrusting me. So I took courage, and I said that times were changed, and I did not think that the allowance he gave you was quite enough for any of his sons, and gave him a few facts to show him why; and he listened and promised to think of it. And then I said that I was sorry for the concealment about coming here, and that, though I had made up my mind to discover Bertha, I ought to have told him my intentions, and that we should have done so if you had been there to tell him.

"Tell me yourself another time, my boy," he said, "and be sure I will listen."

So you see it was very foolish of me not to have spoken out. But all's well that ends well, and I don't think he's sorry now for his miserable journey.

Bertha's fine house and grounds evidently astonish him, and it dawns on him that Marini holds a very good position here, and he means to stay till I am fit to go home. The weather has turned so desperately hot that I don't feel inclined for a move just yet, which would be a good excuse for keeping him; only if we can't mention politics or religion, as affairs are now, it will be very awkward.

My notion is that he had better ask Bertha and her husband to come back and pay a visit at Stokesworthy, and show all the neighbours that we're friends. Wouldn't you like to have Mrs. Bootle asked to meet them ?

Father has been ruminating over all the history of our adventures. He said that he had never taken in the details while he was so anxious, and at last he remarked,

"Algernon Bootle does not seem to have acted so judiciously as I should have expected from him."

"Quite the reverse," said Bertha, rather quickly.

"My dear," said father, "you always judge rather hastily ; he has excellent abilities."

But Bertha looked more pleased than at all his politeness to her.

Then, another thing, he is in a great fuss about my looks, though if he had seen me a week ago he would tell a different story.

"Does he always look so white," he said, "*Birdie ?*"

And oh ! such a look came into her face. I believe she was always called so, and I think father must have indulged and petted her much more than any of *us* can imagine. Then, when she was wilful and our mother had to restrain her, she could not stand it.

And I expect she has thought a great deal more about us than any one ever has of her ; unless it is father himself. *She* knows all the ins and outs of Stokesworthy much better than we do, and I hope she will see it again. But I don't think it would ever do for the girls to come and stay here.

I can't help feeling uncomfortable about Bootle ; he has been so odd lately, and, though I don't think Bertha, under the circumstances, would have said a word to me, one can't feel sure what she might think right about him.

And I hate the feeling of it all on Sunday, though Bertha came last Sunday, and talked about Aunt Dora and the Sunday-school as naturally as possible. But I did not say much, for I thought talking about Mr. Bernard would make her feel ashamed.

I wonder if father would think it wrong to take a drive on Sunday afternoon ; for people drop in here for coffee, and the ladies gossip, and Edgar looks so very foreign when he and all the men rave about Italy, that, on the whole, I think "Sir Vinkvort," as Madame Lecchi calls him, would be better away.

122.—SIR WALTER EDIFIED.

Bertha Marini's Diary.

VARESE, *July* 1.

When one has looked forward very eagerly to some event, and pictured its happening in a dozen different lights, and gone over in imagination all the possible sayings and doings connected with it, it is difficult in looking back to distinguish the imagined event from the actual. At least, I find it so. And perhaps, for once, I am grateful for the confusion; it softens things which otherwise might present themselves in outlines too harsh for endurance.

I ought not to have written those last words; certainly I ought not to complain. I have not had a word or look of reproach from my father,—nothing can be more courteous than his manner,—and he has more than once thanked me for the excellent care that I have taken of his son; only, has he forgotten that his son is my brother? Sometimes I think that he has,—that the old Bertha whom he petted, spoiled, and played with, died to him when she left him, and that I have appeared on the scene like an unknown relative, with whom everybody is conscious of a little awkwardness.

Miles did his best, dear fellow, in that first dreadful moment. He hardly waited a minute for my father to hold him by the shoulders and look at him

T

with that look I remembered so well—proud, glad, satisfied—before he brought him to me.

"Father," he said eagerly, "here is Bertha!"

The expression changed in an instant; I don't know what I stammered, I know it cut me to the heart to see how much older and graver he had become. Absence is like death. I had never been able to picture him different from what he was when last I saw him, and now—he was an old man. He stared at me, too, with bewilderment, I think; perhaps the same impression had come to him, and that he did not know what it meant.

It has lasted ever since, more or less Sometimes a word or a glance seems to bring back the old days, but otherwise it is more like beginning an acquaintance on a new footing. Well, be it so! I will accept the position, and win him again. If I cannot be the old, I will be a new Bertha to him. That is what I say when I am brave, as I am to-day; at other times my heart sinks, and I feel that the past will always lie between us.

I should suppose that by this time poor Mr. Fanshawe had lost those brilliant hopes which he had formed as to my influence. From his looks I fancy that he also is bewildered, and I fear that he thinks gloomily of his prospects. I have had the greatest difficulty in keeping him here; he only yielded when I made it a personal request. I see myself that my father is far from disliking him. I notice that every now and then he is apparently occupied in silently comparing him with Mr. Bootle, and I confess I have the greatest pleasure in doing anything which drives the comparison against that gentleman. There are one or two things which my father can't get over.

Mascherino has an intense dislike to Mr. Bootle, and Mr. Bootle an extraordinary horror of Mascherino; my father, on his part, pishes and pshaws over the precautions with which he surrounds himself, and this morning I heard him mutter something which I do think would have astonished Mr. Bootle if it had come to his ears.

If Miles would throw in his influence *quite* heartily I believe he could carry the day; but—I suppose I have lived out of England so long that I have forgotten the old traditional prejudices.

"Oh yes, he is a thorough good fellow!" Miles assents.

"Well?"

"Well, but all the same one mayn't be exactly prepared for his marrying Zoe."

"Why?"

"Why, to begin with, he isn't altogether——" and then Miles stops, crimson.

"Not altogether an Englishman?"

"I beg your pardon."

"Why should you? Miles, you can see that Madame Lecchi is not very friendly to me."

"I imagined that somehow she didn't quite fancy you."

"That is because she has never been able to forgive me for not being altogether Italian. We can be proud, too, you see."

He reddened again, and repeated, "We?"

"Yes, Miles, you and my father must not forget that I am my husband's wife."

I said this because I was sometimes afraid that Miles was trying to convince my father and himself that I was still more of an Englishwoman than any-

thing else; and with Luigi away I feel that I cannot
allow them to imagine *that*. I feel it the more that
my father so persistently avoids my husband's name.
I sometimes wonder whether he thinks he is a sort
of brigand out for a raid! I believe when he came
here he was prepared for anything,—to see me dressed
as a peasant, and living in a hut,—and that it astonishes him to find us civilised. I laugh at it, but
my heart is very sore; because I ought to be able to
laugh at it with him, and I can't! It is only just
every now and then that he forgets to treat me in a
grand ceremonious fashion. But perhaps he will grow
to forget.

Meanwhile, as he is under the impression that the
Italians are a miserable race, idle, shiftless, and cowardly,
I shall drive him about and show him something of
our high cultivation; and possibly, by and by, he will
believe that our nobles, the Visconti, the Annoni,
Resini, Borromeo, and others, are not altogether of
mushroom growth. Mr. Fanshawe is so good in helping me, in spite of his own thoughts, which are strong
upon him, as I can see. Miles added something about
an artist's being such a poor profession in England
"unless he is at the top of the tree." *Benissimo!* Mr.
Fanshawe will be at the top of the tree, or I am
greatly mistaken. And then——!

July 6.—My father is astonished at what I have
shown him of the country. The heat is so great that
we can only go in the early morning or the evening,
but at either time it is charming. He is impressed
with the way in which all the land—each little bit—
is turned to good account, and with the perseverance
of the people in their labour. From the white mulberry trees—now bearing their second crop of leaves,

for the first has been stripped for the silkworms—
the vines festoon themselves, and underneath mul-
berries and vines maize or corn grows luxuriantly.
Then there is the hemp and the flax. It interests him
to hear statistics as to the produce, and here Mr. Fanshawe comes to my aid. Between us we make the
most of Italy. I have not yet ventured to take him
into a farm. They are splendid old buildings, rich
with every tone of deep full colour; but they are very
unlike Wiltshire, and he might think the colour untidy.

Last evening, however, when there was every promise of a glorious sunset, I drove him and Miles to
Villa Castelbarco. There are certain combinations of
light and shade in which it seems to me the most
beautiful place that I have ever beheld, and I was so
glad that these were just right. All along the road
the flowers were glowing in the grass, clematis hanging from the trees, red lilies shining. I could see that
my father was pleased, though he did not say much.
But Castelbarco itself came upon him with evident
surprise,—the fine house, the great avenue of horse-
chestnuts, the broad terraces, the gardens—thoroughly
well kept and thick with flowers—but, most of all, the
indescribable loveliness of the view,—hills crowned
with white villages, lakes stretched out, the eye carried
on from beauty to beauty until it reached the long line
of Alps, with Monte Rosa rising queen-like above
them, and above her the infinite clear depths of an
evening sky.

We stood on the terrace without speaking a word.
Words, indeed, seemed impossible with this before one's
eyes. It was not until we were driving home again in
the sweet and dewy calm that my father said :   .

"Fanshawe should have been with us; he would

have appreciated such a view. It appears to me,
Bertha, that your country houses beat ours, at least in
their surroundings. And you say the owner has
another great villa ? It really is a remarkable country.
I was not aware that it contained such a spring of
vitality."

" Only wait till it is free and united," I said gladly.

" Ah !" he replied, " I begin to see that that is more
possible than I thought, and to understand better what
your husband and others must feel."

Miles looked at me. As for me, I sent back a little
blessing upon Castelbarco. And that evening, when a
letter came from Luigi, my father actually asked if I
would translate some of it for his benefit !

One never can be *quite* glad. Luigi wrote sadly.
There is a rumour in the air that the French Emperor
means to conclude a peace with Austria,—a peace,
while so much remains unaccomplished ! Surely the
King and Cavour will not consent ! But my husband
hints that Garibaldi has always feared Louis Napoleon
would throw us over or make us pay a heavy price for
his aid. Mr. Fanshawe has been a great deal at the
spezieria to-day ; every one is wild for news. Are we
only escaping from one bondage to be plunged into
another ? God help poor Italy ! I have shown my
father the bright side, but there is a very dark one, for
the ignorance of the people is terrible ; and directly
one plunges a little into the country, prejudices, dirt,
and absolute want of moral perception, meet one in
the most shocking form. It is not only the peasants.
When I hear Miles or Mr. Fanshawe talk about Zoe or
Miss Warburton, or other English girls, their occupations, their intelligence, how can I help contrasting
them with the women who come here to call and

gossip, and, except that just now they are stirred by the great throb of patriotism which beats through the country, can talk of nothing better than dress or petty scandal? Their ignorance, yes, and ignorance in higher places, sadder still, makes Luigi sometimes ready to despair. I used to think I could do something, but I have been a great failure!

That absurd Mr. Bootle! My father wanted him to walk over to Castelbarco to see what made so great an impression upon himself, and it seems he is afraid of brigands! The idea of his ever having come out to look after Miles! Other things make me more uncomfortable about him. Padre Benedetto has confided to me that he has a good hope of bringing him over to the Church. Padre Benedetto is an excellent man, and zealous, but I wish—I wish it had not been just now; it will certainly be such an annoyance to my father; and it is so difficult for me to act, dragged as I am both ways. I believe Luigi would be against Padre Benedetto, but I must consider what to do.

July 9.—Alas, it is too true! An armistice has been signed, and it is said that peace will follow. Imagine the despair of all true Italians, pulled up short just when liberty seemed within their grasp. They say that old Count Baroni is almost mad with the news. My·father has been most kind; he seems to understand something of what it must be to us all, and this morning he said that, if hostilities really ceased, he hoped Colonel Marini and I would come back with him and Miles to Stokesworthy. If it were not for my husband's trouble, how happy this would make me! To see Stokesworthy again, the aunts, the children, the trees, would be delightful. But I don't know whether Luigi would like it. However, when my father had

said this, I was obliged to tell him about Mr. Bootle.
Whatever Padre Benedetto might say, it was impossible
to have another deception growing up between us,
particularly when he had just given such a proof
of forgiveness. He could hardly believe me, and he
was exceedingly angry, calling Mr. Bootle a young fool,
and pacing up and down the *sala*. Then he stopped
suddenly and said :

" Miles is not mixed up in this folly ? "

I could answer truly that, to the best of my belief,
Miles had never spoken to Padre Benedetto, and he
resumed his pacings and his ejaculations, to which I
listened in silence. At last he said :

" He must be sent home ; but I don't believe he
has the sense to get there. A pretty person to have
charge of Miles ! What on earth to do with the fellow
I don't know !"

I suggested that Mr. Fanshawe talked of returning
to England, and my father caught thankfully at the
idea. So it is settled ; and really events are placing
Mr. Fanshawe in the position of guardian angel of the
family as completely as his best friends could desire.
But I must not forget to say that, as my father was
leaving the room, he came back and took my hand
with his old kindness.

" I am greatly obliged to you, Bertha," he said, " for
the straightforward manner in which you have acted.
I trust I have said nothing to hurt your feelings ; but
if so, you must forgive me."

After that Padre Benedetto may say what he likes.

July 12.—Mr. Fanshawe and Mr. Bootle left us
yesterday, that black day for our country on which the
peace of Villafranca was forced upon her. The hate
and passion everywhere shown against the French are

reaching fever-heat, and it is said that Cavour will
resign rather than consent. My poor husband! After
Garibaldi's gallant and successful campaign in the
Valtellina this humiliation will be the more bitter. I
am in great perplexity myself. Miles ought not to
stay much longer, the heat is telling upon him, but he
declares he will not go back to Stokesworthy without
me. My husband has written to press my returning
with my father for a month or two ; peace or no peace,
he says, he must for the present remain with the
General. I cannot, however, leave Italy without seeing
my husband. If hostilities have really ceased, I think
I shall leave my father and Miles here, and go to Lago
d'Iseo, where I expect to find him. Then we will see.

July 14.—It is all settled, and we start to-morrow,
for Madame Lecchi insists upon accompanying me. I
am sorry for it, for we are sure to have rough travelling,
and very likely shall find nothing better than a *timonella*
in which to drive. But there is no arguing with her.
Miles is entertained at being left in charge, but he
knows enough Italian to get on very well ; and just at
this moment the English are at the height of popularity,
and Signora Rossi will look after them. My poor
father submits like a hero.

123.—PATERNAL ADVICE.

Rev. J. A. Bootle to his Son.

HIGH SCALE RECTORY, *July* 2.

My dear Son—Your mother and I have received
your letter announcing the safe arrival of Sir Walter,
who has, I rejoice to think, escaped the dangers incident
to all foreign travelling, and is once more with his

eldest son. I can truly sympathise with his feeling of gratification on this occasion, for I too miss my son sorely, though, doubtless, even the imprisonment and all the troubles which have befallen you have been overruled to your good. And as you are safe we must not complain. At your good mother's especial request I returned thanks at family prayer the night we heard the joyful news of your safety ; and I thought it right to return thanks also on the following Sunday in church. Here, I regret to say, your mother differed from me, esteeming this as a Popish practice lately re-introduced by the Tractarians. I, however, laboured to show her that the church was in truth the proper place wherein to give thanks for so great a mercy, and that the practice was not exclusively Popish ; and, indeed, I was glad I had decided to do it when I saw how moved were our good neighbours, so that my voice would scarce remain firm to the end. But, my boy, there is a passage in your letter which has disquieted me, and that is the one in which you allude to a hope of converting the Popish priest at Madame Marini's.

It were a blessed work, doubtless, could you achieve it, but indeed I much doubt whether you are quite old enough and (pardon me) learned enough in the contro-versy betwixt us and Rome to be successful. On the other hand, I have heard that the web these priests often spread for unwary feet is a show of listening to our teaching in order more surely to delude their victims. Take an old man's advice, Algernon ; be not too self-confident.

Your mother and I will be truly glad to welcome you once more among us.—Until then I remain your affectionate father,   JOSHUA A. BOOTLE.

124.—ALGERNON IN CONTROVERSY.

Miles to Clyffe—continued.

July 14.

So Algy is off with Edgar Fanshawe. Bertha, it seems, had her eyes open and told father. I had just made up my mind to have it out with Algy myself.

He had got a letter from home, and had remarked that foreign travel did enlarge the mind. I said:

"Yes; perhaps you'll ask Padre Benedetto to stay at High Scale?"

"More unlikely things have happened," says Algy.

"Eh?" I said.

And then if he didn't tell me that he was converting the priest! Well, I fell upon him. I haven't pitched into him so for years, and I told him if he didn't take care he would end as a Trappist; and I vowed if he didn't leave off converting Padre Benedetto I'd write to Mrs. Bootle myself, for I wouldn't have such a dangerous intercourse on *my* conscience.

"She wouldn't understand the situation," he said, "from a distance."

So I said no doubt we had enlarged our minds and learned a thing or two, but I didn't mean to go home in a pointed hat and a red shirt, and I hoped he wouldn't make his appearance in a cowl.

He was very angry, but I didn't believe there was anything serious in the matter, and the best way was to laugh at it.

He gave in at once to my father without a struggle and agreed to go home with Edgar.

My father thanked them both magnificently for all they had done for me, and, what is better, asked them

both to meet us at Stokesworthy; but I don't feel sure
if Fanshawe will come.

For, hurrah! we are all going home together. Won't
Zoe be delighted ?   I wish I had seen Marini, but perhaps he will fetch Bertha back.   To prove *I* have
enlarged my mind I send you some bits of translations
from the Italian papers to show you how matters go
here.   So I shall write next from home.   I should be
quite strong now but for the heat, and I mean to come
again when I can go and see everything.——Ever your
affectionate   MILES WINKWORTH.

Emily has been staying with the aunts !

125.—THE FALL OF BOOTLEDOM.

Sir Walter to Aunt Dora.

VARESE, *July* 15.

My dear Dorothea—You have, no doubt, seen my
hurried notes to Zoe, and know from them as well as
from Miles's own letter to her that he is now conva-
lescent, and that I hope to bring him home very soon.
I have been wishing, however, to write to you for some
days, especially since it was decided that Bertha should
return with us for a long visit.

You will understand that there was some hesitation
in my mind before giving the invitation ; but I longed
to see my poor girl in her old home once more, and I
grew more convinced each day that she would do no
harm to Zoe or to any one else.   She is just the
" Birdie " of early days, matured and improved ; and
though at first she seemed to me a sort of brilliant
stranger, unlike the daughter with whom I parted
under such sad circumstances, I now recognise her old

self in her more and more. Her tenderness to Miles
is delightful, and it does him good in every way. He
becomes quite talkative when she is by. And she
speaks of Zoe and of you both with strong affection.

I feel sure if Sophia could see her *now* there would
no longer be any coldness between them. It touches
me to see her love for Sophia's children. I included
Colonel Marini in my invitation, but he seems to think
it impossible to leave his General. So Bertha, accom-
panied by Madame Lecchi, has gone to Lago d'Iseo to
see him. I am not very sorry that he cannot come
with us. It is a serious thing to have a foreigner to
entertain, and yet I should be glad to make some
return for all the kindness Miles has received in his
house. Moreover, I think better of the man than I
did. He is, at any rate, a gallant soldier, and when one
is actually in Italy one sees that what looked like mere
rebellion at a distance has more of patriotism in it
than one fancied. And there is more capability of
improvement in this country than I thought for. I
wish you could have been with us when we drove to
Castelbarco. I must tell you some day how it struck
me.

Perhaps I have been seeing things through Bertha's
eyes in these last few days; at any rate, I feel as if at
High Scale I had lived rather in a corner, and I perceive now what Clyffe meant when he jestingly said—*à
propos* of young Fanshawe, I believe—that my ideal
of a man was " a narrow-minded country squire."

And, by the way, I have seen a good deal of Mr.
Fanshawe lately, and have reason to feel indebted to
him, both for the great service he rendered Miles and
for coming to my help in my smaller dilemma. He
seems to possess all the *savoir faire* in which Algernon

Bootle is so strangely deficient. You will think I am regretting my choice of a tutor, and indeed I don't mind saying in confidence that I have been disappointed in Bootle. His classical knowledge is no doubt quite what was represented, but he seems to be utterly wanting in sound common sense. I am sending him home under Mr. Fanshawe's protection, and shall be glad when I· hear he is safe at the Rectory, though I doubt whether his mother's petting is the best thing for him.

She too has less sense than I used to believe. Sophia had a way of drawing out her best side, but it certainly was not shown in the letters she wrote me before I left England, and I should have been inclined to call the one about Zoe's lace impertinent, only that one shrinks from so characterising a *lady's* letter. I understand now how it was Zoe never took to her.

Give my love to the girls, and tell them I hope soon to be at home again. I know Bertha is sure of a welcome at *your* hands as well as theirs. She is like you in some ways, and I think you will agree with me that, spite of all that has come and gone, she is a woman that one can respect as well as love. I wonder whether you too will think her as beautiful as I do.

Miles desires his love to you both, and I am always, my dear Dora, your affectionate brother,

WALTER M. WINKWORTH.

P.S.—I am glad you have had Miss Warburton with you ; she will be all the better for it. I don't think Miles has forgotten her at all, though he says nothing to me on that subject.

126.—A Dangerous Character.

Algernon Bootle to his Mother.

VARESE.

My dear Mother—A change has come o'er the spirit of my dream, and you may expect me home some day at the beginning of next week. It is as I thought, I am considered too dangerous a personage to be left alone, either by Garibaldi's rebels or the emissaries of the Pope. Madame Marini came into the sitting-room where I was this morning, and with some embarrassment expressed to me that Sir Walter felt he had put me already to much inconvenience, and that, as Fanshawe was returning to England, he thought perhaps I should like to take advantage of his escort as, when they left Varese, they should travel only by short stages for the benefit of Miles. She said this, but I felt, from some hints that Miles and Sir Walter let drop, that there was more behind. When I demurred (as finding myself in good quarters, and doing a great work I naturally did not wish to leave until it was done), both of them pooh-poohed me, and insisted on my taking the advantage of the opportunity, Sir Walter going so far as to assure me that if I did not go off at once, he would not be answerable to you for the consequences. I see it all. The impression I have made upon Padre Benedetto is such, that some of his ecclesiastical superiors—probably, I think, the General of the Jesuits or the Pope himself—dread lest this good man should be converted by my arguments, and are no doubt waiting to entrap me into a worse dungeon than that from which I have escaped; into which, once entered, the Inquisition would take care that I never

emerged alive. Since discretion is usually allowed to
be the better part of valour, I have determined, for
your sake and my dear father's, not to run the risk of
leaving your old age childless, and therefore I say, with
our French neighbours, *"Au revoir !"*—Your affectionate son,   ALGERNON BOOTLE.

127.—EDGAR'S STORY.

Madame Marini to Edgar Fanshawe.

LOVERE, *July.*

My dear Friend—All my life I have thought it
would be the most delightful thing in the world to tell
a real piece of good news to the person interested, and
now that it has come to me I don't know how to
begin ! But don't raise your hopes too high ! It is
not what you would call the best thing, only what I
hope may turn out a step towards it. And meanwhile,
where shall I begin and how shall I work you up to
the proper state of excitement ? I have noticed that
story-tellers always make a long start, so prepare yourself, and I will promise to get quicker at the end.

Some thirty years ago, then (you see I mean to be
very orthodox), an English gentleman wandering
through Italy, and lingering here and there to sketch,
met with a little adventure at Frascati, beginning with
a broken-down travelling-carriage and two ladies in
distress, and ending with an attachment between himself and one of these ladies, strong enough to prevail
against difference of nation, difference of faith, and all
the opposition which these facts conjure up. The lady,
who was young, beautiful, and very delicate, was the
Signorina Claudia, the daughter of a Roman banker.

She was her father's darling, and when he found that her feelings were so strongly awakened that further opposition would probably have a most serious effect upon her health, he yielded to her wishes, and she became Mr. Fanshawe's wife. A year afterwards she died, leaving him the father of one little boy.

That year he had passed happily at Rome, but with her death the love of wandering broke out afresh; what was to become of the baby? His mother solved the question by coming out to him, giving up all English ties, and devoting herself to the care of his child. So the years went by, Mr. Fanshawe restlessly journeying about, the grandmother faithfully fulfilling her charge, the boy growing up with a passionate love of beauty and art, but a yet stronger love for his grand-mother. On one point she was resolute. He should go to an English school and no . other. So it was agreed, and year after year, when the holidays began, she took him herself back to Italy to see his father. You follow my story, do you not? And you remember how, when the boy was eighteen, there came a double sorrow, and both father and grandmother were taken from him.

Then the Italian relations came forward—an uncle, a banker, whose own son was dead, and another uncle, one of our Monsignori—and offered to make their sister's son their heir on condition that he took Italy for his country and our Church for his own. This was ten years ago, and perhaps I need not recall his refusal nor his determination to make the art he loved so dearly his profession. I pass on to the fortunes which went to an Italian cousin, one Angelo Lugani, and in his hands quickly diminished.; they proved a curse to the poor foolish lad, who got into one scrape after

another, until at last, half remorseful and half desperate,
he invested the remains of his money in French *Rentes*,
ran away from Rome, joined the Cacciatori, and was
mortally wounded at one of the engagements in the
Valtellina.

You follow me still ?   My husband had always felt
a certain interest in the young fellow, and when he
was dying he asked him about settling his affairs.
Then—all unconscious of the link—young Lugani
spoke of you as a cousin who should have had the
money he had wasted.   When he found that you were
known to Luigi he was strangely excited, and insisted
upon making his will in your favour.   The poor fellow
only lived another day, and I think you will be glad
to hear that my husband was with him to the last.

There, dear friend, is my news, which Luigi had
already sent to Varese, but it must have been delayed.
I congratulate you with all my heart.   A yearly income of 8000 francs is not a great fortune, but it is a very
pleasant little addition, and may remove some difficulties
out of your way.   Luigi is going to write a dry state-
ment of accounts ; but you will read my letter first, or
if you do not I shall never forgive you.

I go back to Varese to-morrow, and then start for
England.   I could write a volume about things here,
and it is a pity you are not of the party, for you would
certainly paint a whole portfolio of sketches which
might make your fortune at an exhibition.   Do you
know Lovere and its gay little harbour ?   Imagine it
now—lake, woods, vineyards, with a hundred picturesque
elements added to their beauty, and you must long to
be at them.   Perhaps, however, all things considered,
it is as well you are not here.   I would not answer
for the effect Garibaldi might not have upon you ; there

is the most extraordinary power of attraction about that man, gentleness and strength united make him irresistible. No, you are well out of the way, and I advise you to be grateful—if you can—to Mr. Algernon Bootle.

Poor Madame Lecchi has not particularly enjoyed this little journey of ours. It was all very well as far as Bergamo, but there she very unreasonably expected my husband to meet us. Of course this was out of the question, and we had a few difficulties, and a good deal of rough jolting in a *timonella*, where she sat perched the picture of miserable endurance. And she has not met with all the consideration she expected from the Garibaldians, so she says. Poor soul! I think that would be difficult. To tell the truth, they are all naturally greatly taken up with their own affairs, and so wroth at the sudden check put upon the General's successes that they can think and talk of nothing else. You meet little knots of men with gloomy faces at every turn of the road. But Luigi says that, in spite of Garibaldi's deep personal disappointment, he never for a moment loses faith in the future of Italy. I sometimes wonder what my father would think if he were here. I suspect that he would begin to believe too.

Now you may turn to Luigi's dry details, and try to realise your fortune. I hope it is only a step towards something which you will value infinitely more. For that you have our best wishes, and meanwhile believe me very sincerely yours,

BERTHA MARINI.

128.—NOT MUCH GOOD IN IT.

Edgar Fanshawe to Madame Marini.

LONDON, *July.*

My dear Madame Marini—I was very sorry indeed
to hear of Angelo Lugani's death. · I did not even
know that he had enlisted in the Cacciatori. He
never seemed, poor fellow, to care for his relations, and
I think he kept up no friendship with any of them but
Carlo Monti, from whom I used to hear news of him
sometimes, but even they had nothing in common. As
you know, I always got on better with my North
Italian cousins than with the Roman ones, but I liked
Angelo all the same. I am very much surprised at
the poor fellow's leaving his money to me, and I do not
think I ought to have it, being a kind of alien, and
having long ago, and without any trouble, given up all
ideas of the kind. But we shall see what Signor
Marini says about that. I have written to thank him
for his kind letter. I am heartily glad that poor
Angelo had a friend with him. All this time I have
not thanked you for what seemed to me the kindest
letter I ever had in my life; but, knowing you, the
letter did not surprise me. It brought back vividly
all our pleasant talks at Varese, and the patient goodness with which you used to listen to me, and the
sympathy which was so welcome. Here in London I
seem to be among hard facts again, and the world looks
hopeless; for, dear Madame Marini, I quite fail to see,
in spite of your kind words, how this windfall can
possibly be any help towards winning what is just as
far off as ever! But I will not bore you with my
despondencies any longer.

I suppose you are nearly, if not quite, at Stokes-worthy by this time.   I try to imagine it all, but fail. I believe in it so far as to address this letter there.

General Garibaldi is an interesting study—a real enthusiast, and therefore, I think, a hero.   It is a pity that his career is checked.   He might have finished things off and freed Italy.   I knew Lovere well, and have often sketched there.   I was there first with my father, and often since.

Will you remember me to Miles and all of them ? and, with hearty thanks once more, believe me yours most truly,   EDGAR FANSHAWE.

P.S.—Perhaps Miles will write to me one of these days and give me news of you all.   I suppose he is taking the journey as quietly as possible.

129.—MILES'S CONGRATULATIONS.

Miles to Edgar Fanshawe.

HOTEL DU LOUVRE,
PARIS, *July.*

Dear Fanshawe—We are all delighted at the news my sister brought back with her from Lovere.   If my father had heard of it in England, I doubt if he would have appreciated the sacrifice, but he said that "he sees now the advantages offered by a good position in this remarkable country, which could only have been withstood by a high sense of duty and a firm attach-ment to the English Church."   Those are his own words, and he hopes that I shall be able to induce you to come to Stokesworthy.   Do come ; every one will be glad to see you, and don't go off at a tangent about our gratitude ; we'll all be as ungrateful as ever you like.

I want you to tell every one all about it, for I sha'n't
know what to say, and I shall be bored to death by
people's curiosity.   I find the hot journeys more tiring
than I expected, and shall be glad to be quiet.

Poor Clyffe sends you dozens of messages.   He has
almost worried *himself* into a fever about me.   He
doesn't seem to realise Bertha's return or anything else.
But I believe he has written to you.

Come soon and help me through.—Yours ever,

MILES WINKWORTH.

My sister sends kind regards.

130.—EDGAR'S RESOLUTION.

Edgar to Miles.

LONDON, *July.*

My dear Miles—Thank you, but don't give me so
much more credit than I deserve.   The fine word "sacrifice " is quite inappropriate.   One's father's country is
one's own, and must always be so, I think.   It would
have been impossible to give it up for a much larger
bait than was offered me.   I loved Italy, it is true, and
so I do now, but English people were in the other
scale—alive or dead, it does not matter.   The Romans
ought not to have cared for such a half-hearted convert
as I should have been.   As for "a firm attachment to
the English Church," it is good of your father to take
it in that way, but I think the truth was that one felt
it would not do to be anything but honest in these
things, and that it was a man's duty to stay where he
had been brought up, unless *conviction* led him somewhere else.   Excuse this prosing.   I only want to
point out that the temptation and the sacrifice were

neither of them great things.   Your father and you
are very kind in wishing me to come to Stokesworthy,
but I think you, at least, must understand why it is
better for me to keep away.   My affection for your
sister is stronger than ever, if rather less hopeful.   If I
came to Stokesworthy now I could not help showing
her what I feel for her, and I do not suppose that anything has happened to lessen your father's objections to
such a marriage for her; therefore it must surely be
better for me to keep away.   Sir Walter was very
friendly to me in Italy, but I am not such a fool as
to presume on that.   Your friendship and Madame
Marini's is my chief encouragement.   Now let me
enter into business matters a little.   What poor
Lugani left me amounts to between £300 and £400
a year; this brings my income to about £850, besides
what I may do in my profession.   I am afraid your
father would think this nothing, but I should like him
to know the facts; because, in short, I have decided in
my own mind not to come to Stokesworthy at present
unless I have his consent to try my fortune with your
sister.   Let me have an answer as soon as you can.
I do not expect a favourable one, but I have written
myself into a faint glimmer of hope, which, not being
lighted by reason, will of course go out presently.   I
must see you some day somewhere, and tell you all
the active exercise I had in chasing Bootle in and out
of Paris churches.   Pray remember me most kindly to
Madame Marini.   I wrote to her a day or two ago at
Stokesworthy, where I suppose you are all arrived by
this time.   Among the home faces you will soon be
yourself again.—Ever yours,   EDGAR FANSHAWE.

PART VIII.

LOVE BIRDS.

" Do you ask what the birds say ?
The sparrow, the dove,
The linnet and thrush say,
I love, and I love."

Zoe to Clyffe.

THE MIZ MAZE, *July.*

DEAREST CLYFFE—No doubt you are hearing all the
Italian news direct from Miles and all of them, so I
need not tell you how happy they all seem to be.
What a work Mr. Fanshawe has done, and how
blessedly all has turned out in spite of our blunders
and my wrong-doing at first !

Think of Emily being actually in the Dower House
with the aunts. They heard she was hysterical and
altogether upset with the suspense, and they asked her.
Moreover, she came. After that, I don't think she can
ever try to say again that she does not care for Miles.
Perhaps, if one told her so, she would say it was only
common humanity, but we know better than that,
don't we, Clyffey dear ? Miss Madgewick and I
chuckle a little to each other now and then. The
aunts are delighted with her ; she took them by storm
at once, so that they forget that nineteenth-century
young ladies are not what they were forty years ago.
I don't feel half so much afraid of Aunt Dora as I was
till Emily came, in spite of all her kindness. And as
for Emily, she has drawn up, signed, and sealed (in the
presence of Miss Madgewick and me) an act of contri-
tion for having, several times by word of mouth and

once or twice in black and white, called them "old cats." Who but Emily would have thought of doing such a thing ? But you know her way between fun and earnest, and I suppose it really was a relief to her feelings.

She fraternises with Aunt Dora over the family history, and says she never guessed what respectable people we are till she saw what a number of ugly ancestors we are blessed with, only she required them all to have "done something;" and Aunt Dora was delighted, and said she had gone through it all herself, and been so much disappointed that nobody did anything but marry and have lots of children and die, that she wrote a history of the best-looking of them and all his exploits in the Great Rebellion. She lent it to Emily to read—MS. of course—and it really is beautiful. But after all, the man in his Vandyke dress turned out to be a copy of Lord Carnarvon's picture at Wilton, and the Winkworths of that day were only an old man of eighty and his little grandson of four years old. And the only family MSS. to be found are the receipt-books, whereat Emily is very sad, though she says that if our letters are dug up a hundred years hence, posterity will be better off than we are !

It is broiling hot weather, and I am very grateful for the shade of our Wiltshire elms. They are certainly heavy looking, but there is nothing to compare to them for shade. We sit under them a good deal, and talk over our books and work, often about her plans for her collieries, but somehow always working round to Miles. I think I have eradicated the notion that he would not help her in such a duty as attending to them, though, of course, we make no direct allusions. I must tell you one grand symptom. She gave Lisa a photograph of General Tom Thumb in exchange for that one of Miles

which was done before you went away.   I don't think
any one was meant to know of the little transaction;
but Lisa shows off her album, and is asked where she
got the General, and explains at the top of her voice,
while Emily becomes like a peony, and takes refuge in
studying the thermometer, declaring that in this heat it
is a consolation to measure one's sufferings.   Aunt Dora
says it is restlessness carried off with a high hand, and
that she shall devise some expedition or something
pleasant to occupy her.—Your loving sister,

SOPHIA WINKWORTH.

132.—MISS MADGEWICK FOREBODES.

Miss Madgewick to her Sister, Madame Saisset.

MIZ MAZE, *July.*

My dearest Nan—After my last letter you will
have guessed that it *was* Miles and Mr. Bootle whom
you met that evening at Meyringen; and now poor
Miles's minute and anxious inquiries of Henri, about
Italian money, etc., are accounted for.   Having no idea
when I answered your letter that they meant to go
into Italy, I was puzzled, thinking it very unlikely
that Miles should have such a keen interest in the
subject.   Still your "man with the knapsack," who
was so fascinated by the doubtful Austrian countess at
the *table d'hôte*, certainly seemed to have a striking
likeness to the great Algy.   And now it appears that
there *was* an Austrian countess in the case.   How will
Mrs. Bootle take that piece of intelligence?   I am
glad to be able to tell you that Sir Walter has got
safely to Varese, and that Miles is fast recovering;
also, that they are coming home shortly with Madame

Marini, and there seems a fair chance of our all " living happily ever after." What is specially delightful to me is that Emily is staying at the Dower House ; but I have an uneasy foreboding that takes off the edge of my pleasure. Suppose Miles comes home while she is still here, ill, haggard, and melancholy, and of course rather a hero in her eyes just now, when she is only just getting over the shock of hearing he was in danger and her distress at feeling she had encouraged Zoe in urging him to go. Won't she take pity on him in one of her sudden impulses ? and then—oh ! it will be throwing herself away. Miles is a fine fellow ; and from all I have heard lately, through Zoe and the aunts, I begin to think I never quite did him justice. Still he is *not* good enough for Emily, whatever they may think. He would never satisfy her, and he would sooner or later find it out, and grow as moody and miserable as his father used to be at High Scale. But to warn her would probably bring about more harm than good, so there is nothing to be done but to hope that Miles's doctor will keep him away from his native land a little longer. Here come Emily and the children to summon me to croquet, so no more.—Ever, dearest Annette, your affectionate sister,

ESTHER MADGEWICK.

133.—THE SALISBURY STATION.

Miss Winkworth to Mrs. Home.

My dear Mary—Bessie is copying the foreign letters for you, that you may see how much reason we have to rejoice. Meantime we have welcomed our guest. Zoe went to meet her at the station, and it was pretty to see the two bright creatures come in together. There was a blushing grace and shyness about Miss Warburton that was almost deprecating, as if she were asking our pardon or felt herself on sufferance. She is very shy, too, on any mention of Miles. I had feared before that she was shallow, but I do not think so now. Her ardour is not of the light straw-on-fire order. You know Zoe has to be at home to keep guard over her little sisters; but of course the friends are constantly together, either here or at the Miz Maze, and, dear girls, they have quite left off making an ogre of me; but I find myself chattering with them as if I was twenty. Emily gets up at 8 A.M. and comes to church with me every morning, which Zoe has not been permitted to do,—and, indeed, she is too far off. I see that much of Zoe's church feeling has percolated to her through Emily from the Fanshawe family, who must be excellent people, including the Edgar to whom we are under such obligations. There is something very winning about the damsel. She is more of the modern girl than Zoe, and has not the innate dignity that makes such a curious background to our child's sensitiveness and diffidence. Emily is much more impulsive, but with plenty of perseverance. The great scheme of her heart is to do something for the poor colliery children. Zöe begged her leave to tell me about it, and I find that she has already endeavoured to begin building a school chapel on the spot and an orphanage at High Scale for them. Mr. Fanshawe the elder quite approves, but cannot do more for her, and the difficulties in the way are great; for Mrs. Bootle is convinced that the orphanage is the small end of a wedge for introducing a sisterhood into the parish, and has bullied Mrs. Warburton into refusing consent, and

the owner of the ground into breaking his promise to
let her have it. On the other hand, the clergyman of
the colliery parish will not promise to let her pay the
salary of a curate for her chapel; nor does he like her
even to set up a school, lest it should be a rival to his
own. And the people at the place make her feel that
whatever she does is only held as a young lady's fancy,
and that they do not trust it. Then there is all the
difficulty of trying to work from a distance, and with
an unwilling mother. She is only allowed to go to the
place with two servants, man and maid, who, as she
says, are enough to show the absurdity of her attempts.
And yet she perseveres! yet the only thing she can
feel she has really done has been to give one or two
hospital tickets and get a boy into an orphanage. It
is quite refreshing to see such brave young zeal and
sense of duty! And, as Zoe whispered to me that
night, "Won't Miles delight in helping her!"

We are going to have a grand expedition on Monday. It is Mary's birthday, and I am going to take
the whole party of girls to picnic at Stonehenge. I
find Emily has seen Salisbury, and, as it is Mary's day,
and the children infinitely prefer the downs to the
town, we have given in to them. We have to set out
at seven in the break to drive to the station, take a
waggonette at Salisbury, and return at about nine o'clock.
Mr. Bernard undertakes to look in on Bessie. What
fun it will be! I have not seen Stonehenge since
Walter's first courtship, when you were there too, my
Mary. Well, the old stones will be the same, whatever
else is altered.

Zoe and I have a rivalry in the cates we provide,
but I expect to get the better of her with the raspberry
acid I am brewing.

July.—Well, my dear Mary, we have done Stonehenge, and more too.   I am going to begin at the
beginning, though I burn to get to the end; for I
am sure you must be concerned for the health of the
wonder of your native county.   Why, Australia could
scarcely have been baked, or have had time to cool when
those wonderful old circles had begun to get into decay.
Not that it is decay, for who upset them is as mysterious a question as who built them.   How merry we
all were, we six females, I cannot tell you, as we drove
through the lanes and over the downs, with a fresh
soft wind in our faces!   The children had begun by
declaring that they knew exactly what Stonehenge
would be like.   As Miss Madgewick said, Lisa was
ready to build it any day with a box of bricks, and
when we first came in sight the chit turned round
triumphantly with, "There, didn't I say so?"   But
they were awed and amazed when they found how
far we had still to drive, and when the stupendous
stones stood in their mystery beside us.   Happily we
were not infested by other parties, and could enjoy the
grand silence and the fresh breeziness.   Emily and
Zoe thought it almost profane to eat sandwiches and
hard eggs under the shadow of the mighty monolith,
"older than the Druids," as Miss Madgewick and the
guide-book had it.   Poor old Druids! we used to be
quite satisfied with them in my time.   We found some
man-orchids, which the girls thought looked weird
enough to have been used in the incantations they were
sure had been practised here.   And we wandered
about, and made attempts at sketching, and at last
drove back a prettier way, past some of those valleys
that break the downs, and getting more and more
within view of the Cathedral.

x

Well, all this is prelude, for I must keep *the* news
for the last. We came to the station half an hour
before the down train, and had some tea. The train
came up, rather full, and we went running about looking in vain for an empty carriage to hold us all six.
" Nothing but gentlemen," said Emily, after making an
assault on the door of one that looked less unpromising.
And then the door flew open. There was a most
extraordinary sound, like " Ah !" and " Oh !" Emily
disappeared in the depths. Lisa bounded at least two
feet into the air, and her shriek "Papa ! papa ! papa !"
must have amazed the station ; and in one minute
more Walter was bundling in all the rest of us, except
Miss Madgewick, who, as soon as she perceived the
situation, had ensconced herself elsewhere. When I
came to something like my senses, there we were a
mass of rejoicing, eight in number, jammed into a
L.S.W. carriage—a guard unable to repress a grin as
he demanded " Tickets, please !" Farthest in, by the
opposite window, were Miles and Emily. They had
got tight hold of one another's hands, and if there had
been forty people in the carriage, instead of eight, I don't
think they would have found it out. Then next were
Bertha and Zoe, slim creatures, squeezed into one com-
partment. Bertha with those dear, dark eyes of hers full
of liquid softness and feeling, as she held her sister's
hand and looked from one to the other. I was opposite
to them, and then came Walter with Lisa on his knee,
and Mary opposite. They had telegraphed, but Bessie
had it all to herself. There was not much talk, except
Lisa's flow of chatter, for it was a very noisy train,
and looking at one another was enough for most of us.

Bertha is really beautiful, a Winkworth, but with
that sweet mouth you remember in her mother. It

was charming to see her sit hand in hand with Zoe, and meeting her eyes now and then twinkling through her eyelashes with that moist sparkle peculiar to herself, and a tiny, tiny smile at the corners of her mouth as she glanced at the two beyond, who had looked out of the middle window together at the advertisements of elephants standing on their heads till the last moment, and then, at the jerk of starting, subsided into their opposite seats, Emily pertinaciously gazing from her little window. Miles was on my side, so I did not see him till we tumbled out at Stokeshill Road, and then I saw a somewhat gaunt shadow, going red and pale every minute, but with a glory in the eyes of him which made him such as I had never seen before.

Bessie had done her best by sending the pony carriage and the cart for the luggage, besides the break. It was 8.30 o'clock, quite light, and very beautiful, and so refreshing, for it had been so hot in the train that if they had all been strangers we should have pitied ourselves to a savage extent. Bertha at once told her father that Miles should have as little excitement as possible, and Walter at the same time decreed that he would himself drive the boy home with the ponies, and on they swept past us.

Bertha sat between Zoe and me. She told us about the journey, but broke off every now and then with little cries of delight and recognition at the outlines of the hills, the cottages, and the trees, treating as old friends what seemed new to her sisters, and quite astonishing Lisa, who had begun to patronise and tell the names of everything. There was all the calm, pale, gold loveliness of a summer sunset, the church-spire rising into it when they put us down at the Dower House, with *such* a kiss from Bertha and from Zoe.

Emily had not spoken all the way home. She ran up at once, and when Bessie had heard all, I followed.

"Oh! please excuse me; I can't come down," she gasped.

"No, my dear, you shall not," I said rather doubtfully, opening the door; "but you must let me come and kiss you and rejoice over this return—your work, you know."

Poor child! she let me come in, and flung herself upon me, nestling into my arms.

"Oh! it was in such a moment," she said, sobbing and panting, "but I couldn't help it. He was so dear, and he looks so dreadful."

"I suspect that you have cured him," I said. "For my part I never saw him with such a pair of eyes."

That brought me a fresh squeeze; but, poor child, how she did want her mother! She broke out as she let me loose: "Oh! I could beat myself. I never thought to have done it in such a silly way."

I told her I had no doubt that Miles would have no objection to see her "do it" over again to-morrow with full honours, but that she was tired to death, and I should put her to bed, and give her some supper, like my own very dear child. We had one little outburst again: "Oh dear! the colliers! And I had promised myself I'd never be hampered with a man till I had set them to rights."

"My dear," I said, "you will be of ten times the service to your colliers with a man like Miles to act for you. Make it *his* duty to attend to them, and see how he will do it."

And the last of the murmurs was: "Oh, I have been very foolish; but then I never understood half what he was!"

So she had a little wine and water, for she could not eat, and I read her a Psalm and tucked her up; and then I found, even after telling Bessie, I was much too excited to sleep; so here have I been working it off to you to be ready for the mail to-morrow morning. You'll get a solemn and dignified announcement from Walter by the next. But you can't think how much of the High Scale he has shaken off on the road.— Your loving   D. W.

134.—MILES FINDS HIMSELF A HERO.

Miles to Clyffe.

CLARIDGE'S HOTEL, LONDON, *July.*

Dear Clyffe—As if any one would not have been tired out with these hot, long, baking journeys, father wouldn't be content unless a London doctor looked at me. So we had to stop here last night, and all for nothing, for Dr. A. says I only want rest, and after hearing my adventures, he wondered at my being well enough to travel at all. But "rest" at Stokesworthy, with nothing to do, and every one making a fuss and asking ridiculous questions—how I hate the thought of it! One could forget one's self sometimes at Varese, where it is all so bright and new; but at home, to be hearing of her, perhaps seeing her—though that's not likely—and yet to be so far from her, how shall I bear it? And when no one will let me alone! I wish I was Frank; I'd go to the end of the world out of the way!

I declare it's too bad of me, and I won't send this. You have had enough worry about me already. But you'll know it's only Miles grumbling as usual, and if

I could just hear your jolly old voice and see your eyes twinkling at me I should cheer up directly, and pick up heart for all the worries. And you would answer all the questions that every one will ask ! Well, I won't give in, I *will* fight through it somehow, and stick to all I must learn to do at Stokesworthy. My father has been much too kind to be vexed and disappointed by seeing me out of sorts. We go down this afternoon.

Miz Maze, same evening.—Oh, Clyffe ! Clyffe ! She was there, and I have seen her, and she *will !* It was all a mistake and my own stupidity. The look in her eyes was enough, and Salisbury Station will be in a golden glory of sunlight for ever !

Miz Maze, July.—Well, I don't know which end of all that is the maddest; but they swept me off in such a hurry, I could not speak to her again— as if one could be tired then ! Or as if one could sleep. However, I did go to sleep in the morning, after Bertha paid me a visit, and never woke up till past twelve; wasn't it disgusting of me ? Then there was a tremendous row in the passage, and there was a frightful quarrel between Smut and Mascherino. (Bertha presented him to me, as he had taken such a fancy to me.) Smut in a state of frantic jealousy. Then I got off to the Dower House at last, and she was in the garden, and we had it all out. She says it was all my own fault for being so stupid as to think she knew her own mind, and then she laughed at me and said that she knew I was going to say Clyffe would have known better. She wanted to hear about the prison; but I did not tell her much, as she was ready to cry at the thought of it ; only she declared she had always wanted a hero, and now she had got one. They all seem to have got

an idea that being shut up in prison is a heroic proceeding. I can't imagine why, unless from Algy. I
know, if I had had the "command of foreign languages,"
as he called it, which I have since acquired, I would
have taken good care to keep out of the scrape.

Then we got upon the colliers, and she poured out
all her hopes and longings for them. How few girls,
brought up as she has been, would have given them a
thought! I said how could she suppose that I could
think it less my duty to look after them than after the
people here, if I came to it? No doubt it will be
troublesome work, but after all what would be too
much to do for *her*, and because I am so thankful to
have her? I think she has frightened the clergyman
by trying to be too independent of him; and, of course,
it is not fit for her to have such arrangements to make
at her age.

She has been the making of Zoe. Poor little Zoe!
she looks as if she had had a very hard time, and I
wrote her such savage letters from Switzerland to comfort her. However, this afternoon, while Emily was
making Bertha's acquaintance, I told her all Fanshawe
had done, and she listened, and I think she felt that
here *was* a hero for her!

"Will he come—he will come, I suppose, and see
you?" she said presently.

"Well—I don't know!" I said. "I hope he will.
But I don't feel quite certain." Zoe coloured up very
much, and did not ask why.

Mrs. Bootle seems to have offended father somehow
over all this business. I can't say that it is altogether
a misfortune; and yet I shouldn't like, after all these
years, to quarrel with any of them. I think I shall
go, when I am able, down into those parts and see

them, and tell them how kind old Algy was to
me.   But, of *course*, I shall go to Triermain!   It
makes my head turn round to think of it.   I cannot
believe how the world is changed for me.   If I can
only be fit to make her happy!—Yours ever,

· MILES.

135.—MISS MADGEWICK OUT IN THE COLD.

Miss Madgewick to her Sister, Madame Saisset.

MIZ MAZE, *July.*

My dear Nan—She has done it! and exactly as I
expected.   After my last letter, and when I tell you
that Miles and Sir Walter arrived yesterday, you will
know what I mean.   They flashed upon us in the most
utterly unexpected manner at the Salisbury Station, on
our way home from Stonehenge, where we had just had
such a pleasant day.   We went in force—a whole
waggonetteful of us, in honour of Mary's birthday.
Emily, Zoe, the children, and myself, conducted by
"Aunt Dora," who is a most agreeable companion for
an expedition of that kind.   She and I had a trifling
passage of arms on the subject of the Druids, to be
sure, but it did not produce a lasting rupture; and I
was backed up by Emily and the guide-book.

All this, however, is a parenthesis.   Well, we were
all on the platform at Salisbury looking for an empty
carriage, when I suddenly saw a lady whose face I
seemed to know, and before I had taken in that it was
Miles on the farther side of her, Emily had shot into
the carriage, and Sir Walter shot—yes, he absolutely
shot out; whereupon I saw that the only thing to do
was to jump into the next, and (like Punch's old man

and his meals) "let 'em fight it out between 'em."
One look at Emily when we got out at our station
made it clear that the deed was done.   She hardly
spoke all the way home, and then, as we dropped her
at the Dower House, of course I saw her no more last
night; nor Miles either, for he was pronounced by his
father too much over-tired to appear at the very late
dinner which we all had together.   I need not say
that the rest were all perfectly bubbling over with
satisfaction at the state of affairs.   *I* am not, however,
as you may suppose.

My poor little Emily!   I can't bear to think that,
after all, she has done such an irrevocable thing as this
just in an impulse.   Though I did forebode to a certain degree, who would have thought of its coming all
in a moment, in this breathless way?   If she could
but have had a little time to be with Miles in a quiet,
every-day sort of way, after the glamour of his adventures had gone off a little.   But if they had all been
scheming in cold blood to catch her unawares, they
could not have pounced down upon her at a more
opportune moment.

Zoe is so ecstatic that one must feel sympathetic,
and it is very nice to see them all so happy; still I
can't help feeling sad and disappointed.   But then I
never yet have seen the ideal man that I should call
quite good enough for Emily ; and perhaps I am looking
at things with a jaundiced eye to-day.   Perhaps I do
feel more than a little jealous of Miles taking possession of all her thoughts and confidences and castles-in-
the-air.   And then, perhaps too, I feel just a little bit
out in the cold, now that the whole family are so entirely absorbed in each other ; for didn't I tell you
Madame Marini came home with her father and brother

last night ? and, as a matter of course, the children
have a holiday ; and they are all wandering about the
house and grounds together, so that I have the whole
day to myself to write to you and relieve myself of
my misgivings about Emily, which naturally I could
not breathe to any one hereabouts. · How unaccount-
able Zoe would think them !

But now for Madame Marini. She is a very
beautiful woman still, though she must be at least
eight-and-thirty, I suppose ; and, as a girl, I should
say she must have been handsomer than Zoe. There
is more variety of expression in her face. She is not
so stately and statuesque, but she is one of those people
who couldn't go into · an ungraceful attitude if they
tried. If both their heads were on a coin, you would
say they were wonderfully alike ; but after you have
watched Madame Marini a little, you find that the
likeness has almost vanished, as family likenesses often
do when you get used to the faces. Hers has never
the same expression for two minutes together. There
is rather a sad one, which is perhaps the most constant;
but I have not seen Zoe's " severe " look, that makes
people misunderstand her so, poor child ! Now
Madame Marini's face expresses what she is feeling in
a quite unusual way. Probably having lived so long
amongst Italians may have something to do with this,
but it is certainly not a Winkworth idiosyncrasy. I
suppose she is like her mother, who, Miss Dorothea
says, was a charming, lovable woman, and that is
exactly how Madame Marini strikes one. Her manner
is like nothing I ever met with before. Even in
the very few snatches of talk I have had with her,
it struck me that there was something peculiarly
sweet and courteous in her way of speaking. One felt

as if she was genuinely interested in what one said, and went *with* one, as it were.   I should say that Zoe's face had more thought in it, but Madame Marini's has so much of what the old books call "sensibility" that one can quite imagine how all the troubles of her young days came about.   It is very odd to watch her with Sir Walter.   His way to her is more what it is to Lisa than to any of his other children, possibly because there is less of himself in those two.   But it is really pathetic to see how anxious he is about Miles, who did not appear at breakfast this morning, and whom nobody has yet seen but Madame Marini.   She reported that he was asleep after a wakeful night, and her father actually went out himself and locked up Smut, because he barked under Miles's window.

Sir Walter's sentiments on the Italian question seem extraordinarily modified by his experiment in foreign travel.   This morning when I responded to Madame Marini's reprobation of the armistice, he said, "Ah, Bertha! you must go to the schoolroom for sympathy in these matters;" and then he quoted to me certain speeches of Mr. Fanshawe's, concerning the slipperiness of the French Emperor, with "an unprecedented urbanity" (as the *Wilts Chronicle* observed in a report of Sir Walter's speech at a tenants' dinner).

Now, as Zoe has gone to fetch Emily to lunch, and I must, if possible, secure her to myself for a few minutes, I will say good-bye, dear Nan.——Ever your affectionate sister,   ESTHER MADGEWICK.

Looking out of window, behold Miles striding, not with the air of an invalid, in the direction of the Dower House.   No hope of a *tête-à-tête* at present.

136.—Relic-Worship.

Fanny to Annie.

THE MIZ MAZE.

My dear Annie—You will pardon the liberty, but you ain't a got the right tale. Miss Lisa told me all about it when I was doing of her hair. It was her half-sister, the lady as I told you of, who got the pardon, and Mr. Edgar took it; but there was not no shooting, only Mr. Winkworth has had a fever,—and no wonder.

th.—I could not finish my letter last week, and now here they be, all come home on a heap. And Mr. Winkworth have made it up with your Miss Warburton, and they are as sweet as sweet. We shall all go out of mourning, and Mrs. Pearson says she will recommend me as lady's-maid; and if you could be housemaid we would be together again like doves, dear Annie. The other lady, Madame Marini, is come home. They say she is a Papist, but she is a very nice, civil-spoken lady, and you would never think it of her. To be sure I did see her a kissing of an old china dog as stood in her room, and she stands up in the window like one in a maze gazing out. Is that the way they tells their beads?—Your affectionate friend,   FANNY.

137.—Earthly Paradise.

Miss Winkworth to Mrs. Home.

THE DOWER HOUSE.

My dear Mary—There is a sort of paradise going on all round us, not inhabited only by one solitary pair! I had not gone farther than my first look from

my window when I caught sight of Birdie on the lawn.
Her early Italian hours had brought her out long
before breakfast, and there she was, smelling to every
flower and spending a little adoration on the Lamarque
over the wall towards the churchyard, which she remembered in an infant state.   I knocked at the window
and in she came, with the present Zeenab in her arms,
declaring that she is the very Zéenab she left, and, in
fact, she really has the same tabby pattern on her nose
that her grandmother possessed (I have written this in
the style of the advertisement: "Lost, a pony, the
property of a lady with a piebald nose").   But really
it is all confusingly delightful.   Bertha is just the
Birdie of old, only more so.   People talk of her likeness to Zoe, but I only see it so far as they are both
Winkworths.   What I do see is the winning sparkle
of the eyes and deprecating smile of her mother, and
a thousand little tricks of manner and gesture that
must bring back his younger days to Walter.

She roamed about my room, recognising everything
and gloating over it, saying she had dreamt it all so often
that she is only half sure of being awake now, till the
church-bell rang, and we had to feel the rift between
us.   I went very thankful to church with Emily, and
she returned to breakfast; but my Bird she was back
again by half-past ten, as soon as she thought Aunt
Bessie would be ready, and with the children after her.
She is all over the place, and they go roaming after
her just like a schoolboy the first day of the holidays.
Miles was reported fast asleep; but Zoe and her father
came down to take possession of Emily, and make us
all come up to luncheon, for the young lady had a shy
fit, and would not come up without us.

Walter is exceedingly pleased about it all.   He

shows it, dear old fellow, by heartily wishing Sophia
could have seen all that he has seen ; and I ventured
to tell him what Zoe read to me once from a letter of
Emily's about what she owed to his wife. I never saw
him so much overcome. The forgiveness of Bertha
seems to have taken a load off his mind and spirits,
and he only longs that Sophia could have shared it
with him. " She had pardoned," he said, " and if I had
given the smallest opening she would have been the
first to take it up." They have almost made a Garibaldian of him. He has begun to find fault with the
Congress of Vienna as much as he can with anything
in which the Duke of Wellington had a share. " But
no doubt it was all done by those villains Metternich
and Talleyrand ; and the last ten years have educated
the Italians a little."

Another thing has had a great effect on him—the
discovery that Mr. Edgar Fanshawe was not, as he had
always believed, a lazy, dawdling fellow, who preferred
his brush and palette to a respectable desk and ledger,
but a man who had sacrificed wealth, ease, and position
at Rome rather than be untrue to his country and
Church. He was greatly astonished to hear that I had
known this from Zoe, and said it would have made a
great deal of difference in the way the young man was
regarded. Now it seems that Mr. Fanshawe has come
into some property, which will put him at ease. Walter
has asked him here, and likewise that young Bootle,
feeling gratitude due to both, though he declares the
latter young gentleman to be " an unmitigated ass !"
and his dear mother not much better.

Miles seems much better to-day, and these long
summer days are made for lovers. They are a pretty
sight.—Your loving sister,   D. W.

138.—EMILY'S ANNOUNCEMENT.

Emily to Mrs. Warburton.

THE DOWER HOUSE, *July.*

My dear Mamma—I know you will be glad to hear what I have now to tell you, but I beg of you, for many reasons, not to tell anybody before I come home. I am engaged to Miles. He came home suddenly last evening. We met at Salisbury Station, and, after all he has gone through so nobly, and with such self-devotion, I could not but feel that it is an honour that he should have ever cared for me. It all was settled very suddenly; I cannot tell you how; but nothing can exceed the kindness of Sir Walter and all of them. I never guessed before how kind Sir Walter could be, and you know how I looked up to dear good Lady Winkworth. Madame Marini is *so* delightful. Please, please, dear mamma, not a word to Mrs. Bootle.—Your affectionate daughter,

EMILY BROOKE WARBURTON.

139.—EMILY'S RECANTATION.

Emily to Charles Fanshawe, Esq.

THE DOWER HOUSE, *August.*

My dear Cousin Charles—It is due to your great kindness that you should know at once of the great happiness that has come to me. It might have come sooner, only then perhaps I should not have known the full nobleness of Mr. Winkworth. You know we grew up together, and last autumn I began to see that he cared for me, but I thought the thing was a good

deal arranged as a desirable affair between mamma and
his father. I thought, too, that he was, though always
good, rather commonplace, and might hinder me in my
higher schemes of life. But I know now how foolish
I was not to perceive all that was hidden under his
shy, reserved manner. His heroism and patience in
this expedition, undertaken from a strong sense of
duty, have brought out all that he is, and I see now
that with him lies my only hope of at all fulfilling my
stewardship towards those poor people. I am so happy,
and they are all so kind and good. Sir Walter says
he shall write to you, but, dear cousin Charles, will
you take care they don't tie all my money up so that
no one can have any good out of it ? Is not Edgar's
inheritance delightful ?—Your affectionate

E. B. WARBURTON.

140.—MR. BOOTLE'S PROMOTION.

Mrs. Bootle to her friend, Miss Dumbleton.

HIGH SCALE RECTORY, August.

My dearest Penelope—You say your old school-
friend has not written to you for a long time. Well,
my love, I have great news, and so you will say when
you have read it. News of Deaneries and Baronetcies,
news for the Clergy List and the Peerage, Church and
State. I must explain myself. What do you say
when I tell you that I—yes, your old friend Maria
Bootle, am to be Mrs. Dean ? There, my dear ! It's
true. Mr. Bootle has been made Dean of Tully Cleogh
in Ireland, and I am all in a flutter, for I don't know
anything about Deans, having never lived among the
worldly, thank Heaven ! The last Dean was single, and

I hear there is only room for one where he sits in the cathedral, so I think of sending orders to have the stall enlarged for two.   Then, Penelope, you who live in London, can tell me what sort of clothes he'll have to wear.   Just step down to Westminster, there's a dear, and send in your card, to ask the Dean for a contribution to one of your societies, and take notice whether he wears robes and whether he has an apron, and if you could find out who was his tailor, we might order a suit just like his for Mr. Bootle, who will never think of it for himself.   And now, I dare say, this is only a first step to a bishopric, perhaps to Canterbury itself.   Then I should die happy.   Now I have another piece of news.   My Algy, who was so persecuted for his faith in Italy, is about to be married to a young lady of good family and fortune, Miss Sophia Winkworth, daughter of that esteemed nobleman, Sir Walter Winkworth, whose family came over either with William the Conqueror or with William III., I'm sure I forget which—never thinking much of such vanities.   The young people have been attached from infancy; and Algy says the way she avoids him is quite beautiful, so modest and retiring.   I am sure she will feel deeply what an honour it is to be allied to my Algernon, like the lady who said she wished she had two necks to bring as an offering to such a husband—one of our kings, was it Henry VIII.?— because he defended the Protestant Faith.   And he replied, "Would that all my people had but one neck!" meaning one just like hers; which, no doubt, was his way of paying a compliment.   Now I must conclude. Don't you think it will sound well if Algy's life is written, "Son of a dean and son-in-law to a baronet"? —Your old friend,   MARIA BOOTLE.

141.—ALGERNON'S GRACIOUS PROPOSAL.

Algernon Bootle to Sir Walter.

HIGH SCALE, *August.*

Dear Sir Walter—I thank you exceedingly for your most kind and flattering invitation, which it will give me (and, as I hope, others of your family) the greatest satisfaction to accept.

As, however, I have always believed and acted upon the principle that perfect candour is the distinguishing attribute of a gentleman, I think it my duty to inform you that there is one member of your family for whom I have long felt an attraction—may I venture to hope it has been reciprocated?—and that in coming to the Miz Maze, it is my chief hope to enter into a closer alliance with your amiable family.

Need I say that your daughter Sophia is the person to whom I allude? Do not, dear sir, think that this is a hasty and ill-considered step on my part. I have grown up from infancy with Zoe; I know her character thoroughly, and, although I am not blind to her imperfections, I feel at the same time that, under wise guidance and sober training in the principles of the Protestant religion, she will grow up worthy of her lot as an English pastor's wife and daughter-in-law to my dear mother, whom you, I know, so highly value. I speak with more confidence on this point, because I know the touch of romance in your dear daughter's nature. At one time, I confess, I feared that I might not have proved a sufficiently striking and romantic figure to take her fancy; but now that the halo of my past imprisonment for my principles and my narrow escape from a violent death hangs around me, I trust

that this deficiency may be removed. I venture, therefore, to lay my hand and heart at the feet of one whom
on this occasion I feel it right to call, not my playmate
Zoe, but Miss Sophia Winkworth.

You will naturally ask (and far be it from me, dear
sir, to blame such parental anxiety) what are the prospects which I offer to your daughter to share ? It is
the fact that these are considerably superior to what
until now they would have been which has made me
(with my father's and mother's full approbation) choose
this moment for taking the step I now do. My father
yesterday received, and this morning accepted, the offer
of the Deanery of Tully-na-Cleogh, in the Sister Island;
and until the decease of the worthy man who holds the
living of Combermere in Westmoreland, which has been
promised to me at his death, he will be enabled to give
his only son (myself) a comfortable allowance, such as
will enable me to offer to my wife a refined and elegant
home.

Allow me, dear sir, to conclude this letter by re-
marking that, although you may have higher views for
your daughter than to see her the wife of a country
clergyman, riches and grandeur are not happiness ; and
even if a coroneted earl should come forward to apply
for her hand, there would be no certainty that her
higher welfare or even her earthly comfort would be
so considered as by, dear sir, yours most sincerely,

ALGERNON BOOTLE.

142.—Sir Walter's Refusal.

Sir Walter to Algernon Bootle.

THE MIZ MAZE, *August.*

Dear Algernon—I was wholly unprepared for the purport of your letter, having expected merely an acceptance of the invitation I had so much pleasure in sending.

My daughter Sophia shares my feeling of gratitude for the friendly care you took of her brother during his illness, but she is quite unable to reciprocate the sentiments you express. She is not aware—nor am I —that there has ever been anything in her manner to give encouragement to the hope you have made known to me, and we both trust that you will dismiss it altogether from your thoughts. We cannot, of course, expect you under these circumstances to come to us here at present, but I shall always be glad to hear of your welfare.

Pray present my sincere congratulations to your father on his ecclesiastical promotion, and with best regards to him and Mrs. Bootle, believe me yours faithfully,   WALTER M. WINKWORTH.

143.—Zoe's Suitors.

Miss Winkworth to Mrs. Home.

My dear Mary—The plot thickens. Of course all the world is rapturous over Miles and Emily, so much so that my young ladies make faces and laugh over Emily's having refused him once for being groovy and desirable. But here is Walter encumbered with two

suitors for his daughter.   Mr. Bootle has got an Irish
deanery, whereupon the great Algernon desires permission, in a letter almost equal to the immortal Mr.
Collins's, to lay his hand and heart at Miss Sophia
Winkworth's feet.   "The puppy!" cries Walter.   And
as to the young lady, she does nothing but laugh.

But there is another rock ahead.   Mr. Fanshawe
has written to Miles that he cannot feel it honourable
to come without making known to Sir Walter his
affection for Zoe, explaining his means, etc.

Poor Walter!   It is a blow.   He says it is nonsense, and that Zoe is a mere child; but he can't get
any one to agree with him that she is perfectly indifferent.   He tells Birdie that she has lived in Italy
and is romantic, to which she retorts that the English
are far more romantic than any Continental people.
Miles and Emily won't give him any comfort either;
but he says it is partiality to Emily's cousin.   "Any
way," he says, "we must have it over.   The fellow has
acted honourably, and we cannot forbid him to come
and have it out.   And then we shall be done with it,
and settle down in peace."   Poor old Walter!   I doubt
it.—Your loving   D. W.

144.—A Cordial Invitation.

Sir Walter to Edgar Fanshawe.

.THE MIZ MAZE,
STOKESWORTHY, *August.*

Dear Mr. Fanshawe—We have brought our invalid
home safely, and, though he was rather knocked up
at first, he is now rapidly improving.   We are all in
good spirits at being together again, and I write to ask

if you could be induced to join us for a week or two.
At this time of year one has no attraction to offer in
the shape of shooting and so forth, but if you can put
up with our country dulness, it will be a great pleasure
to us *all* to welcome you among us. Your cousin, Miss
Warburton, is staying with my sisters, as no doubt
you are aware, and she and my daughters are together
every day. Miles begs me to tell you that he will
take no excuse, and I assure you it will be a personal
disappointment to me if you cannot come down. I
fear I did not half convey to you my deep sense of the
kindness you displayed on our behalf, but you must
let me say now how truly I felt it.

Let us hear soon that you are coming, and tell us
by what train, that we may send to meet you at the
station.—With best regards, very faithfully yours,

WALTER M. WINKWORTH.

145.—COME, CONQUERING HERO.

Emily to Edgar Fanshawe.

My dear Edgar — You have been the *Deus ex
machina* to us all along. (Miles won't let me call
it, in a sensible way, machine—a—— and, after
all, I don't know what the machine was, unless it
was the railway.) And I cannot help hoping that
you are going to be as happy as all of us, so don't
you be desponding and proud and stand-offish when
Sir Walter writes to invite you, as Miles tells me
he is doing or going to do. There's no fear but
that he will be conformable when he sees that Zoe's
heart is in it. He has an immense respect for you,
and considers you as the genuine Protestant martyr,

or at least, confessor, while Algy was the imposition;
so you had better strike while the iron is hot.   The
odd thing is that he should never have understood the
real objection to your doing at Rome as Rome does, but
thought it mere Bohemianism, while we young ones
all knew it well.   Only if you come, put it off, I warn
you, till after Thursday, when there is to be a great
and awful state-dinner to show Bertha reinstated,
and, I am afraid, to show me off likewise.   The real
conquering and rescuing hero would be too much; or
rather, the hero would find it a bore.   And Zoe had
better not be distracted in her calculations as to which
goes first, a knight's eldest son's wife or a baronet's
youngest daughter; and whether to have her ice from
London or Salisbury.   Mamma comes on Wednesday,
and will take me away on Monday, but it would be
jolly to meet you here and see it all right first.

You cannot think how nice it all is.   Somehow Sir
Walter is so much more natural and easy to get on
with than at High Scale, I fancy it is the being in his
proper home and with the aunts.   I don't think anyone can be long with Aunt Dora without coming off
the high horse.   He is so kind!   I feel it a strange
privilege.   I never deserved that a silly little flighty
ape like me should belong to such good people, thinking so much of duty.   I cannot imagine how I ever
was so foolish as to think Miles would be an obstacle
to anything that seemed right.   There is a peaceful
dignity about this whole place that I know you will
appreciate.—Your affectionate cousin,   E. B. W.

146.—COMING.

Edgar Fanshawe to Sir Walter Winkworth.

LONDON, *August.*

Dear Sir Walter Winkworth — I am extremely obliged to you for your most kind invitation to Stokes-worthy, and nothing could give me greater pleasure than to accept it. If Friday is convenient to you, I shall be very glad to come down on that day, reaching your station at 6.15.

I am glad to hear so good an account of Miles. Pray remember me to him, and, with thanks for the kind expressions in your letter, believe me yours sincerely, EDGAR FANSHAWE.

147.—PRESUMPTION.

Edgar Fanshawe to Emily Warburton.

LONDON, *August.*

My·dear Emily—Why did you write to me? do you want my good wishes all over again? These things become monotonous, and I have sent them twice already. I have just written a note to Sir Walter, which I flatter myself is neither desponding, proud, nor "stand-offish." I hope, among other correct habits, you will acquire that of writing English. Sir Walter's letter is most kind, and I have done my best to answer it in a proper spirit, cordially, yet without too much confidence. But if you know what I said in my letter to Miles the other day, which of course you do, it must be plain to you that Sir Walter's writing to me has only one meaning. Still your encouragement is not at

all wasted.   One sentence in your letter amazed me.
I wish to be respectful; but are women ever presumptuous in judging each other?   And do they ever
say more than they are justified in saying?   If that
sentence is true, dear Emily—and I ought not to
distrust your experience—then, indeed, my last fears
are groundless.   But I think that was only an
amiable slip of the pen.   You did not write intending
to tell me that; but to warn me against Thursday and
the dinner.   I am most grateful.   How I shall exist
till Friday afternoon I don't know, but business keeps
me in town till then.

Has she a talent, do you think, for ordering ice
and sending people in to dinner?   What a pity it will
be wasted, as it will be, at least till I am P.R.A.!
But now I am presumptuous.   Are you in love with
Madame Marini?   You will do me the justice to
remember that I stood up for Miles long ago, and told
you he was not such a bad fellow as you thought.   I
am not afraid to write this, for I cannot imagine you
weak and slavish enough to show your letters to him.
A rivederla.—Your faithful cousin,

EDGAR FANSHAWE.

It was neither I nor the railway.   It was the
engine-driver.   What should we do without him?

148.—SHE LIKES THE MAN!

Miss Winkworth to Mrs. Home.

August.

My dear Mary—The dinner came off with all the
impressiveness that Walter could desire.   It was good
to hear the gusto with which he presented "My

daughter, Madame Marini," and begged to introduce
Miss Warburton. George Thorburn was the first of
the guests, and his satisfaction could only find vent in
kissing Emily, and nearly crushing all our fingers.
He has already announced that the wedding must take
place from Dallington. Mrs. Warburton is a perfect
cushion of contentment, and spends her time in con-
fiding anecdotes of Miles's juvenile preference for
Emily. I think the good lady was rather disappointed
that they refused to make themselves entertaining, and
acted, as she confided to Bessie, "not at all like lovers ;
oh no ! quite the reverse." Indeed, Miles was so shy
that he would not even turn over Emily's music, but
got behind a curtain till he was routed out by George
Thorburn. Poor George, there's one drawback to his
satisfaction. "I protest, Bessie," says he, "Winkworth   actually   has   come   back   declaring   there's
something to be said for those rascally fellows in
Italy ! I don't want to alarm you, but 'tis very hot
there. Are you sure the sun has not had any effect
on his head ?" And on the other hand, Walter wishes
George Thorburn would take a journey on the
Continent ; it would do him so much good. Zoe
managed charmingly, but looked a little anxious and
oppressed.

Mrs. Warburton and Emily are spending a few
days at Dallington before going to Brighton. The
ecstacy of George Thorburn will not be satisfied
without a visit from them ; and of course Miles must
ride over every day.

th.—Mr. Fanshawe is come. He *does* look
foreign ; but he has good honest eyes, and I like the
ring of his voice. His sketches are lovely, and bring
Birdie's Italian surroundings before us. He makes

himself pleasant; but I pity the poor young man, for he must know that the entire company of us are looking round wondering when the deed is to be done; all but Zoe, the victim, who goes about unconscious, but with a light in her eyes and a spring in her step I never saw before.   There, even while I wrote, the thing was accomplished.   Walter made his appearance with, "Why, Dora, I never expected this.   She likes the man!"   I am sorry to say I laughed.   He did so look as if he had been caught in a trap, having only had him here to "get it over."   Of course Zoe might have higher expectations, and the word artist is sorely against the grain with him; but I do not think that if all things suit he will refuse consent.   Indeed he cannot, having been fully told beforehand the purpose of Mr. Fanshawe's coming.

This must go at once, so you must wait till next mail.—Your affectionate   D. W.

149.—HAPPY ZOE.

Zoe to Emily.

THE MIZ MAZE, *August.*

Dearest Emily—I hardly know how to write.   Life seems too beautiful; but nobody knows what Edgar really is so well as you do, so you will not say mine is a rhapsody.   How humbling it is to be taken for so much more than one is worth, and by such a man!   All that can be done is to try to live up to the ideal he has before him.   By his side I feel such a narrow little English girl, and my heart sinks lest I should disappoint him, and try his patience.   Yet how can I speak of my heart sinking?   Why, it dances!   I feel

as if I had never known before what happiness is.
And yet how true it is that "we cower before the
heart-searching Eye in rapture as in pain."

Sometimes, when I am alone, a fear of my own joy
comes over me, and then as soon as he comes in sight
doubt or fear seems as far away as the recollection of
the winter's cold.

It seems hardhearted not to be more sorry at
leaving papa and the children, but somehow I never
see it from that point of view ; and I do trust Aunt
Dora entirely to make them happy.   It is very good
of him to give me up.   I hear them coming in.—Your
loving   ZOE.

150.—HAPPY EMILY.

Emily to Zoe.

DALLINGTON, *August.*

Dear One — Now everything is doubly delicious.
Not but that my prophetic mind knew what was
coming when mamma snatched me away on Monday
morning.   I had not been without intelligence either
(to say nothing of Miles), for some good folks arrived
yesterday who had called at the Miz Maze the day
before, and who imagined Edgar to be Signor Marini.
There was a young lady who was disappointed that
he did not wear a red shirt, and wondered that he
spoke such good English !   But she thought him rather
young for Madame Bertha !   The fun was that Mrs.
Thorburn was so excessively angry at any cousin of
hers being taken for a trumpery Italian rebel and
Papist.   Though, to be sure, it is a misfortune that
poor dear Edgar would look so foreign, whatever they
could do to him.   She hopes *you* will take him in hand.

Indeed, my dear, folly apart, I am glad and thankful that we shall all be so closely united, and such true brothers and sisters. As to your being narrow, insular, etc., don't you know that a clever man's ideal is to have a wife whom he can teach,—a blank sheet to draw upon. No, no! you sha'n't be a stupid blank sheet, but one of those nice ones, with just the lightsome blue sky toned off put in ready to hand, and all the rest ready to receive whatever he chooses to put on. Do you know that the Thorburns are raving to get the wedding from Dallington? I should not mind at all, for there will be a stranger by that time at High Scale, and perhaps we may combine. That would be nice, would not it? You see we must any way have two bridesmaids in common. I am afraid Bertha will not stay for it, but Miles says he will take me to see her, for he wants to know how the Italians are getting on. As to your father, never mind about him. It is not complimentary to you, but Aunt Dora can manage Sir Walter ever so much better than you can. He has always thought much of her judgment, and it is not in the nature of things that he should leave off thinking you a little girl. As to Polly and Lisa, she will mother them capitally with good sense, and Aunt Bessie with tenderness. I don't pity anybody but Clyffe, and he has got his regiment. Dear Zoe, how can we be thankful enough for so much happiness?— Your loving EMILY.

We go to Brighton to-morrow. Don't let Miles work too hard and fancy it is to please me; I don't care a rush for degrees.

151.—BERTHA IN ENGLAND.

Bertha Marini to Colonel Marini.

THE MIZ MAZE, *August.*

Patience, patience, *caro mio!* Rome was not built in a day, and it will take many a day to win her; but somehow or other the day will come which will reconcile irreconcilables, and show the world Italy free and united and great. You will laugh when I tell you that I am a better patriot now than when I was in Italy. My thoughts are seldom long away from you, and I am ashamed to remember how often you had cause to think me indifferent to what you cared for so dearly. Now I read every word which the English papers say about the campaign, and get so provoked over the stupidity of some of them! It is odious of them when they will not see that the Italians only ask for a few of those blessings which come as freely to English people as the air they breathe. I get Mascherino into a corner, and grumble to him—in Italian. There is no one else. Mr. Fanshawe would understand; but the foreign element has to be repressed in him just at present. He is comically anxious to keep it under.

No, my Luigi, you need not fear that my visit will disenchant me with Italy. It has been the greatest joy to me to come, the kindness and love shown to me are beyond all I dreamt about, but—I could not live here. Life seems to me so cramped, one is hedged about by conventionalities, the days pass in a groove, so many things offend people, what is small looks disproportionately big. Our people have a hundred faults, but there is a spontaneous grace and freedom about them which must always be delightful. They are like children, as tiresome and—as fascinating.

And now having, I hope, reassured your mind, and proved to you that I shall be ready to return directly you recall me, how am I to give you an idea of the general atmosphere of bliss in which we live at present ? Zoe's face is a study ; the child moves about as if she were in a wonderful dream, but the person who most completely enjoys the romance of it all is Aunt Dora. She has said once that she wished Mr. Fanshawe had been an English squire. If he were, she would not have cared for him half so much, and, when Mary marries the typical man, as she will, being a sentimental little maid, and abhorring prose, Aunt Dora will not throw herself into the affair with half of her present enthusiasm.

Well, *caro mio*, you will understand that I am very happy, but longing for a sight of you. At this moment I wonder what you are looking at and what you are thinking of. I am thinking of you and Italy. I see, when I lift my eyes, something as different as possible from our blue skies and snowy mountains. Do you remember it ? The great sweep of grass, with tall trees feathering down into the rhododendrons to the left, the farm lying snugly in other and more distant trees to the right, beyond a peep of the downs, overhead gray clouds, neither stormy nor threatening, but touched with silver lights and promise of sunshine. And there, yes, there go Zoe and Edgar ; Aunt Dora, who is in the garden, making a barefaced pretence of not seeing them, and calling to Lisa, who, not so discreet, is following. As for Miles, he is, of course, at Dallington.—Your own   BERTHA.

You love me as well as ever, don't you, Luigi ?

152.—CLYFFE'S OPINIONS.

Clyffe to Zoe.

MONTREAL, *August.*

My dearest Zoe—All's well that ends well, but I wouldn't go through the last six weeks again for something. I knew Miles was wretched and out of sorts before I found out what he had been putting up with on my account. It was enough to make one dream about him, and we had rather nothing more was said about that part of the story. Of course I knew what the newspaper paragraph meant, and I don't think his first letters did much to relieve one's mind, though I couldn't help laughing to think of him out there in Italy, the centre of so much excitement. I gather, however, that he rose to the occasion, and found he could use his own tongue for himself. I may remark in passing that *I* have had to learn to do a great many things for *my*self which belonged to his share of the concern generally. We never were meant to have the Atlantic between us. But, however, *he'll* be all right now, and I hope Emily really knows what the old fellow is worth. They were always fond of each other, and I always thought Miles took No for an answer much more easily than I should. I never have got to realising that you all live at Stokesworthy ; if I think about you, it is always at dear old High Scale. As for Bertha, I don't think I quite believe in her. Give her my love, however, in a proper way ; she seems to have been very kind to Miles. Does she speak English ? But of course she does. I have written to Fanshawe. I *was* glad of his letter, he seems to be a famous fellow. The downfall of Algy is a pure and entire delight to me! What rises *I* would have got out of him if I had had him abroad with *me!* Of course I have written flaming congratulations to Miles. I always knew he'd marry Emily some day, so there's nothing new about it. I wish they would come out here for their wedding tour, it would be satisfactory to see the old fellow all right again, and would put all the misery out of one's head.

August 28.—Ha, ha! Miss Zoe! So it has all come out now, has it? This is the way you all go on when my sober presence is removed from you. Refusing the excellent Algy and accepting a wild Bohemian foreigner! So he used to be described in *my* time! Oh, the sublime indifference which you and Emily always thought it correct to show to any unfortunate fellow that tried to be civil to either of you! So the conquering hero has come. I couldn't think what had happened now, when you and father and Miles all wrote at once; late events have made me quite nervous. And you haven't even the honour and glory of being persecuted for your true love's sake; a convenient fortune and the wonderful luck that attends some people have set it all straight. As for Algy, he'll get over it and marry a rich widow!

Thanks for Bertha's photograph; she cuts you out, my dear child. Poor dear father! What will he do? He must come out and pay me a visit. I could take him to a fancy ball in the great skating rink!—Ever your loving brother (a little homesick),

CLYFFE WINKWORTH.

Z

153.—A NEW POET.

Algernon's Diary.

HIGH SCALE.

This morning, the last but one before I leave the home of my childhood for other scenes, I have received a blow. ' Yes, a severe blow, and from the hand of one whom I should have thought so far my inferior in every way that I need have had no fear. Sophia Winkworth is engaged to Edgar Fanshawe! How the proud Winkworths can have bowed their pride to accept an artist for the husband of Zoe passes my comprehension, especially when, as my mother says, they might have done so much better! To be refused for the sake of a duke or an earl (not that I ever heard of such wooers for Zoe) would have been intelligible. I should have lamented the worldliness of the family, but at the same time I should have taken courage from observing the power of wealth to blind the eyes to true merit. Now I have no consolation of this nature. I cannot even assure myself that worldliness has caused my rejection, since I am surely a far better match in the eyes of the world than a landscape painter! I am bewildered; nor does Miles's friendly little note which accompanies his father's clear up the mist of my ideas. He writes that it is an attachment of old standing, though only recent events have put Fanshawe in a position to ask for Sir Walter's consent; and that, though of course I shall not wish to pay my visit now, he hopes I shall do so at some future time after the wedding, which is to be next Easter. But how could she, as Shakespeare says, on this mountain cease to feed, and batten on that moor? O Miss Winkworth, shallow-hearted! O my Zoe, mine no more!

Rejected love, I have often heard, tends to call out the latent poetry in a man. In one breath I find myself quoting Shakespeare and Tennyson. What if this blow should be the inauguration of new powers in this breast! What if from this bitter pang should arise the birth of a new poet, before whose name the light of Tennyson, Longfellow, even Tupper, shall fade! Rhymes, before unknown, seem to rise and float in my brain.

> Farewell the false, the vain, the showy!
> Farewell, farewell, deluding Zoe!

Deluded, however, would perhaps be more true, for I will not wrong my old playmate so much as to accuse her of coquetting with my affections. Poetry and truth are said to be incompatible. " Bootle's Poems " shall be renowned for both. Some day I will send her a copy, chastely bound in dark-green morocco, with her name in gilt letters on the outside. If I tried, could I not get them ready as a wedding gift before Easter? I will make up my mind to write at least two every week until Christmas. They can then be printed and published before Easter. Fame will follow, and perhaps fortune! Who knows but that at some future day I may be glad that this blow fell upon my tender heart to call out its latent song?

Farewell, Zoe!

154.—A Good-natured Grumble.

Miss Winkworth to Mrs. Home.

My dear Mary—You will be glad to hear that all is settling itself as happily as possible. Walter hummed and hawed, and said that it would never have happened if his daughter had had any one to, look after her, and that a girl who had never had a season in London did not know what she was throwing away; but, when all had been said, he finally consented on condition that Bessie and I shall come back to the Miz Maze and look after him and the two young ones. Of course we consented, though—it shows how one changes in growing old, or else it is perverseness—by no means with the same feelings as those we had prepared when we hoped and expected he would take us back on his first bereavement. Then we had not quite divested ourselves of the sense that we were the young ladies of the Miz Maze, and had the best right there; and now—well, we are very thankful to be useful to him, and to mother the dear children; but it *is* a surrender of home and of freedom! There, I've had my grumble out, and I see you shake your head at discontented Dora. As to Miles, Mr. Bernard has a nephew coming to him who will act tutor as far as is advisable, and the boy will go up for his degree when term begins. Emily says she will forgive him if he takes no honours. Meantime High Scale will be put in order. It will eventually belong to Clyffe, but my brother has it for his life, and the young people can live there and attend to the welfare of Emily's colliers, a matter she has much at heart. It will give Miles something to do; and, as we hear that the new rector is the very opposite in opinions to Mr. Bootle, it will be well for him to have some old inhabitants to act with him. Mrs. Warburton talks of living chiefly at Brighton, but Emily wants to keep up Triermain, with hopes of getting Zoe there in time, though I think Edgar will make her at home in Italy before he even takes a house in London. Walter says he shall keep the Dower

House for them against the time when Edgar has got
tired of his painting nonsense; and, as it is a consolation to him, they don't absolutely say nay.   Meantime,
Signor Marini has got an appointment, and Bertha
doubts whether he will be able to stay more than a
day or two when he comes to fetch her.   It is a relief
to some people, as you may guess.   D. W.

PART IX.

WOO'D AND MARRIED AND A'!

"You, to a love which your true faith doth merit,
You, to your land, and love, and great allies."

155.—Miles's Degree.

Miles to Clyffe.

Well, it is all over now, and I have pulled through after all; but I didn't expect it, and I really hadn't time or sense even to scribble to you till the examination was over. I think I am nearly as glad as when I got out of prison, and I feel as if I never wished to open a book again, at least not for months. They all thought I should be nervous, for Emily's letters (which somehow helped me through) always declared that she shouldn't mind a bit if I was plucked. However, the deed's done, and I have written to poor old Algy and told him that all his coaching was not thrown away. He was a great ass to think of Zoe; but there's no reason the poor old fellow shouldn't get the bit of credit that is his due.

Now, I have some news for you. Of course it was rather soon to have to grind after the fever, and I have had such frightful headaches and still feel so good for nothing in and out, that they say I must have a thorough change and holiday, and, in short, I am coming out to pay you a visit. What do you say to that? Shall you be glad to see me? We shall have just a few things to talk over! You don't feel quite up to date with the home world, do you? And I—

nothing can be complete for me without you, and there
will be plenty of time to get a sight of you and home
again before Easter.   There are to be great festivities,
which I think Edgar hates the notion of more than I
do.   Then I shall take Emily to see Varese before we
settle down at dear old High Scale.   I am so glad
though that she has got something rational for me to
do.   I should get as stupid as old Thorburn if I was
let alone ; and, on the whole, I think there might be
room in one's life for something besides hunting,
though I wish it wouldn't take the opportunity of
freezing hard just now when I *might* take a day with
a clear conscience.   I'll write again to let you know
when I sail.   I must go to Triermain for a few days
before Christmas.—Ever yours,

MILES WINKWORTH.

156.—MILES IN CANADA.

Miles to Zoe.

—— STREET, MONTREAL,
January 1860.

Dearest Zoe—I have sent off a packet for Emily ;
but must find time for a few lines to you.   What a
relief it was to feel that the strain was over, and the
examiners floored at last !   Certainly Italian fevers
are a bad preparation for taking a degree ; but the sea
air blew away all my headaches, and I was as jolly as
possible before we got to land and Clyffe joined me.

My dear, I don't think, as you say, that I *do* wish
that Bertha lived in England.   Depend upon it, all the
different ideas which she suppressed so carefully during
her visit would break out, and spoil her intercourse
with father certainly, if not with all of us.

Well, as to Clyffe, poor boy! I am so thankful I came. He suffered so dreadfully last summer that I don't think he has ever quite got over it. He looks very handsome and soldierly, much less boyish; and father would be proud to hear how every one speaks of him; but he didn't seem at first to have a laugh left in him. He is of course very popular, and his chief friend, Kirkland, seems a very nice fellow. He told me that he noticed something amiss with Clyffe quite suddenly, but that he never confessed to it till the newspaper came, and then, poor fellow, he could not conceal it, and of course it was weeks before he got Edgar's letter. And Bertha and all the new interests have been like an uncomfortable sort of dream to him, and sometimes he was anxious about me, and sometimes felt as if I had got away from him into a world of my own. He never was bothered before in his life without our being able to talk it over. But we had it all out—how wretched he had made himself over father's mistake, and then hearing bad news of me directly afterwards. I said that I did not think that the *idea* of an accidental detention would have frightened me very much, and he heard I was better before he knew I was ill. He said " Yes, but somehow something took the life out of him ;" and that curious dream, whatever it may have been, had a lasting effect on him, how deep, his letters gave one no idea. I believe he thought I should never get here safe and sound. However, he is all right again now, and it *is* jolly to be together again. We had such a day of skating yesterday that was like old times, only I felt myself a very awkward Britisher on the ice, though at Oxford one's lakeland training made one quite a swell. Clyffe has greatly improved; but it is a marvel to see the

young ladies skate. I need not say that he knows a
good many, but I think at present there's safety in
numbers. Every one is exceedingly civil, and no
doubt we shall be very gay; but I don't care, with
Clyffe to protect me. He wants to finish with a few
lines before we go to dine at the mess, where, happily,
I sha'n't be accosted by hospitable strangers in mistake
for Clyffe.

Clyffe, in addition.

Yes, here he is, and every one is delighted with
him. He makes himself quite agreeable, and is not a
bit too shy. There never was half as much " *to* him,"
as the Yankees say, before. He seems very well, and
has grown quite distinguished-looking ; and it's "Emily,
Emily " every other word. It is glorious to have him
once more, and when we have made the most of the
fun here I shall get leave, and we shall go for a little
tour through the States; jolly ! And I don't think
that after he goes back it will be so very long before I
come and see you all in your new spheres, for every
one thinks the regiment will be ordered home before
the end of the year. Give my love to the children.
Tell Polly to practise her dancing and learn to behave
pretty before I come home in time for a grand ball to
celebrate her coming out; she mustn't get *too* superhuman. Poor Lisa, just ready to fly, must have her
wings clipped and be shut up tight. What a time she
would have in this land of liberty for precocious little
girls !

Well, good-bye; Miles thinks we sha'n't catch the
post.—Your affectionate brother,

R. WINKWORTH.

157.—LETTERS TO A CHRISTIAN BRIDE.

Mrs. Bootle to Zoe.

HIGH SCALE RECTORY,
March 1860.

My dear young Friend—With every good wish for the approaching auspicious event in your life, accept from your late mother's best friend the accompanying wedding-gift, *Letters to a Christian Bride,* which I trust you will feel is of greater value than gold or pearls or worldly adornments.   I trust, indeed, that you and your young friend Emily will not make so awful and solemn an event as your wedding-day an occasion for displaying your poor perishable bodies (which may ere long be a prey for the worm) decked out in worldly gew-gaws; for happiness does not consist in wedding-dresses or wedding-cakes, but lies altogether out of this world and as much beyond the reach of the worldly as the sword that hung over Robert Bruce's head when he exclaimed : "If happiness were banished from all the world it should still find an abode in the hearts of kings."   That that happiness may be yours, my dear Zoe, is the wish of your sincere friend,

MARIA BOOTLE.

158.—ALGERNON'S FAREWELL.

Anonymous Poem received by Zoe on her wedding-day.

O LADY, who hast left me lorn,
Upon thee breaks thy marriage morn,
And from the ancient steeple swells
The pealing of thy marriage bells.

But ah ! those marriage bells so dear
(Which distance doth forbid me hear)
Sound but a dirge, as they ring on,
Within the breast of Algernon !

'Mid prisoners' chains and captive cords,
'Mid dungeons foul and rebel hordes,
My heart beat firm, and full, and free,
Because I knew 'twas all for thee.

But when I felt the cruel blow
Which laid my hopes for ever low,
From out the lowering, stormy heaven
Flashed forth the poet's burning levin !

Be happy !   May the hand of art
Adorn thy home and cheer thy heart !
My feet have pressed the muses' mount !
My lips have drank Castalia's fount !

                              A WELL-WISHER.

159.—MISS MADGEWICK IS NOT OF THE SAME OPINION.

Miss Madgewick to her Sister, Madame Saisset.

THE MIZ MAZE, *April* 1860.

My dear Annette—*It* is over, and we are in a limp, spiritless, and altogether demoralised condition ; and all agreed in feeling that the only thing possible under the circumstances is to sit down and write to somebody. Lisa is scribbling away to Madame Marini ; Mary, I verily believe, to Zoe—already !   Clyffe is stretched on a garden-bench with a writing case and a cigar ; and

Miss Winkworth, I have no doubt, is despatching letters to everybody not likely to be written to by any-body else; and I suppose we shall all say the same thing to begin with: that there could not have been a more perfect day or a prettier wedding. But before I describe the wedding I want to tell you of two conversations that I had the day before.

The first was in the morning, when I was in the garden considering one of the sketches I promised to make for Madame Marini—a view of the house, bringing in the sun-dial. Miles came out to ask whether I would drive with "Aunt Dora" to Dallington to say a private good-bye to Emily. Presently, after he had stood leaning against the sun-dial for a few minutes, he said, with a twinkle in his eyes that made him look like Clyffe: "Miss Madgewick, be frank and own that you think Emily is throwing herself away." This came unexpectedly, and I didn't answer for a moment. Then I said:

"Well, frankly then, if you had asked me that-a year ago, I don't say I wouldn't have admitted it." Miles laughed a little, and began again:

"Ah! but if you meant to be *quite* frank, you would admit that, though you are determined to stand by Emily and make the best of it, you feel that

'A woman convinced against her will
Is of the same opinion still.'

But of course I never expected you to think me good enough for Emily, only I should be sorry—— In fact, I don't want you to think I can't appreciate her, or that I should ever want to cramp and mould her into a sort of conventional country squiress, like—well, Mrs. Thorburn for instance."

Here neither of us could help laughing, "It never struck me to be afraid of that," I said, "and indeed I am *not* of the same opinion still. I know you better now than I did in those days. And honestly, though I had doubts once as to whether Emily quite knew what she was doing, I am really satisfied and happy about her now, and that means a good deal from one who cares for Emily as I do."

"Thank you," said Miles; "I know it does." So we shook hands, and talked about Emily till the lunch-bell rang.

The other colloquy was at Dallington, when Emily carried me off to her room and hugged me in her old way.

"Oh! Madgy, Madgy!" she said, "isn't it horrid and base of me and Zoe to desert you after all? After all my castles in the air about our being nursing-sisters to my orphanage and hospital!"

"It *would* have been unpardonably base," I said, "only that there is something I am going to confess which I am afraid will make you accuse me of being the basest of the three."

And then I told her about Tom, much to her surprise and excitement.

My own little castle in the air at present is that, when I have (as Mrs. Bootle would say) "finished" Mary,—say in about two years,—I should go to take charge of Emily's orphanage for the colliers' children (which she hopes to have set on foot by that time). I might be a sort of Mother-Superior there till—well, you know Tom *talks* of five years hence, when both his brothers will have left school and be doing something for themselves; but he is always sanguine. Boys don't get "something to do" so easily. However,

Emily, who was perfectly aghast at discovering that we
had been engaged seven years and that I had never
told her, had a host of plans ready on the spot.   Her
cousin Charles should supply Tom's brothers with
lucrative appointments, and Tom himself should have
charge of the future hospital for disabled colliers ; for
Miles, she said, had promised to help her in all her
plans, and I must not think he was not quite as much
in earnest as herself.   So then I told her of the little
explanation which Miles and I had had in the morning,
after which the conversation continued to dwell upon
that topic until Miss Dorothea summoned me to go
home.

Not much room left for a description of the wedding, is there ? and all this time I have said nothing of
Zoe.   She has been growing lovelier every day.
Happiness has been very good for her, and leaving
home is not the wrench it would have been in her
mother's time.   But, beautiful as she looked yesterday,
she did not extinguish Emily.   At all events, I am
sure Miles, Mrs. Warburton, and myself, were of one
mind on that point.   Most girls don't look their best
in bridal dress, but she was at her very prettiest.   As
for Sir Walter, he rose to the occasion, and said more
in his speech at the breakfast than I have heard from
his lips in a year, since I first entered his house.

But *the* speech was Mr. Thorburn's, and the gist of
it was that, however radical a young man's opinions
may be in his bachelor days, marriage and advancing
years never fail to turn him into a conservative, which
encouraging sentiment was evidently not lost upon
either Mr. Fanshawe or Emily.   Now I must write to
Tom, as the Indian letters go to-night, and Emily
insisted on my telling him of her hospital *en Espagne*.

2 A

She thinks an army surgeon will be peculiarly well
adapted to the curing of wounded colliers. Well, she
is a dear child. Who but she would be thinking of
orphanages and hospitals and the matrimonial prospects
of governesses on the eve of her own wedding ?—Ever,
dearest Nan, your very affectionate sister,

ESTHER MADGEWICK.

160.—LISA AT THE WEDDING.

Lisa to Birdie.

THE MIZ MAZE,
Easter Week, 1860.

Dearest darling Birdie—The wedding was great
fun. We wore white dresses and veils with wreaths
of scarlet geraniums and jessamine leaves. Zoe's dress
was *moiré antique*, and her wreath was made of real
orange-flowers. Emily's was artificial—prettier, I think.
I liked all the fuss people made and the civil things
they said, and Charlotte Thorburn and the boys are
very jolly. Miss Skinner told me " Zoe was very
pretty, but she liked *my* style better; it was less severe."
Was not she silly ? Edgar gave us each a little picture ;
mine was of High Scale, but Polly's was a head of Zoe,
with which she is so pleased. She almost says her
prayers to it.

It is great fun having both the boys at home, and
I am just going out riding with papa and Frank, so I
shall have to stop suddenly. You never saw such
creatures as some of Emily's cousins (not the Fanshawe
cousins, but on Mrs. Warburton's side). They blazed
with jewels and wore all the colours of the rainbow.
Even Mr. Thorburn seemed quite a quiet nobody com-

pared to them.   He made a long-winded speech about politics at the breakfast, as if politics had got anything to do with weddings.   Here comes Frank, so good-bye. —Your loving sister,   LISA.

161.—WEDDING-CAKE.

Fanny to Annie.

My dear Annie—I hopes you will receive this safely. It is a bit cut with the bride's own hands out of the wedding-cake, as it would have done your heart good to look at, standing up in the middle of the table, quite heavenly with ciphers of W. and F. and doves and flowers, which Miss Lisa have got in a glass case.   We servants all had new dresses—I send you a bit of mine, real sweet, ain't it ?—and favours, and we was able to get down to church, which was all full of primroses and hot-house plants, and looked like magic.   There was four bridesmaids, my two young ladies and two Miss Thorburns, all in white, with scarlet geranium tied with green.   And then came Miss Winkworth, just like a queen, on her papa's arm, and Miss Warburton with old Mr. Thorburn.   They was such a pair as no one ain't often seen, both in white corded *moiré* silk, at fifteen-and-six the yard, and Honiton veils just alike.   I must tell you that the lace as was lost is come back.   It was Miss Winkworth which sold it to rise a ransum for her pore brother when he was in prison, but Miss Warburton recovered it, and now they would neither of them wear it, but old Miss Dorothea did over a fawn-coloured brocade, and every one said what a fine figure of a woman she is. But Mrs. Warburton's dress was the sweetest, an amber colour, with a real bird of paradise in her bonnet.

I send you the account of the wedding and the breakfast out of the paper. A young gentleman of the press came from Salisbury, and was very civil, and I told him who every one was and who give all the presents, and he sent me the paper in return, which I calls very proper. You may show it to friends, but be sure you returns it. Sir Walter's speech filled my eyes with tears, and Mr. Thorburn he was as good as if he had been in the pulpit. Mr. and Mrs. Winkworth are gone to the Rhine, and Mr. and Mrs. Fanshawe to Switzerland, and they be to meet at Madame Marini's. I wonder that Mr. Winkworth should go there again, but Miss Lisa says there is no danger now, for Mr. Marini is one of the king's advisers, and would not let no harm come to them. Mrs. Fanshawe would not take no maid, and it goes to my heart what will become of her lovely trusoe without no one to fold up for her.

The old ladies is come to live here and keep house, which if they turns out strict, I shall give warning.— Dear Annie, I remain your affectionate friend,

FANNY.

162.—AUNT BESSIE'S SECOND SPRING.

Miss Winkworth to Mrs. Home.

THE MIZ MAZE, *April* 1860.

My dear Mary—Here we are in the reaction! Our weddings are over! Poor dear little Zoe had many heart-searchings about leaving her father and the children. "Oh, Aunt Dora, when I couldn't help liking Edgar, I never thought it would come to this, leaving all I promised mamma to do for her! I couldn't do it if I did not see papa was comfortable with you, and the children too. I think he is really more satisfied about them with you than he ever could be with me." And that is to a certain extent true, for Walter fidgeted over Zoe's management. Clyffe came home with Miles. He pretends to be uproarious, but, poor laddie! it must be rather sore work for him to have two old aunts substituted for his young brother and sister. I hope we shall not be a check on the young spirits. We have our old rooms and our mother's morning-room which Bessie means to use when there is too much going on for her downstairs. However, I am not sure that she is not going to develop a second spring, she has done so much of late, and seemed to enjoy it. She was quite equal to the occasion when I went to London with Zoe to buy wedding clothes and persuade Mrs. Warburton to have the weddings together and give up her ideal of St. George's, Hanover Square, and she has gone through the day of bustle and excitement quite cheerily. She dressed Zoe herself. You know nobody ever could put on a dress and give the last touches as Bessie's dainty fingers could, and the very last thing she fastened on that Trichinopoly chain and the cross, which had been her first and only wedding-present, and said, " Please wear it, my dear. I do so like it to go to one whose bridegroom comes from Dallington." It nearly overcame Zoe, though she was very good throughout, and looked—though I say it as should not say it—nearly as lovely as you did, my Mary, in spite of her crinoline. As to Emily, she might have been the White Cat at the moment of transformation, and Miles looked at her as if he was afraid she would melt away! George Thorburn was in his glory, and all went off well, and I am thankful it is over, and that we can settle down into our new old life.

There is Walter calling me to come down to the farm with him and admire the new cows.—Your affectionate sister,

D. W.

THE END.

Printed by R. & R. CLARK, *Edinburgh.*

www.ingramcontent.com/pod-product-compliance
Lightning Source LLC
Chambersburg PA
CBHW021712110726
47902CB00005B/1154